THE GREATEST MARIAN TITLES

Visit our web site at
www.albahouse.org
(for orders www.stpauls.us)

or call 1-800-343-2522 (ALBA)
and request current catalog

The Greatest Marian Titles

Their History, Meaning, and Usage

ANTHONY M. BUONO

ST PAULS

Library of Congress Cataloging-in-Publication Data

Buono, Anthony M.
 The greatest Marian titles : their history, meaning, and usage / by Anthony M. Buono.
   p. cm.
 ISBN 0-8189-1247-2
 1. Mary, Blessed Virgin, Saint—Titles—History. 2. Mary, Blessed Virgin, Saint—Titles—Meditations. I. Title.

BT670.T5B86 2007
232.91—dc22
                                        2007004270

Acknowledgment: The author is very grateful to the Catholic Book Publishing Corp. for graciously granting him permission to use in the present book (as part of chapters 9, 15, 16, 19, 20, 21, 22) some of the material that he originally wrote and included in the *Dictionary of Mary,* © 1997 by Catholic Book Publishing Corp. All rights reserved.

Produced and designed in the United States of America by the
Fathers and Brothers of the Society of St. Paul,
2187 Victory Boulevard, Staten Island, New York 10314-6603
as part of their communications apostolate.

ISBN 13: 978-0-8189-1247-4
ISBN 10: 0-8189-1247-2

© *Copyright 2008 by the Society of St. Paul / Alba House*

Printing Information:

Current Printing - first digit	1	2	3	4	5	6	7	8	9	10
Year of Current Printing - first year shown										
2008	2009	2010	2011	2012	2013	2014	2015	2016	2017	

Table of Contents

Introduction xiii
   Mary's Present Mission xiii
   The Value of Titles xv
   Biblical, Conciliar, and Traditional Sources xvi
   The First Centuries (Second and Third) xviii
   From the Fourth to the Sixth Centuries xx
   From the Seventh to the Eleventh Centuries xxi
   From the Twelfth to the Fifteenth Centuries xxii
   From the Sixteenth to the Twentieth Centuries xxiii
   The Most Frequently Used Title xxvi

1. Advocate of Grace 1
   A Title from Earliest Times 1
   Early Prayer to Mary's Patronage 1
   Most Gracious Advocate 2
   Endorsed by the Church 3
   All-powerful Advocate 4
   Application to Us 6
   Prayer to Mary Our Advocate 7

2. Associate of the Redeemer 9
   A Modern Term 9
   Based on the Bible 10
   A Title Not Usually Found among the Fathers 11
   Favored by Vatican II 12
   Universal Association 13
   Integral and Dependent Association 14
   Application to Us 15
   Prayer in Honor of Our Lady, Associate of the Redeemer 16

3. Blessed Mother 17
   Development of This Title 17
   "Our Mother" 18
   Characteristics of Mary's Motherhood 19
   "Blessed Mother" 21
   Application to Us 22
   Prayer to Our Lady, Mother and Teacher 24

4. Daughter of Zion 25
   A Title Revived by Vatican II 25
   Based on Old Testament Texts 27
   Alluded to in the New Testament 28
   The Daughter of Zion and the Poor of the Lord 29
   Piety Rooted in the Scriptures 30
   The Magnificat and the Psalms 31
   The Scriptural Bases of the Magnificat 32
   Meaning of the Title 35
   Application to Us 36
   Prayer to Our Lady, Daughter of Zion 37

5. Exemplar 39
   The Human Need for Models 39
   Christian Models 40
   Mary as a Singular Model 41
   Meaning of "Model" in This Case 42
   Imitation of Mary 43
   Model of the Church 44
   Model of Christians 45
   Application to Us 47
   Prayer to Our Lady, Exemplar of Christians 49

6. Handmaid of the Lord 51
   A Title Mary Applied to Herself 51
   "Servant" in the Old Testament 51
   "Servant" in the New Testament 52
   Mary, Servant of the Lord 53

Jesus, Servant of the Lord 55
Mary's Servant Activity 57
Mary — the Poor of Yahweh par Excellence 58
Application to Us 59
Prayer to Our Lady, Handmaid of the Lord 61

7. Help of Christians 63
A Title Used from Earliest Times 63
Primitive Appeals to Mary's Help 64
From the Fifth to the Eleventh Centuries 65
Vanquisher of the Devil 67
Vanquisher of Heresies 69
Vanquisher of the Church's Enemies 70
Application to Us 72
Prayer to Mary, Help of Christians 73

8. Immaculate Conception 75
The Name Mary Gave Herself at Lourdes 75
A Doctrine of the "Sense of the Faithful" 75
"You Are All-Beautiful, O Mary" 76
Mary's Physical Beauty 77
A Spiritual Portrait of Mary 79
Lourdes and the Immaculate Conception 81
Implied in Sacred Scripture 81
The Fathers and the Teaching 82
The Medieval Theologians and the Teaching 84
The Popes and the Teaching 85
Application to Us 86
Prayer to the Immaculate Conception 87

9. Mary the Virgin 89
The Name of Mary in Scripture 89
Meaning of the Name Mary 90
Feast of the Name of Mary 91
Mary's Virginal Conception of Jesus 93
Mary Ever Virgin 94

A Teaching of the Church 97
Application to Us 98
Prayer to Mary the Virgin 100

10. Mediatrix 101
    Mediatrix in Three Ways 101
    History of the Title 103
    1921 to the Present 105
    The Doctrine and the Magisterium 106
    Mass of "Mary, Mother and Mediatrix of Grace" 107
    Christ: The One Mediator 108
    Application to Us 110
    Prayer to Our Lady, Mediatrix of Graces 111

11. Mother of the Church 113
    Championed by Pope Paul VI 113
    History of the Title 115
    The Title in Scripture 117
    Meaning of the Title 118
    A Teacher of the Spiritual Life 120
    Application to Us 122
    Prayer to the Mother of the Church 123

12. Mother of God 125
    The Fundamental Title 125
    Based on the Scriptures 127
    The Title and the Magisterium 128
    The Title and the Liturgy 130
    Meaning of the Title 132
    Application to Us 134
    Prayer to Mary, Mother of God 136

13. Mother of Mercy 137
    Mercy — Compassion for the Misery of Others 137
    History of the Title 138
    Basis in Scripture 139
    Meaning of the Title 142

Table of Contents

The Pact or Covenant of Mercy 144
Application to Us 146
Prayer to Mary, Mother of Mercy 148

14. Mother of the Savior 149
    Centrality of the Paschal Mystery 149
    The Center of the History of Salvation 150
    A Title Emphasized by Vatican II 151
    A Title Based on Scripture 153
    History of the Title 155
    Meaning of the Title 157
    Application to Us 159
    Prayer to Mary, Mother of the Savior 160

15. New Eve — New Woman 161
    A Title Used by Vatican II and Pope Paul VI 161
    Mary, the New Eve 162
    The New Woman 163
    The Ideal Human Instrument 164
    Teaching of the Church 165
    Mary and the Modern Woman 166
    Revealer of the Transforming Design of the Christian Economy .. 168
    Application to Us 169
    Prayer to Our Lady, the New Woman 170

16. Our Lady of the Blessed Sacrament 171
    Mary, "Woman of the Eucharist" 171
    Presence of Mary in the Eucharist 173
    The Church's Reason for Honoring Mary 175
    Devotion to Mary in the Eucharist 175
    An Intrinsic Element of Christian Worship 177
    Mary in the Eucharistic Celebration 178
    Liturgical Marian Celebrations in the United States .. 178
    Celebrations of Mary outside the Proper Calendar ... 179
    Our Model in the Celebration of the Mysteries 180
    The Magnificat in a Eucharistic Key 181
    Devotion to Mary in Private Prayer 182

Mary and Prayer 183
Application to Us 184
Prayer to Our Lady of the Blessed Sacrament 185

17. Our Lady of the Rosary 187
    A Title Given Us by Mary 187
    What Is the Rosary? 188
    The History of the Rosary 189
    Mystery and Meditation 191
    The Magisterium and the Rosary 192
    John Paul II and the New Luminous Mysteries 195
    Praying the Rosary during the Liturgical Year 196
    The Rosary and the Liturgy 197
    Application to Us 198
    Prayer to Our Lady of the Rosary 199

18. Perfect Disciple of Christ 201
    The Meaning of "Disciple" in the Ancient World 201
    Christ's Requirements for His Disciples 202
    The Title and Scripture 204
    The Title and the Fathers 206
    The Title and the Magisterium 207
    The Great Believer or The First Among Believers 209
    Application to Us 210
    Prayer to Mary, Perfect Disciple of Christ 211

19. Queen of Angels 213
    Mary's Queenship 213
    Church Teaching about Angels 215
    The Angels in Human Life and in the Church 216
    Mary's Awareness of the Angelic World 218
    Mary's Experience of Angels in Her Life 219
    Angels at Mary's Assumption 220
    Church Documents about Mary and Angels
        After the Eighth Century 220
    Scriptural Basis of Mary's Heavenly
        Queenship of Angels 222

Table of Contents

Application to Us 223
Prayer to Mary, Queen of the Angels 224

20. Queen of Families 225
    Meaning of the Title 225
    The Family — First and Vital Cell of Society 226
    The Christian Family — A Miniature Church 227
    Christian Parents: Educators in Prayer 229
    The Family and Liturgical Prayer 230
    The Family and the Liturgical Year 231
    The Family and Private Prayer 232
    Mary, Mother of Every Christian Family 233
    Mary, Queen of the Home 235
    Application to Us 236
    Prayer to Mary, Queen of Families 237

21. Queen of Peace 239
    A Modern Title 239
    An Outgrowth of the Title "Help of Christians" 240
    Meaning of Queenship of Mary 241
    Reasons for Mary's Queenship 243
    An Understanding of Mary's Queenship
        in Accord with Our Time 245
    Application to Us 248
    Prayer to Our Lady, Queen of Peace 249

22. Seat of Wisdom 251
    Wisdom in the Old Testament 251
    Wisdom in the New Testament 252
    History of the Title 253
    Mary's Words of Wisdom 254
    Power of Mary's Words 255
    First Word: Childlike Wonder 256
    Second Word: Obedient Service 257
    Third Word: Biblical Knowledge 259
    Fourth Word: Joyful Praise 260
    Fifth Word: Gentle Authority 261

Sixth Word: Tender Charity 262
Seventh Word: Deep Faith 263
Seven Words for Eternity 264
Mary Shared in the Wisdom of the Father 265
Mary Shared in the Wisdom of Her Son 266
Mary Shared in the Wisdom of the Holy Spirit 267
Application to Us 268
Prayer to Mary, Seat of Wisdom 269

23. Temple of the Holy Spirit 271
    The Temple Theme in Scripture 271
    The Title in the Fathers and the Liturgy 272
    The Contributions of Vatican II and Pope Paul VI 273
    Close Union of Mary and the Holy Spirit 275
    The Spirit Prepared Mary for Her Role in the Divine Plan .. 276
    The Spirit Overshadowed Mary to Enable Her to Become the Mother of God's Son 277
    The Spirit Proclaimed Mary's Divine Motherhood through Elizabeth 278
    The Spirit Established Mary's Spiritual Motherhood at the Foot of the Cross 279
    The Spirit Descended on Mary and the Disciples at Pentecost ... 280
    The Spirit Works in the Hearts of Mary's Children 281
    Application to Us 282
    Prayer to Our Lady, Temple of the Spirit 284

24. Queen of All Hearts 285
    The Culmination of All Marian Titles 285
    Christ, the King of All Hearts 285
    Mary, the Queen of All Hearts 286
    Meaning of the Title 288
    Application to Us 291
    Prayer to Mary, Queen of All Hearts 292

Appendix: Selected List of Marian Titles 293

Introduction

Mary's Present Mission

After his Resurrection and Ascension, Jesus was freed of space and time and is now ever present and present everywhere. His presence cannot be seen by us, but it remains nonetheless. And he continues his mission of redemption for each one of us.

Something similar is true of Mary after her Assumption. She is no longer bound by space and time. She is present always to each of us to exercise her Spiritual Motherhood, which Jesus assigned to her. She possesses a presence and a particular mission different from that of the Saints who pray for us and obtain graces for us.

Mary's work on earth is not finished. Vatican II says that this work continues until every one of the faithful is led to the beloved homeland.

Thus, Mary is living and truly our Mother standing by each of us with an active presence — even though we do not see her. Her presence is a maternal and effective one and lays the groundwork for the titles accorded her by the Church. In the words of Pope John Paul II:

"For every Christian, for every human being, Mary is the one who first 'believed,' and precisely with her faith as Spouse and Mother she wishes to act upon all those who entrust themselves to her as her children.

"And it is well known that the more her children persevere and progress in this attitude the nearer Mary leads them to the 'unfathomable riches of Christ' (Ephesians 3:8).

"And to the same degree they recognize more and more clearly the dignity of the human being in all its fullness and the definitive meaning of the human vocation" (*Redemptoris Mater*, no. 46).

Strictly speaking, devotion to Mary is not absolutely necessary for our salvation, for there is only one Mediator —Jesus. However, in God's plan Mary has an important though secondary role in the Redemption, and those who have devotion to her are enriched in a way that others are not.

"Devotion to Mary is the surest and shortest way to reach Christ. By meditating on all phases of the life of Mary, we learn how to live for and with Christ in daily life in a perfect inner union" (Hans Urs von Balthasar).

Perhaps Pope Paul VI put it best in his Apostolic Exhortation *Marialis Cultus* on Devotion to Mary (no. 57):

"Christ is the only Way to the Father (see John 14:4-15), and the ultimate example to whom the disciple must conform his own conduct (see John 13:11), to the extent of sharing Christ's sentiments (see Philippians 2:5), living his life, and possessing his Spirit (see Galatians 2:20; Romans 8:10-11). The Church has always taught this, and nothing in pastoral activity should obscure this doctrine.

"But the Church, taught by the Holy Spirit and benefiting from centuries of experience, recognizes that devotion to the Blessed Virgin, subordinated to worship of the Divine Savior and in connection with it, also has a great pastoral effectiveness and constitutes a force for renewing Christian living....

"Mary's many-sided mission to the People of God is a supernatural reality that operates and bears fruit within the body of the Church. One finds cause for joy in considering the different aspects of this mission and seeing how each of these aspects with its individual effectiveness is directed toward the same end, namely, producing in the children the spiritual characteristics of the Firstborn Son. The Virgin's maternal intercession, her exemplary holiness, and the Divine grace that is in her become for the human race a reason for Divine hope."

The Value of Titles

Modern society makes great use of titles. We have titles for people in the public eye, such as movie stars, ball players, and politicians, and even for members of our family — titles such as "The King," "Mr. October," "The Gipper," and "The Breadwinner." The important thing about these titles is that they immediately impart an essential fact about the person to whom they refer.

Clark Gable, "The King," was the most popular actor of his generation. Reggie Jackson, "Mr. October," was one of the greatest clutch hitters during his years in baseball. Ronald Reagan, "The Gipper," was an outstanding leader and communicator. "The Breadwinner" (whether Mom or Dad, or both) is the person who brings home the paycheck.

Just as in secular life, Christians have from the beginning utilized titles to identify the great men and women of their Faith. We use many titles to designate aspects of our Lord — some of which are: "Messiah," "Lamb of God," "Son of Man," "Son of God," and "Sun of Justice."

We also have titles for Mary referring to some dignity, honor, distinction, or preeminence attached to her by reason of rank, office, precedent, privilege, or attainment. In short, each of Mary's titles in the Liturgy and in piety ultimately emphasizes some aspect of her relationship to God or to us.

The titles may even refer to a place or need or some reality where people work. They constitute a kind of sacramentalization of aspects where people live and experience the suffering and the joy of their Faith.

No matter what the title used, every one of them recalls the person to whom it is applied, and we give our veneration to that person. In the present case, each title recalls for us the person of Mary under some aspect that is dear to us.

In the eyes of her devout clients, Mary possesses a surprising element of universality and historicity. She is above everyone, from everyone, and for everyone and as such is present in various historical situations.

This explains Mary's titles which, beyond the Mystery of the Mother of the Lord and Mother of the Church, detail her presence, her action in some place, situation, or concrete experience. Indeed, the variety of her titles is a veritable encyclopedia and one that is neither useless erudition nor mere folklore. Rather, it is an indication of indefinite ways of encountering the unique and loving countenance of this Mother in diverse situations.

The titles of our Lady are rich and numerous and filled with meaning for us today. They call us unerringly to venerate her person under some beloved aspect.

Biblical, Conciliar, and Traditional Sources

The Word of God was set forth in the Bible to sinful humankind for its salvation. In the New Covenant, that Word has revealed the Mystery of Mary.

In particular, Luke shows us how the message of God in the annunciation of the Messianic Incarnation has inaugurated the praise of Mary by the greeting that the Angel addressed to her (Luke 1:28). The Gospel of John then completes this Biblical portrait of the Mother of Jesus, presenting her as the woman of faith become the Mother of the disciples (John 19:25-27).

Departing from these evangelical titles ("Full of Grace," "Servant and Mother of the Lord," "Mother of Jesus," "Blessed Believer") as well as from the Old and New Testament contexts from which these titles arise, the Church has refined and explained Marian doctrine and devotion.

Introduction

Doctrinally, faith in the Mystery of Mary is a Christological affirmation; and faith in Christ has, in turn, developed as faith in God and in the Trinity of Divine Persons. This development flows from the professions of faith such as the Baptismal Formulas.

In the most famous professions, we say that we believe in God the Father, in the Son and Savior, in the Holy Spirit, and in the Church. And we affirm that the Son is true God and true Man, "conceived by the power of the Holy Spirit and born of the Virgin Mary."

The text of St. Cyril of Alexandria approved by the Council of Ephesus (431) is a much more complete explanation of the doctrine of the Church and focuses on the title "Mother of God." Defining the doctrine of the Incarnation, it states:

"It was not that an ordinary man was born first of the holy Virgin, on whom afterward the Word descended; what we say is that, being united with the flesh from the womb, [the Word] has undergone birth in the flesh, making the birth in the flesh his own."

The text continues:

"Thus [the holy Fathers] have unhesitatingly called the holy Virgin 'Mother of God' [*Theotokos*]. This does not mean that the nature of the Word or his divinity received the beginning of its existence from the holy Virgin, but that, since the holy body, animated by a rational soul, which the Word united to himself according to the hypostasis, was born from her, the Word was born according to the flesh" (J. Neuner, S.J. and J. Dupuis, S.J., editors, *The Christian Faith*, no. 605).

This passage from Biblical language to the language of the Councils and the Fathers of the Church came about through Tradition. This term "tradition" designates the voice of the Church, which is infallible through the voice of the Holy Spirit who guarantees, for example, that St. Leo I, in his Letter addressed to St. Flavian during the Council of Chalcedon (451), has spoken as Peter himself would have spoken.

The voice of infallible Tradition must be distinguished from that of the fallible tradition in which it is manifested. The teaching about Mary is a privileged terrain, which facilitates the correct interpretation of the faith of the Church in a Divine revelation transmitted through Tradition. In this the Sacred Scriptures are the inspired element, guaranteed as Word of God.

The First Centuries (Second and Third)

We have few documents concerning the faith of the Christians of the second century — i.e., from the death of the last Apostle to the year 199. The texts that we do have are based closely on the Bible with few references to Mary.

In this century, St. Ignatius of Antioch — who was the second successor of St. Peter in the See of Antioch and who died a martyr at Rome in 107 — has left us seven letters. These bear ardent witness to his love for Christ and his faith in the Divine Plan of salvation: God really became man to suffer and die for us.

Ignatius calls Mary Virgin and Mother of God our Savior in order to demonstrate the truth of the Incarnation. He also sets forth three Mysteries that have been "hidden from the devil and that need to be proclaimed": Mary's virginity, her act of giving birth, and the Death of the Lord.

The person of Mary takes on great importance in the apologist St. Justin Martyr (d. 165). He calls Mary "the Virgin" and makes a parallel between her and Eve that is inspired by the Bible but not derived directly from it.

The *Protevangelium of James* (sometimes called the *Gospel of Mary*) is a noncanonical work written in Egypt between 150 and 200. It is a kind of Life of Mary, with nice touches that became the inspiration for the Marian art of the Middle Ages. It emphasizes Mary's perfect holiness and virginity, which were the result of God's providence and grace, and goes so far as to attest to the virgin birth at Bethlehem through the testimony of the midwife Salome.

St. Irenaeus of Lyons (d. 202) develops the Eve-Mary parallel (Mary is the new Eve). As a disciple of St. Polycarp (d. 156) of Smyrna in Asia Minor, Irenaeus represents the tradition of both East and West. For him, Mary has become "the cause of salvation for herself and for the whole human race."

In the third century, Tertullian (d. 230) further develops the identity between the Mystery of Mary and that of the Church. However, he does not indicate any knowledge of Mary's virginity, asserting that she had other children.

This century was instrumental in developing the title *Theotokos*: Mother of God. Origen, the ecclesiastical writer (d. 253), is the first known exponent of this title, commenting on it in his lost work *Letter to the Romans* — a fact indicated by the fifth-century historian Socrates (d. 450).

Origen is also the source of another important spiritual tradition, namely, that Mary is the *model of the perfect disciple of Christ*.

An Egyptian papyrus from the third century found at the beginning of the twentieth century reproduces a very important text of a prayer to Mary known as the *Sub Tuum* ("Under Your Patronage"), which contains the words "We fly to your protection and your mercy, O Mother of God."

Finally, it is worth mentioning that the latter part of the third century also marks the first recorded appearance of Mary to someone on earth. According to St. Gregory of Nyssa (d. 395), our Lady appeared (in the company of St. John the Apostle) to St. Gregory the Wonderworker (d. 270), Bishop of Neocaesarea in Asia Minor who was known for his miracles of healing and his propagation of the Faith.

From the Fourth to the Sixth Centuries

The fourth to the sixth centuries constitute the Golden Age of the Fathers of the Church. The beginning of the fourth century signals the end of the persecutions against a constantly growing Church. In 313, Emperors Constantine and Licinius grant the Church the freedom for a development that rapidly accelerates, so that even Constantine and his family become Christian.

The first four Ecumenical Councils (Nicaea, 325; Constantinople, 381; Ephesus, 431; and Chalcedon, 451), among many other accomplishments, make Marian doctrine more precise, e.g., calling Mary "Mother of God" and leading to a more ardent love for Mary.

St. Ephrem the Deacon (d. 378) inaugurates a poetic theology in which the praise of Mary is extraordinary in quality. Mary is "sister, spouse, and handmaid of Christ." Her beauty lies in her holiness.

St. Gregory of Nazianzen (d. 379) sets forth the classic line: "If someone does not believe that Mary is the Mother of God, he is outside of the Divinity."

St. Ambrose (d. 397) affirms that Mary is the worthy Mother of the Lord, of the Son of God: "What is more excellent than the Mother of God?"

St. Epiphanius (d. 403), a native of Palestine who was Bishop of Salamis (Cyprus), adds to the titles of "Mother of God" and "Ever Virgin" those of "Mother of the Living" and "Cause of Life."

St. Augustine (d. 430) indicates that Mary is the Mother of Christ and the Church is the Mother of the members of Christ. If Christ is the Head of his Body, Mary is its most holy and most eminent member. Indeed, Mary conceived the Son of God "first in her heart and then in her womb."

St. Romanos the Melodist (d. 500) in his great poems sings the praises of the Mother of God, her dignity, and her intercession. She is the Mediatrix of Adam and Eve, "the voice and the honor of our race." He places Mary at the foot of the Cross and has her receive the first appearance of the risen Christ.

At the end of the sixth century appears the magnificent Akathist Hymn, which magnifies the Mystery of the Incarnation and the Mother of God, whom the end of each of the 24 stanzas invokes as the "Bride [of God] ever virgin."

From the Seventh to the Eleventh Centuries

St. Ildephonsus (d. 667) invokes Mary as our Sovereign and asks us to pray to the Holy Spirit to obtain the grace to love Mary and serve her.

St. Bede the Venerable (d. 735) develops the Augustinian Marian tradition and sees in Mary the extraordinary work of the Holy Spirit.

St. John Damascene (d. 749) celebrates Mary as the "new heaven" in whom the Son of God dwells. He even speaks of consecration to Mary.

Ambrose Autpert (d. 784) successfully formulates the Spiritual Motherhood of Mary: If Christ is the Brother of believers, why not call his Mother the "Mother of the Faithful"?

And the unknown writer of this time dubbed Pseudo-Jerome — because of his pseudonymous letter *Cogitis Me*: "You Know Me" — states that we must glorify Mary, Queen of Heaven, next to her Son, imitate her, and call upon her.

St. Paschasius Radbertus (d. 865) stresses the virginity of Christ's Mother.

From the Twelfth to the Fifteenth Centuries

At the beginning of the twelfth century, the great Marian Doctor St. Anselm of Canterbury (d. 1109) comes to the fore, attributing to Mary her proper place in theology: "O lovable reality. In how sublime a place do I contemplate Mary! None is equal to Mary and none superior to Mary, outside of God! God has given Mary his only Son whom he loved as himself, having alone generated him, from his heart, as his equal!"

The twelfth century can justly be termed a Marian century, and it is best summed up by the celebrated sermons of St. Bernard of Clairvaux (d. 1153) on the Mysteries of Christ and his Mother, especially the Annunciation, and the Assumption, which indicate that Mary is our Mediatrix with the Mediator Christ.

The growing number of religious orders assign Mary a place in their Liturgy, Homiletics, and Books. The cathedrals begin a program of religious education that guides the Church on her earthly pilgrimage by means of catechetical announcements on their doors and the illustrations of the History of Salvation on their windows and on their walls. These identify Mary as the type of the Church. Just as Mary is Mother, Queen, and Mediatrix, so is the Church.

The "Hail Mary" prayer becomes more widespread with the two parts coming together only in 1496. St. Thomas Aquinas (d. 1274) and St. Bonaventure (d. 1274) make Christology more precise and so prepare a true deepening of Marian teaching. Mary's Divine Motherhood becomes even more understood and explained not simply as a physical one but in the spiritual perspective enunciated by St. Augustine ("She conceived Jesus first in her heart and then in her womb").

Blessed Duns Scotus (d. 1308) develops the arguments of his predecessors and concludes that the redemption of Mary is real and perfect insofar as it is a prevention — laying the ground-

Introduction

work for the popularity of the title "Immaculate Conception."

In his classic work *The Divine Comedy*, Dante (d. 1321) is guided by his companion Beatrice toward the contemplation of the Mother of God, toward whom all the blessed like children stretch out their arms.

We see a new evolution in popular piety in the description and representation of the Virgin with the Child. These stress the humanity of the Child. Later, there will appear the suffering Christ, with his Mother sorrowing at the foot of the Cross. This leads to works like that of Michelangelo's Pietà (1498) and to the Spiritual Motherhood of Mary.

From the Sixteenth to the Twentieth Centuries

The Council of Trent (1545-1563) limits itself to endorsing devotion to Mary and asserting that in the matter of original sin its intention is not to include Mary in it.

Treatises on Mary are written by Francisco Suarez (d. 1617), St. Peter Canisius (d. 1597), Cardinal de Bérulle (d. 1629), and his disciple, John Olier (d. 1657). St. Francis de Sales (d. 1622) and Bossuet (d. 1704) write pages about love for the Mother of God, and St. John Eudes (d. 1680) promotes devotion to the Immaculate Heart of Mary.

Titles of Mary continue to abound, but not too many catch the fancy of the people. The Litany of Loreto is completed and approved for use, and in 1631 the Sacred Congregation of Rites prohibits the addition of any invocations to the Litany without the explicit authorization of the Apostolic See.

The eighteenth century belongs to St. Louis Grignion de Montfort (d. 1716), with his magnificent body of Marian work culminating in the classic *True Devotion to Mary*, and to St. Alphonsus Liguori (d. 1787), with his classic work *The Glories of Mary*. Both authors make use of many Marian titles, such as "Mother of Mercy," "Queen of Heaven and Earth," "Cause of Our Joy," "Help of the Sick," and "Dispenser of God's Gifts."

The nineteenth century witnesses a proliferation of Marian congregations (more than 700 women's congregations alone). These bear the name of some Mystery of Mary, especially the Immaculate Conception, the Assumption, the Holy Family, and the Rosary as well as the Name of Mary.

At the same time, and into the twentieth century, a number of Marian shrines spring up and become the centers of pilgrimage in places where apparitions of Mary occur to children and the poor. Some of these are: Rue du Bac at Paris (Miraculous Medal: 1830), La Salette (1846), Lourdes (1858), Pontmain (1871), Fatima (1917), Beauraing (1932-1933), Banneux (1933), and the Shrine of Our Lady of Tears in Syracuse, Italy (1953) — leading to new titles, such as "Our Lady of Lourdes" and "Our Lady of Fatima."

In more recent times, there have been apparitions that are in various stages of approval by the Church: Medjugorje (1981), Cuapa (1981), Akita (1984), and Kibeho (1988). In all, scholars have identified some 232 cases of Marian apparitions between 1930 and 1975. And that number increases greatly as we reach the twenty-first century.

The nineteenth and twentieth centuries have also brought forth two main dogmatic definitions: the Immaculate Conception (1854) and the Assumption (1950). The former proclaims that Mary was preserved free from original sin because of the foreseen merits of Christ. The latter defines that Mary has been brought into glory both in body and in soul at the end of her earthly existence without indicating whether or not she died.

The Decrees in which the definitions are given also contain titles of Mary, such as "Enclosed Garden," "City of God," "Temple of God," "Ark of the Covenant," and "Woman Clothed with the Sun."

Introduction

At the same time, Cardinal John Henry Newman (d. 1890) looks upon Mary as the "New Eve" and "Mother of the Living." M.J. Scheeben (d. 1888) — followed by a host of other writers into the twentieth century — makes Mariology an organic part of Christology.

The epoch-making Second Vatican Council (1962-1965) issues a masterful document on Mary in the Church, inserted as chapter 8 in its *Dogmatic Constitution on the Church* (nos. 52-69). It integrates the Mystery of the Mother of God into that of the Church. In particular, it highlights the Biblical and traditional basis of Marian teaching, taking account of recent results of exegesis, patristics, and later theologies.

The Council has given rise to such titles as "Finest Fruit of the Redemption," "Perfect Disciple of Christ," "Queen of the Universe," and "Helper of the Redeemer."

In 1974, Pope Paul VI issues the Apostolic Exhortation *Marialis Cultus* ("Devotion to the Blessed Virgin Mary"). He explains Mary's place in the liturgical year and the meaning of her feasts. The Pope also sets forth that Marian devotion entails a fourfold character: Trinitarian, Christological, Ecclesiological, and Pneumatological. It must also follow four doctrinal orientations: Biblical, liturgical, ecumenical, and anthropological.

Mary must be shown as the model human person, the responsible woman, in conformity with the Biblical reality and in accord with the concrete requirements of the phenomenon of the liberation of women and the recognition of their insights in modern society.

In 1981, Pope John Paul II approves another Litany to the Blessed Mother, which has thirty new invocations, some of which can be regarded as new titles of Mary, e.g., "Advocate of Grace," "Queen of the World," and "Helper of the Redeemer."

The same Pontiff also continues the nineteenth- and twentieth-century tradition of Popes adding new invocations to the

Litany of Loreto that has seen the addition of "Queen Conceived without Original Sin" (1854); "Queen of the Most Holy Rosary" (1883); "Mother of Good Counsel" (1903); "Queen of Peace" (1916); and "Queen Assumed into Heaven" (1951). In 1980 he adds "Mother of the Church," and in 1995 "Queen of Families."

The Most Frequently Used Title

The most frequently used title is "Blessed Virgin Mary." The Latin version of this title (*"Beata Virgo Maria"*) is how Mary is ordinarily named in official Church documents.

It is a title that has given offshoots in many languages. In English we have: "Our Blessed Lady," "Our Blessed Mother," and the "Virgin Mary." In other languages, there are translations of "Holy Virgin," "Most Holy Virgin," and "Mother of God" as well as the Italian "Madonna" ("My Lady") and the French "Notre Dame" ("Our Lady").

In addition to these titles that may be regarded as having to do with her Name, there are others that have to do with Mary's function, such as "Associate of the Redeemer," "Daughter of Zion," and "Glory of the Holy Spirit."

The following chapters will set forth a commentary on twenty-four of what may be termed the most important and popular titles of our Lady in our time. A better knowledge of the history, meaning, and usage of such titles will help keep them alive in the hearts, minds, and lives of Catholics today.

Even more important, by dwelling on some aspect of Mary's personality we can get to know her better and imitate her more closely. In turn, such reflection may in some small way lead us to have greater love for and devotion toward our heavenly Mother — so that we may go *through Mary to Jesus!*

1
Advocate of Grace

A Title from Earliest Times

Advocate is a title that has been given Mary from the earliest of times in the Church. Already in the early part of the third century, St. Irenaeus of Lyons described Mary as the "Advocate of Eve."

This term "advocate" was used in the same way as it is today — "someone who pleads the cause of another."

However, Mary's action on behalf of Eve is not to be taken as a personal act of intercession for Eve alone. Rather it refers to the action that Mary accomplishes in favor of the human race with full adherence to God's plan in faith and obedience.

Mary's action rectifies and annuls the consequences of Eve's (and Adam's) unbelief and disobedience and constitutes a true defense of Eve. Eve can no longer be accused of the ruin of the human race because that ruin has been dispelled by Mary's obedience.

Early Prayer to Mary's Patronage

Toward the end of the third century, the Church succeeded in formulating a prayer of invocation to Mary's patronage or defense. The prayer is called by the Latin name *Sub Tuum* ("We Fly to Your Patronage"), and it has come to light only in recent times:

> *We fly to your patronage,*
> *O holy Mother of God;*
> *despise not our petitions in our necessities,*
> *but deliver us always from all dangers,*
> *O glorious and blessed Virgin.*

The words take for granted that Mary has the power to protect her children. They also imply that Mary is our Mother. And as St. Alphonsus Liguori (d. 1783) declared, "When Mary's clients call her Mother, they are not using empty words. She is our Mother — not by flesh, of course, but spiritually; the Mother of our souls, of our salvation."

The text of this brief prayer expresses with rare efficacy the people's faith in the intercession of Mary. The Mother of God, who is glorious and blessed, is a refuge of mercy for the Christian community.

In the Blessed Virgin, the community feels secure and thus expresses its conviction that she will not reject the supplication of all who invoke her in the hour of necessity and danger.

The Saints, says St. Augustine (d. 430), are our advocates because they share Christ's advocacy. This is most true of Mary. Hence, she is our Advocate beyond compare.

Most Gracious Advocate

The *Hail, Holy Queen*, a favorite prayer from the Middle Ages on, shows this very clearly. Mary is called a "most gracious Advocate" who has the power to save all. It is impossible for Mary not to be heard by her Son or by the Father. For her prayers are those of a Mother and contain something of a command.

All this is summed up in the classic saying: "What God can do by commanding, you can do by praying, O Blessed Virgin."

In addition, Mary is a compassionate advocate for even those who have strayed very far from the right path. She is much more powerful than all the Saints. And to that same degree she is more tender and solicitous for our happiness.

Our Lady is the singular Refuge of the abandoned, the Hope of the miserable, and the Advocate of every sinner who turns to her.

In his eagerness to show us mercy, God has given us his Son as our Advocate. And then to make our confidence even stronger, he has made available to us another Advocate, who obtains through her prayer whatever she asks.

Endorsed by the Church

In modern times, this title was used by Popes Pius VII, St. Pius X, Pius XI, and Pius XII. The Fathers of the Second Vatican Council also alluded to it:

"In her maternal charity, Mary cares for the brothers and sisters of her Son who are still journeying on earth surrounded by dangers and difficulties, until they are led into their blessed homeland. Therefore, the Blessed Virgin is invoked in the Church with the titles of Advocate, Helper, Benefactress, and Mediatrix.

"This, however, is to be understood in such a way that it neither detracts from nor adds anything to the dignity and efficacy of Christ the one Mediator" (*Constitution on the Church*, no. 62).

The Council also set forth an official explanation of the meaning of this title:

"In fact, no creature can ever be compared with the Incarnate Word and Redeemer. However, just as the priesthood of Christ is shared in various ways both by the sacred ministers and by the faithful and as God's unique goodness is communicated to his creatures in various ways, so also the unique mediation of the Redeemer does not exclude but rather gives rise among creatures to a manifold cooperation that is but a sharing in this unique source.

"The Church does not hesitate to profess this subordinate role of Mary" (Ibid.).

Indeed, the Church utilizes the title in the new Litany of the Blessed Virgin that forms part of the *Order of Crowning an Image of the Blessed Virgin Mary*: "Advocate of Grace."

Thus, Mary, besides testifying to our ultimate future with Christ, cooperates to bring it into effect in us. In relation to us, who are enmeshed in the weaknesses of the world, she is constituted as an intercessor.

All-powerful Advocate

The Saints go so far as to regard Mary as an *all-powerful* Advocate, but they are very careful to indicate what they mean by this.

Since the power of a son and that of a mother are the same, a mother is made all-powerful by an all-powerful son. Thus, Jesus, who is all-powerful, has also made Mary all-powerful. However, it is always true that, while Jesus is all-powerful by nature, Mary is all-powerful only by grace.

St. Bernard (d. 1153) stated that the Eternal Father, wishing to show all the mercy possible, besides giving us Jesus as our principal Advocate with him, also gave us Mary as our Advocate with Jesus:

Advocate of Grace

"There is no doubt that Jesus is the only Mediator of justice between human beings and God. By virtue of his merits and promises, he can and will obtain for us pardon and Divine favors.

"But because human beings recognize in him the majesty of God, since he is God, and because they fear his Divine Majesty, it was necessary to assign us another Advocate to whom we can appeal with less fear and more confidence. This Advocate is Mary."

We can always have recourse to Mary with confidence, for she will defend us! In the words of St. Thomas of Villanova (d. 1555):

"This great Mother, who is the Mother of your God and Judge, is also the Advocate for the whole human race. Moreover, she is the proper person for this office, because she can do with God whatever she wills.

"Mary is all-wise, for she understands all the ways to appease God. And her solicitude is really universal, in the sense that she welcomes everybody and refuses to defend no one."

St. Louis Grignion de Montfort (d. 1716) added:

"St. Bernard strongly recommended to those he was guiding along the way of perfection: 'When you want to offer something to God, to be accepted by him, make sure to offer it through the worthy Mother of God if you do not want to see it rejected.'

"Human nature suggests this way of proceeding to those who are less important in the world with respect to the great. Why should grace not do likewise with respect to God! He is infinitely exalted above us. We are less than atoms in his sight. But we have such a powerful Advocate that she is never refused anything.

"Mary is so resourceful that she knows every secret way to win the heart of God. She is so good and kind that she never bypasses anyone — not even the lowest and most sinful."

The Saint goes on to exhort the faithful to know, love, and honor Mary more and more. If they do so, "they will have recourse to her in all circumstances as their Advocate and Mediatrix with Jesus. They will see clearly that she is the safest, easiest, shortest, and most perfect way of approaching Jesus and will surrender themselves to her, body and soul, without reserve in order to belong entirely to Jesus."

Application to Us

Most Catholics have become imbued with the knowledge of Mary as our Advocate from the time when we learned the *Hail Mary* as children. We are keenly aware of Mary's advocacy of grace: "Pray for us now and at the hour of our death."

At the same time, familiarity with frequently uttered invocations to Mary reinforced our belief in her as our powerful Advocate: "Mary conceived without original sin, pray for us who have recourse to you"; "Pray for us, O holy Mother of God, that we may be made worthy of the promises of Christ."

For most of us, Mary is *the* Advocate with her Son. She is regarded as the best of humankind, the one who knows our lives through and through. Even though we believe Jesus was human, we do not feel this same confidence from his likeness to us in all things human (except sin).

It just seems easier to have recourse to the Lady of Sorrows who shared our afflictions in this valley of tears. When our end is near, we know she will be our Advocate of grace to save us from temptations of all kinds and lead us to our heavenly home.

Prayer to Mary Our Advocate

> O blessed Lady, you found grace,
> brought forth the Life,
> and became the Mother of salvation.
> May you obtain the grace for us to go to the Son.
> By your mediation,
> may we be received by the One
> who through you gave himself to us.
>
> May your integrity compensate with him
> for the fault of our corruption;
> and may your humility, which is pleasing to God,
> implore pardon for our vanity.
> May your great charity cover the multitude
> of our sins;
> and may your glorious fecundity confer on us
> a fecundity of merits.

2

Associate of the Redeemer

A Modern Term

The term "associate" is a modern one. It was used by Pope Pius XII in place of the word *Coredemptrix*: "[Mary is] the noble Associate of the Divine Redeemer" (Apostolic Constitution *Munificentissimus Deus* ["Most Munificent God"] defining the Dogma of the Assumption).

The title *Coredemptrix* originated in the fourteenth century and has been used by Catholic bishops, theologians, and spiritual writers ever since. However, in recent times the Church seems to have shied away from its use, preferring to substitute the title "Associate."

Together with Christ (*although in complete subordination to him and by reason of his power*), Mary atoned or satisfied for the sins of the human race, merited every grace for the salvation of all human beings, and united herself with the Redeemer's sacrifice on Calvary to satisfy God's justice.

By reason of this joint operation of Son and Mother, God canceled the debt of all human beings and took them back into his friendship that had been lost by sin.

Based on the Bible

This Marian title is based on Scripture. The Old Testament has a recurring theme about a Woman close to the Messiah. The noted Scripture scholar F.M. Braun has stated: "For [Isaiah] and the Yahwist, the Savior and the Woman called to give birth are closely united: they form the predestined group on which the hope of salvation rests."

In addition, the Old Testament scholar and Mariologist Henri Cazelles, after studying the mother figure in the patriarchal society and kingly tradition, concluded: "Mary is the Associate of her Son born of God, in his earthly birth, in his royal governance, and in his glory."

Indeed, Mary was associated with Christ from the beginning of his saving event until Calvary and the Resurrection. With her explicit "Let it be done" (*Fiat*) at the Incarnation of the Son of God and with her implicit "Let it be done" on Calvary, she consented to her Son's saving sacrifice.

Hence, our Lady was associated in the Redemption wrought by Christ basically through her consent, as the noted Marian scholar René Laurentin has said: "At the Cross as at the Annunciation, Mary's activity is essentially a *consent* in which her faith and love are committed. At the Incarnation, the consent is a consent to life, the human life that she gives her Son. In the Redemption, her consent is a consent to death, the human death that Christ was to undergo (Luke 24:46) to save the world.

"But these two consents are in reality only one: the consent of the Incarnation, which unconditionally and irrevocably concerned everything that would be involved."

A Title Not Usually Found among the Fathers

Although there are hints of this title in St. Augustine, it was not one found in the Fathers of the Church. It was only in the eighth century that the title was explicitly stated by Ambrose Autpert — and then only in verb form, not as a noun.

The first one to use this title as a noun was Ekbert of Schonau in that same eighth century: "[Mary,] the Lord is with you, assisting you in all things, uniting you to himself as an Associate, completing with and in you the work of the redemptive Incarnation, which cannot be accomplished without him, nor fittingly so without you."

But it was in the works of the so-called Pseudo-Albert (an unknown writer of the thirteenth century) — once thought to have been written by St. Albert the Great — that the title was fleshed out:

"The Blessed Virgin was not a vicar but a helper and Associate, sharing in the Kingdom as she shared in the sufferings for the human race when, as all the ministers and disciples fled, she stood alone beneath the Cross and received in her heart the wounds that Christ received in his body, so that a sword pierced her soul."

From that time on, the title was used in one way or another but was never really prominent until the twentieth century.

In the sixteenth century, St. Thomas of Villanova called Mary Christ's "partner": "How faithfully she stands by to help her Son, how steadfastly she bears the torment with him! Not so did even his beloved Apostles support him, for they were not given as partners to the new Adam as was the new Eve.

"God said, 'Let us make him a helper fit for him' (Genesis 2:18): fit for him by her purity, her virginity, her innocence and freedom from sin; a helper like himself in poverty, in humility, and in suffering; like him by her immaculate conception, his *partner* by grace and now his *partner* in glory."

In the twentieth century, the world-renowned Scripture scholar Ferdinand Prat wrote: "Simeon's prophecy [see Luke 2: 34-35] intimately associates the sorrows of Mary with the persecutions which her Son is to undergo. The passion of Jesus and the compassion of Mary always go hand in hand and reach their peak on Calvary.

"Mary's sorrows will be solely or principally caused by the sufferings of Jesus, while the most excruciating torment of Jesus will be to see his Mother's anguish at the foot of the Cross. Jesus saves the world by his sufferings; Mary is to be *associated* in the work of redemption by the sword that pierces her heart."

Favored by Vatican II

Pius XII stated that Mary cooperated in our Redemption "in such a way that our salvation flowed from the love of Jesus Christ and his sufferings intimately united with the love and sorrows of his Mother..." (*Acta Apostolicae Sedis*, no. 48, p. 352).

The Second Vatican Council used this title as a substitute for Coredemptrix:

"The Blessed Virgin ... was on earth the loving Mother of the Divine Redeemer, and above everyone else and in a unique fashion the generous *Associate* and humble Handmaid of the Lord.

"Mary conceived, brought forth, and nourished Christ. She presented him to the Father in the Temple and was united with him in suffering as he died on the Cross. In this completely special manner, she cooperated in the Savior's work by her obedience, faith, hope, and ardent love in restoring supernatural life to souls. Accordingly, she is our Mother in the order of grace" (*Constitution on the Church*, no. 61).

This text sets forth three important points about Mary as Associate. (1) She cooperated *in a special way* in the work of the Redeemer. (2) She was not a mere passive instrument in God's hands but cooperated in the salvation of the world *with free faith and obedience*. (3) She is truly the *Mother of the members of Christ* because she cooperated with Christ in the birth of the faithful in the Church, who are members of Christ her Head.

In short, Mary is actively associated with Christ the Redeemer in the work of salvation of the world in a *universal, integral, and completely dependent manner.*

Universal Association

Mary's association with Jesus is universal in time, extending throughout the whole History of Salvation from the "Gospel before the Gospel" in Genesis (3:15) to the Second Coming announced in the Book of Revelation (22:7). She is essentially united with her Son by force of her physical Motherhood for the grand purpose of the Redemption:

"Redeemed in an especially sublime manner, in consideration of the merits of her Son, and united with him in a close and indissoluble bond, she is endowed with the high office and dignity of Mother of the Son of God" (*Constitution on the Church*, no. 53).

This statement of the Council stresses the basis for Mary's collaboration in the redemptive work of her Son: she is above all one of the redeemed. And as such she is associated with the redemptive work in the name of the redeemed.

Even though Mary's role was not strictly speaking necessary for salvation, it was a real role for the realization of the redemptive sacrifice. She freely participated in the Divine Plan of salvation.

Mary took part in the Mysteries of the Infancy: virginal conception, visitation to Elizabeth, birth of Jesus, presentation in the Temple, and finding of Jesus in the Temple. She also took part in the Mysteries of Christ's Public Life: marriage feast at Cana, life of miracles and preaching, and Calvary.

Such an association continued at Pentecost when our Lady prayed for the coming of the Spirit, who had already overshadowed her in the Annunciation. And it still continues with her glorious Assumption and her life in heaven. Assumed into heaven, she did not set aside this saving role, but by her manifold acts of intercession she continues to win for human beings gifts of eternal salvation.

Integral and Dependent Association

Mary's association is *integral*. She participates in the salvation of all the redeemed and for the whole of salvation. She obtains for the faithful the graces of salvation and cooperates with a maternal love in their rebirth and formation.

Our Lady adds her contribution of faith, obedience, prayer, and suffering during her earthly life and now her maternal intercession in her life in heaven.

Finally, Mary's association is *completely obedient to and dependent on Christ*. Her full participation does not alter the fact that Jesus is the sole Redeemer of the world and, first of all, of his Mother. He alone is the incarnate Son of God and he alone died and rose again for our sins.

Mary's maternal duty toward human beings in no way

obscures or diminishes *this unique mediation of Christ* but rather shows its power. All the saving influences of the Blessed Virgin on human beings originate not from some inner necessity but from the Divine pleasure.

These saving influences flow forth from the superabundance of the merits of Christ, rest on his mediation, depend entirely on it, and draw all their powers from it. In no way do they impede union of the faithful with Christ. Rather they foster such a union.

Application to Us

Although the title "Associate of the Redeemer" is a bit vague as to what Mary actually did, it is a title that says something to contemporary people. We think of an *associate* as a person who *works with* another — for example, an associate pastor, associate professor, associate lawyer, associate justice, associate producer.

What distinguishes the associate in each case is that he or she in one way or another takes part in the work of the other.

Thus, we see immediately that as an associate Mary shared in Christ's work of the Redemption. Indeed, she was an integral part of it — in God's plan it was through Mary that Christ would become man and be in a position to redeem humankind.

This title also reminds us that we too can somehow take part in this sharing. With Mary we can be "associates" of Christ every hour of all our days. All we need do is fill them with prayer, conscientious works, and kindness toward all we encounter as well as offer up the trials that each day brings.

In this way we will also be doing what St. Paul the Apostle intimated should be done — making our sufferings fill up the sufferings of Christ: "I rejoice now in the sufferings I bear for your sake; and what is lacking to the sufferings of Christ I fill up in my flesh for his Body, which is the Church" (Colossians 1:24).

Prayer in Honor of Our Lady, Associate of the Redeemer

Blessed are you, O Mary,
Virgin Mother of Christ
and the generous Associate of our Redeemer.
You conceived, bore, and nourished Christ,
you presented him to the Father in the Temple,
and you were united with him in his work,
especially in his Death on the Cross.
You thus cooperated
by your obedience, faith, hope, and love,
in the work of the Savior
in giving back supernatural life to souls.

Help us to share in the Redemption
by uniting our sufferings to those of Christ.
Grant that we may even rejoice in them,
so that we may be filled with joy
when he comes again in glory.

3

Blessed Mother

Development of This Title

One of the favorite titles of Catholics for Mary is "Our Blessed Mother" or "The Blessed Mother." It is used constantly by preachers, teachers, and lay people when speaking of the Mother of Jesus.

In some respects, this title has a strong affinity with the title "Mediatrix." However, in many others, it offers its own special meaning.

In the Fathers of the Church, there are insights that refer to Mary's Spiritual Motherhood (for example, in Sts. Irenaeus, Epiphanius, Ambrose, and Augustine). St. Augustine, for one, wrote in the fourth century:

"According to the body, Mary is Mother only of Christ. But insofar as she carries out the Will of God, she is spiritually sister and mother. Hence, this unique woman is mother and virgin not only in spirit but bodily.... She is really Mother of the members [of Christ's Body] whom we are, because she cooperated by charity so that there might be born in the Church believers, of whom [Christ] is the Head."

And in the eighth century, Ambrose Autpert asks: "If Christ is the Brother of believers, why should she who brought forth Christ not be the Mother of believers?"

However, it was only with the advent of the Middle Ages that this title was developed. At the time of St. Bernard, St. Anselm, and Scholasticism in the eleventh century, almost every theologian makes his own contribution to the belief in Mary's Motherhood of all human beings. As St. Bernard states, "The Mother of God is our Mother!"

It is almost as if Christians *experienced the reality* of Mary's Motherhood before they *defined it* in a logical manner. The presence and action of our Lady upon their lives led inevitably to the picture of her as Spiritual Mother of Christians.

In the twentieth century, the title of Mary our Mother has come to full development spurred on by Popes, theologians, and ordinary faithful, starting with Leo XIII: "Just as we call God Father, so we have the right to call Mary Mother and truly regard her as such."

The Second Vatican Council endorsed this title wholeheartedly: "The Church does not hesitate to profess this subordinate role of Mary. *She experiences it continually and recommends it to the hearts of the faithful,* so that encouraged by this maternal help they may adhere more closely to the Mediator and Savior" (*Constitution on the Church,* no. 62).

"Our Mother"

The word "Mother" has to do with transmission of life and its nurturing. In this case, it refers to our life in Christ — specifically to his Mystical Body, which is the Church. The Head of this Body is Christ, and the faithful are its members.

Another way of saying the same thing is found in the Parable of the Vine and the Branches narrated by Jesus (John 15: 1-10). It clearly shows that the same life links members to the Head (branches to the Vine): "I am the Vine, and you are the

Blessed Mother

branches. Those who remain in me and I in them will bear much fruit, because you can do nothing without me."

The Church, from the earliest days, was regarded as "Mother Church." In time, Mary's relationship to the sons and daughters of the Church also came to be conceived as a maternal one — a Spiritual Motherhood. Mary is *physically* Mother of Christ the Head; hence, she is *spiritually* Mother of the members of Christ.

It was from the Cross that Jesus gave Mary to us as our Mother when he said to the Apostle John (who symbolized us): "Behold your Mother" (John 15:26).

Mary is also the Mother of all human beings because Christ died for all. As the Second Vatican Council indicated, she received the Word of God into her heart and her body at the Angel's announcement and thereby *brought life to the whole world.*

Mary conceived in her heart, with her whole being, before she conceived in her womb. First came her faith and then her Motherhood. By her faith she became the perfect example of what the Gospels mean by "Spiritual Motherhood."

Characteristics of Mary's Motherhood

Some of the characteristics of Mary's Motherhood are the following:

(1) It is in and through service to her Son that Mary, during her life on earth, exercised her maternal activity toward us. The Second Vatican Council gives the extent of Mary's maternal devotion to Jesus personally:

"Embracing the salvific will of God wholeheartedly ... [the Mother of Jesus] consecrated herself totally as the Handmaid of the Lord to the person and work of her Son. In subordination to him and with him, by the grace of Almighty God she served the

Mystery of the Redemption" (*Constitution on the Church*, no. 56).

Moreover, everything she did for Christ and with him concerns us in our life as children of God:

"Mary conceived, brought forth, and nourished Christ. She presented him to the Father in the Temple and was united with him in suffering as he died on the Cross. In this completely special manner, she *cooperated* in the Savior's work by her obedience, faith, hope, and ardent love in *restoring supernatural life to souls*. Accordingly, she is our Mother in the order of grace" (*Constitution on the Church*, no. 61).

(2) Mary continues today to live her Spiritual Motherhood. "Beginning with the consent that she voiced in faith on the day of the Annunciation and that she sustained without vacillating beneath the Cross, this Motherhood of Mary in the economy of grace continues without interruption until the perpetual crowning of all the Elect. Indeed, taken up to heaven ... by her manifold intercession she continues to obtain for us the gifts of eternal salvation" (Ibid., no. 62).

Mary's maternal love leads her to care for "the brothers and sisters of her Son who are still journeying on earth surrounded by dangers and difficulties" (Ibid., no. 62).

(3) The purpose of Mary's maternal activity is to unite us with Christ so completely that each of us may say: "The life I live now is no longer my own; it is Christ living in me" (Galatians 2:20).

Mary's Spiritual Motherhood derives from her Divine Motherhood and is "explained" by it. Her Spiritual Motherhood is like an extension of the Divine because it consists in forming us in Jesus and Jesus in us!

(4) Mary's maternal function toward us is entirely the fruit of Christ's saving action; it flows from it and depends on it in everything.

(5) Mary conceived the Word of God in her heart and flesh

by the power of the Holy Spirit who overshadowed her (Luke 1: 35). And it is by the same power of the Spirit, who is the soul of her soul and life of her life, that she attains the spiritual fruitfulness that makes her our Mother.

"Blessed Mother"

In the Bible, "blessed" is the preferred description of the Mother of Jesus. This designation is evidence of the veneration in which the early Church held her.

The Beatitudes (Matthew 5:1-12) that Jesus pronounced at the beginning of his Sermon on the Mount can help us to understand how the word "blessed" is particularly appropriate when applied to Mary. The qualities they set forth are those that we see in Mary.

The early Church believed in Mary's unique holiness: "All ages to come will call me blessed.... God who is mighty has done great things for me" (Luke 1:48). In her, above all others, was realized Christ's promise, *"Blessed* are those who hear the Word of God and keep it" (Luke 11:28).

The Fathers of the Church called Mary "all holy." She was declared to be "free from all stain of sin," "fashioned by the Holy Spirit into a kind of new substance and a new creature."

St. Sophronius of Jerusalem, who lived in the sixth and seventh centuries, gave a nice summary of why Mary is "blessed":

"Truly, you are blessed among women, for you have changed Eve's curse into a blessing; and Adam, who hitherto lay under a curse, has been blessed because of you.

"Truly, you are blessed among women, for through you the Father's blessing has shone forth on human beings, setting them free of their ancient curse.

"Truly, you are blessed among women, because through you

your forebears have found salvation. For you were to give birth to the Savior who was to win them salvation.

"Truly, you are blessed among women, for without human concurrence you have borne, as your fruit, him who bestows blessings on the whole world and redeems it from the curse that made it sprout only thorns.

"Truly, you are blessed among women, because, though a woman by nature, you will become, in reality, God's Mother. If he whom you are to bear is truly God made flesh, then rightly do we call you God's Mother. For you have truly given birth to God.

"Enclosed within your womb is God himself. He makes his abode in you and comes forth from you like a bridegroom, winning joy for all and bestowing God's light on all."

Vatican II declared that Mary was "enriched from the first instant of her conception with the splendors of a totally unique holiness" (*Constitution on the Church*, no. 56).

Thus, the present title is made up of two of the greatest of Mary's privileges — her Divine Motherhood and her Immaculate Conception.

Application to Us

Cardinal Gabriel-Mary Garrone has said: "We see the providential role this Mother was to play in enabling us to become, in God's sight, the 'little child' from which we are so far removed, and enabling us to say at last 'Our Father.'

"Within us there is a limitless capacity for self-deception and lies. Mary teaches us this difficult humility and childlike simplicity. She forms the heart of a child of God when she forms the heart of her own Son."

As for us, we must be careful not to use the word "Our" without reference to Christ. When we say that Mary is our Mother, we do not mean to deny that she is also the Mother of God.

Indeed, her Motherhood in our regard derives from her Motherhood of Christ, is inserted in that of Christ, and has a bearing on union with Christ. As Vatican II indicated, Mary gave birth to Christ to make him be born and grow in the hearts of the faithful by means of the Church (*Constitution on the Church*, no. 65).

We must also be careful not to use the word "Our" without reference to the Church. Just as it is true that we cannot have God for our Father if we do not have the Church for our Mother, so we cannot have a right attitude toward Mary as our Mother if we separate her from the Church that is her family.

We must not interpret the word "Our" as if Mary belonged exclusively to our group or our Church. The word must signify "of all human beings," so that in Mary every child of hers must become brother or sister to all other human beings in the world.

The word "Our" must lead neither to an excessive trust in Mary nor to an excessive distrust in ourselves. True Motherhood neither impedes action nor takes away personal responsibility. It makes true children and adults.

We must not adopt a spiritualistic interpretation of Mary's maternal function, making it disincarnate from the human and the earthly. Neither should we adopt a sentimental interpretation that fails to harmonize our life with our personal commitment.

This title should tell us that in her present union with the Risen Christ Mary is solicitous for our welfare and desirous that we become even more like Jesus, her firstborn. The Mother of Jesus wishes all her other children to reach that maturity of the fullness of Christ (see Ephesians 4:13; Colossians 1:28).

Prayer to Our Lady, Mother and Teacher

Blessed are you, O Mary,
Mother and Teacher in the Spirit.
You are a Teacher
who keeps the Word of the Lord
in her heart.
You are a Mother
who gently invites us to go up
to the mountain of the Lord,
which is Christ himself.

As our Teacher,
instruct us in the fear of God,
to live by the Spirit of the Gospel,
to look up to you in prayer,
to love God above all things,
to be rapt in contemplation of his Word,
and to serve the needs of others.

As a Mother,
watch over us
and keep us under your protection.
Make us imitate your virtues
and reach our heavenly home with you.

4

Daughter of Zion

A Title Revived by Vatican II

The title "Daughter of Zion" was revived, so to speak, by the Fathers of the Second Vatican Council based on the Christian reading of the Old Testament Books, i.e., their rereading and fuller understanding in the light of the New Testament:

"The Books of the Old Testament describe the History of Salvation and the gradual preparation for the coming of Christ into the world. These primitive documents, as they are read in the Church and understood in the light of further and fuller revelation, bring the figure of a Woman, Mother of the Redeemer, into a gradually clearer light.

"Under this light, the Woman is already prophetically foreshadowed in the promise of victory over the serpent that was given to our first parents after their fall into sin (see Genesis 3:15). Similarly, she is the Virgin who will conceive and bear a son, whose name will be called Emmanuel (see Isaiah 7:14; Micah 5:2-3; Matthew 1:22-23).

"She stands out among the *humble and Poor of the Lord*, who with full confidence hope for and receive salvation from him.

"And finally with her, the exalted *Daughter of Zion*, after a long period of waiting for the promise, the times are fulfilled in her and the new economy is established. All this occurred when the Son of God took a human nature from her so that, in the Mysteries of his flesh, he might set human beings free from sin" (*Constitution on the Church*, no. 55).

The conciliar document gives no Scripture reference, either explicit or implicit, for the relationship between the phrases "humble and Poor of the Lord" and "Daughter of Zion." However, an explanation is provided by Gerard Philips, who played a large role in the formulation of the document:

"None of the two phrases is accompanied by a reference because of the fact that both form a kind of common locus for Old Testament piety. The 'Daughter of Zion,' a type of the chosen people, bears the promise that will be fulfilled in the fullness of time."

The principal promise is that of the Messiah, who is Jesus Christ. The entire economy of the Old Testament speaks of him and is directed toward him — persons, institutions, events: from Adam, Abraham, Moses, and the Servant of the Lord to the Passover lamb, the Prophets, and various types of the Messiah.

And in the Old Testament, in addition to the current that prepares for the Messiah, there is a lesser and parallel current that prepares the Messianic people of the New Covenant. The latter has one of its most characteristic expressions in the Daughter of Zion.

Thus, the Council stresses that our Lady, who undid the sin of Eve by her sinlessness, is by nature the daughter of Adam. She is the true child of Abraham for in *believing* the Angel's message she conceived the Son of God in her womb. She is by descent the branch from the root of Jesse, for she bore the *flower* that is Jesus Christ the Lord.

Daughter of Zion

Based on Old Testament Texts

In the Old Testament, the term "Zion" designated the rock of Jerusalem between the Kidron Valley and the Tyropoean Valley. It appears for the first time in the account of David's conquest of Jerusalem (2 Samuel 5:6-10). It came to be used for all Jerusalem and eventually for all Israel (Isaiah 46:13; Psalm 149:2). Scholars tell us that the term Zion is used 152 times in the Old Testament and except for a single case is always connected with *God's action toward his people*. It is thus at the heart of the History of Salvation.

The phrase "Daughter of Zion" is an example of the usage dear to the Old Testament. Many times in the Poetic Books a region is called by its proper name preceded by the term "daughter": *Daughter of Babylon; Daughter of Tyre; Daughter of Edom.*

This personification sometimes indicates the region or city and at other times its inhabitants. When applied to Jerusalem, it gives us "Daughter of Zion" (Isaiah 10:32; Jeremiah 6:2), "Daughter of Jerusalem" (Isaiah 37:22; Lamentations 2:13; 2 Kings 19:21). In time, because of the centrality of Jerusalem, with the Lord residing in her, it came to designate all Israel.

The phrase "Daughter of Zion" is found first in Micah (1:13; 4:10, 13) and then comes into frequent use. Three texts are especially important: Zephaniah 3:14-17; Joel 2:21-27; and Zechariah 9:9-10. They are all addressed to the "Daughter of Zion," i.e., Israel personified, and have as their object the announcement of the Messianic joy whose most characteristic expression is "Rejoice" followed by the words "Do not fear." For the Lord comes to reside in Zion as King and Savior!

Furthermore, from Micah onward, the phrase "Daughter of Zion" begins to signify not all Israel but a part, a *Remnant* that has been tested and continues to be the bearer of a new hope in the midst of giving birth in sorrow to a liberated people (4:9-10).

Zephaniah (3:12-20) exhorts the Daughter of Zion to rejoice. Jeremiah speaks of a "Daughter of my people" and applies the expression to Jerusalem (4:11).

Alluded to in the New Testament

In the New Testament, Luke and John make use of this theme of the Daughter of Zion and apply it to Mary. In chapter 1:26-35, Luke follows the teachings of the Prophets as he sets forth the Annunciation: (1) everything comes only from God (v. 26); (2) God is with the Daughter of Zion (as he always has been) and active with his omnipotence (v. 35); (3) his activity is in favor of a Davidic Messianism, for the promises of God are without repentance (v. 32); (4) Mary's response to God's invitation as well as his presence and his promises is the source of Messianic joy (v. 28).

John seems to model the episode of Cana (2:1-11) on the central event of the Old Testament — the great theophany at Sinai recounted in chapters 19 and 24 of Exodus. Corresponding to this Exodus event are the computation of the days (John 1: 19—2:12) and the salient word of Mary: "Do whatever [Jesus] tells you" (John 2:6), which corresponds to the pledge of the people of the Covenant: "We will do whatever the Lord has said" (Exodus 19:8; 24:3, 7).

Hence, we are in the presence of an indirect identification of the community of the Exodus with Mary at the beginning of Jesus' ministry. Indeed, the Evangelist has Mary express the profession of faith that the whole community of the chosen people proclaimed one day at Sinai.

The word "Woman" by which Mary is called by Jesus (John 2:4) could have been selected to highlight the personification of ancient Israel that has reached the fullness of time. Even on

Daughter of Zion

the Cross, at the moment when the ingathering of the dispersed children of Israel is taking place (John 11:51-52), the "Woman" is again highlighted, hearing Jesus announce the Mystery of her Spiritual Motherhood of his followers (John 19:25-27). She is the new Zion of the Messianic times who gives birth to a new people. There returns the theme of the motherhood of the Daughter of Zion joyous at Bethlehem and sorrowful on Calvary.

Hence, it is quite evident that the term "Woman" in John represents the equivalent of the "Daughter of Zion" in Luke.

The Daughter of Zion and the Poor of the Lord

As the Daughter of Zion, Mary was the greatest representative of the "Poor of the Lord," the pious Jews from ancient times who believed in the Lord and placed their hope in him alone. Theirs was a "poverty of being," not simply one of money.

They were those of whom the Prophets spoke, the "Remnant," who would remain faithful to the Lord and inherit the promises he had made (Isaiah 6:13; 37:31; Micah 4:6-7).

Thus, Mary was at the head of the New Testament community of the Poor of the Lord that included Zechariah, Elizabeth, the Shepherds at the crib, the afflicted, widows and orphans as opposed to the proud and the self-sufficient who trusted in their own strength and showed no need of the Lord.

These pious ones did not trust in themselves but in the Lord. They knew that just as the Spirit of God worked in the primeval darkness to produce all that exists, so the Lord worked on his "poor" to produce all that is good for them.

It was the Lord who created a *land* for that people by uprooting the inhabitants of Palestine before them. And it was the Lord who gave them the *Law* through Moses. In all these cases, human power would have availed them nothing.

Piety Rooted in the Scriptures

The source of Mary's piety was the Scriptures as is shown by her grand canticle of love and thanksgiving, called the *Magnificat*, which she uttered at the time of her visitation to her cousin Elizabeth in the hill country of Galilee (Luke 1:46-55).

The *Magnificat* is filled with references to the Old Testament (the only Scriptures in Mary's time), especially the Psalms, which were known as the Prayerbook of the Poor of the Lord.

The Psalms do not speak of Mary. They contain no comparable passage to the text of the so-called Protoevangelium of Genesis (3:15):

> *I will put enmity between you and the Woman,*
> *and between your offspring and hers.*
> *He will strike at your head,*
> *while you strike at his heel.*

Neither is there in the Psalms any comparable passage to the text announcing the Virgin Birth in Isaiah (7:14):

> *Therefore, the Lord himself will give you this sign:*
> *the Virgin shall be with child*
> *and give birth to a son,*
> *and shall name him Emmanuel.*

Nevertheless, the Psalms formed the web and woof of Mary's meditation and her prayer. Like many of the Poor of the Lord, Mary knew the Psalms by heart. They were not only in her mind but also in her heart and her innermost being.

By uttering the *Magnificat*, Mary inscribed herself deeply into the traditions of the Psalms. We can say that the Canticle of Mary is the "Christian Psalm" beyond compare.

The Magnificat and the Psalms

The *Magnificat* is closely akin to many of the Psalms by its form. Like all Hebrew poetry, it contains rhythm, which is the recurrence of accented or unaccented syllables at regular intervals. But its outstanding trait is the parallelism symptomatic of all Hebrew poetry — the equal distribution or balance of thought in the various lines of verse.

Synonymous parallelism is the repetition of the same thought with equivalent expressions:

> *My soul proclaims the greatness of the Lord;*
> *my spirit rejoices in God my Savior* (Luke 1:46f).

Antithetic parallelism expresses a thought by contrast with an opposite:

> *The hungry he filled with good things;*
> *the rich he has sent away empty* (Luke 1:53).

Synthetic parallelism occurs when a second line completes the thought of the first by giving a comparison:

> *He has come to the help of his servant Israel*
> *for he has remembered his promise of mercy,*
> *the promise he made to our fathers,*
> *to Abraham and his children forever* (Luke 1:54f).

The *Magnificat* is also like the Psalms in its *inspiration*. It renders praise to God who loves the poor and the lowly and is faithful to his promises.

Even more, this powerful hymn of thanksgiving is like a mosaic of ancient Psalm texts and other Scripture texts, as can be seen from the arrangement given below. We give first the text of the *Magnificat* that is used in the *Liturgy of the Hours* and is that of the International Consultation on English Texts. Next to each part of it — *in italics* — we give the text of the Scripture that each recalls.

The Scriptural Bases of the Magnificat

Magnificat	Psalms and other Scriptures
My soul proclaims the greatness of the Lord,	*(My heart exults in the Lord - 1 Samuel 2:1.)* *(Let my heart rejoice in your salvation;/let me sing of the Lord, "He has been good to me" - Psalm 13:6.)*
my spirit rejoices in God my Savior.	*(I greatly rejoice in the Lord,/and I exult in my God;/for he has clothed me in garments of salvation - Isaiah 61:10.)* *(Glorify the Lord with me;/let us extol his Name together - Psalm 34:4.)*
For he has looked with favor on his lowly servant.	*(O Lord of hosts, look with pity on the misery of your servant - 1 Samuel 1:11.)* *(He will respond to the prayer of the destitute - Psalm 102:18.)* *(He lifts up the poor from the dust - Psalm 113:7.)* *(I will leave a Remnant in your midst,/a people humble and poor - Zephaniah 3:12.)*
From this day all generations will call me blessed:	*(May the Lord Almighty bless you,/forever and ever - Judith 15:10.)* *(I will extol your Name through all generations - Psalm 45:18.)*
the Almighty has done great things for me,	*(You have done great things; O God, who is like you? - Psalm 71:19.)* *(Then they said among the nations,/"The Lord has done great things for them./The Lord has done great things for us;/we are glad" - Psalm 126:2-3.)*
and holy is his Name.	*(He has sent deliverance to his people/and ratified his Covenant forever;/holy and awesome is his Name - Psalm 111:9.)*

Daughter of Zion

He has mercy on those who fear him in every generation.	*(I show kindness to the thousandth generation of those who love me and keep my commandments - Exodus 20:6.)*
	(The Lord proclaims peace to his people and to his faithful ones - Psalm 85:9.)
	(The kindness of the Lord is from eternity/with those who serve him - Psalm 103:17.)
He has shown the strength of his arm.	*(His right arm has won victory for him - Psalm 98:1.)*
	(Behold, the Lord God is coming with might;/his own arm has won him the victory - Isaiah 40:10.)
He has scattered the proud in their conceit.	*(He frustrates the hands of the cunning - Job 5:12.)*
	(With your strong arm you have scattered your foes - Psalm 89:11.)
	(The haughty he knows from a distance - Psalm 138:6.)
He has cast down the mighty from their thrones, and has lifted up the lowly.	*(God is the judge;/he humbles one and exalts another - Psalm 75:8.)*
	(He lifts up the poor from the dust;/he raises the needy from the refuse heap/to make them sit with princes - Psalm 113:7-8.)
He has filled the hungry with good things,	*(He satisfied the thirsty spirit,/and the hungry heart he filled with good things - Psalm 107:9.)*
	(They shall not hunger or thirst - Isaiah 49:10.)
and the rich he has sent away empty.	*(Those who were filled have hired out for bread - 1 Samuel 2:5.)*
	(The great grow poor and suffer hunger/but those who seek the Lord lack no good thing - Psalm 34:11.)
He has come to the help of his servant Israel	*(You, Israel, my servant...,/whom I have taken from the ends of the earth ... /I will strengthen and help you - Isaiah 41:8-10.)*
for he has remembered his promise of mercy,	*(He has revealed his kindness and his faithfulness/ to the house of Israel - Psalm 98:3.)*

	(With an everlasting love have I loved you;/ therefore, with kindness will I draw you to me - Jeremiah 31:3.)
the promise he made to our fathers, to Abraham and his children forever.	*(Through your descendants all the nations of the earth shall invoke blessings on one another - Genesis 22:18.)*
	(The Lord swore to David/a firm oath that he would not withdraw - Psalm 132:11.)

Even a cursory examination of the lines above will indicate how greatly the piety of Mary, the Daughter of Zion, was nurtured by the Old Testament, especially the Psalms. She makes use of expressions that she has repeated in her prayer a thousand times. But she so skillfully weaves them into a Psalm-like prayer that she can be looked upon as an author of a Psalm herself.

Indeed, like the authors of the Psalms, she makes use of prophecy to prophesy her own glory throughout the ages: "From this day all generations will call me blessed." She thus affirms God's extraordinary attention toward her: "The Almighty has done great things for me." As far as she is concerned, she remains a lowly handmaid of the Lord, but she is very aware that the privileges and role he has conferred upon her are incomparable!

God has been pleased to prepare her to be the Mother of the Incarnate Word, who will bring to completion God's saving plan for his people. Henceforth, it is the Incarnation that will reveal — more than any other sign or miracle of God — the holiness of his Name and his great mercy from age to age.

However, Mary stresses that this salvation given by God in Jesus Christ is not automatically inscribed upon each person in the course of human history. It has to be received "humbly" anew from age to age.

Far from thinking only of herself, Mary expands the horizon of her thanksgiving to include the whole People of God. Her canticle is a thoroughly new and original meditation on the history of the People of God and all humanity called to salvation.

By his present action, God is showing himself to be faithful to his promises made to his people in the past. He is thus readying a blissful future for all who are close to him, all who possess the characteristics of the "pray-ers" of the Psalms — all who are the Poor of the Lord!

Meaning of the Title

In the Divine Plan of salvation, God called the Patriarchs, united them to himself in a Covenant of love, established the Law through Moses, raised up the Prophets, and chose David as the king from whose line the Savior of the world was to be born. In foretelling the coming of Christ, the Old Testament gradually brings into clearer focus the figure of a Woman, the Mother of the Redeemer — Mary, the Joy of Israel and the noble Daughter of Zion.

God has constantly revealed a maternal aspect in his people and then in his Church. Hence, the Old Testament is dominated by the great figures of the Mothers of Israel: Sarah, Rebekah, Rachel, Tamar, Judith, Miriam sister of Moses, and the Daughter of Israel.

In Mary, the Daughter of Zion, it is the Messianic community that brings forth the Messiah. In Jesus, who entrusts his disciples to his Mother (John 19:26-27), it is the Messiah who gives his salvation to the new people.

By calling Mary the Daughter of Zion, we signify that she is the most pure realization of the Mystery of the Church, the Church of the Old Testament that prepared for the coming of Christ and the Church of the New Testament that prolongs in time and space the presence of Christ among human beings.

Mary's mission is to be a "pray-er." Through her intercession, asked of God, she becomes a privileged instrument of grace, because the children of God are born not of flesh and blood (John 1:13) but of water and the Spirit (John 3:5). The great revelation of the new times is the Daughter of Zion, Mother of a kingly, priestly, and prophetic people. Mary's privilege and her mission always have Jesus as their goal.

Application to Us

The title "Daughter of Zion" has a great instructive and operative value for us. It is the affirmation of the communality of the Redemption. The Christian community has in Mary more than just a model. It has a relationship of life.

God willed to express his maternal love toward human beings by raising up the Church - Mother in all times. The Daughter of Zion has represented the chosen people's vocation of perennial Motherhood.

Mary is the Mother *in* the community of the last times. She is also the Mother *of* that community. In Mary is realized the promise of the birth of a new people of whom Christ is the Head and Christians are the members.

It is through Mary that Zion has brought forth a new people and has numerous children that their Mother feeds and consoles (Isaiah 66:11-13) thanks to God and his Holy Spirit (Isaiah 61:1). She is Mother of the members of Christ as the Council stated in the *Constitution on the Church* (no. 53).

Every one of us in the Church enjoys the Divine gift, but at the same time we must also participate in the maternal mission of the Church. Every time the Church works, proclaims, celebrates, or sanctifies with the Sacraments, all the members of the Church are involved in it. *Each with his or her own charism and proper function.* This is the continuation of the Daughter of Zion.

Prayer to Our Lady, Daughter of Zion

Blessed are you, O Mary,
Daughter of Zion.
You were chosen by God
as the crown of Israel
and the beginning of the Church
to reveal to all peoples
that salvation is born from Israel
and that the new family of God
springs from a chosen root.

By nature you are the daughter of Adam
who by your sinlessness undid Eve's sin.
By faith you are the true child of Abraham
who first believed and so conceived.
By descent you are the branch
from the root of Jesse
bearing the flower that is Jesus.

Obtain for us
to follow your example
by offering you the homage of our heartfelt faith
and placing in you alone our hope of salvation.

5
Exemplar

The Human Need for Models

History shows that human beings have a real need for models on whom to pattern their lives. Most peoples have a number of models of life who are handed down through epic accounts, songs, images, popular sayings, and the like.

Such models vary according to a particular era, culture, or socio-cultural situation, but they are ever present. Life models run the gamut from exceptionally gifted persons to divinized ancient forebears or ideal personages endowed with qualities that people desire to possess. And they are kept before the people by philosophy, literature, the arts, and the other means of communication.

In addition, new models are always being sought in order to replace those that get old by going out of fashion or out of favor. This increases the need for those who work for the betterment of human beings to come up with more relevant models, i.e., those that respond to the needs of modern-day people.

At the same time, every religion has models of its own that it offers its adherents to help them get in touch with God. Some such models may be priests or ministers or founders of a religious school or heads of a movement. In the case of families, the prime models are the parents or forebears.

Christian Models

It is no surprise then, that the Christian religion also has its models. First of all, Christians are urged to take God as their model of perfection by Christ himself: "Be perfect because your heavenly Father is perfect" (Matthew 5:48). Going further, Christ indicates how God is to be imitated: "Love your enemies and pray for your persecutors so that you may be children of your heavenly Father" (Matthew 5:44-45).

In Leviticus (11:44), the Lord himself tells the priests to take him as a model of holiness: "Sanctify yourselves, therefore, and be holy because I, the Lord your God, am holy." Then Jesus extends to everyone the Father's command to the priests: "Be merciful, as your Father is merciful" (Luke 6:36). Later, St. Peter puts it even more broadly: "In the image of the Holy One who has called you, become holy yourselves in your whole conduct" (1 Peter 1:14).

In addition to his coming on earth to introduce us to the Father, to speak about him and show us his countenance, Jesus came to help us be children of God through imitating the Father. In order to bring this about, he who is the image of the invisible God, begotten before every creature (Colossians 1:15), became man in order that humans might be conformed to himself inasmuch as he is the perfect image of the Father (Romans 8:29; Colossians 3:10).

Thus, Christ addresses himself to the believers and says: "Learn from me" (Matthew 11:29), and again: "I have given you an example so that as I have done you also may do" (John 13:15); "Love one another as I have loved you" (John 15:12).

To be a Christian means to follow Christ, to be like him, to imitate him, to put on his sentiments and his will, in accord with what God himself said when he uttered the words: "This is my beloved Son; hear him!" (Mark 9:7).

Accordingly, every Christian who reflects Christ bears the image of God into the world and becomes at the same time a model for his brothers and sisters — as St. Paul says: "All of us, with faces unveiled and reflecting as in a mirror the glory of the Lord, are being transformed into his very image from glory to glory, in accord with the action of the Spirit of the Lord" (2 Corinthians 3:18).

That is why Paul dares to say to his Christian converts "I exhort you to become imitators of me as I am of Christ" (1 Corinthians 4:16). And Peter directs the attention of the first Christian community to the need for behavior that is worthy of the vocation one has, because in it the light of Christ is reflected and becomes visible (2 Peter 1:3-11).

Mary as a Singular Model

Thus, all Christians are called to be models realizing in themselves their vocation. Indeed, Paul and Peter recommend to Timothy (1 Timothy 4:12) and to the elders (1 Peter 5:3) that they should become models for their flock. It was only natural, then, for the first Christians to turn to Mary as a model for them (as it was later for them to turn to the Saints, especially the martyrs: "For our own greater good and that of the whole Church, we seek from the Saints *example in their way of life*, fellowship in their communion, and aid by their intercession'" — Vatican II: *Constitution on the Church*, no. 50).

Meditating on the Infancy Gospels, in which the Mother of Jesus plays a huge role, they saw in Mary the exceptional riches of holiness: the image of the Father becomes, in her, fullness of grace and greatness of gifts. They discerned in Mary not only the physical countenance of the Lord, her Son, but the spiritual one too. As the first among believers, the first of the saved, and a member of the Church, Mary participates in Christ's saving mission maternally as a model.

Indeed, Mary was faithful to the Lord God as were her forebears, faithful to the laws of the Jewish community in which she lived, faithful to the demands of the Father's Will and to those of her motherhood toward her Son. She thus was present and available at Bethlehem, in the Temple, at Nazareth, at Cana, beneath the Cross, and in the Upper Room — saying with her whole life, "Do whatever he tells you" (John 2:5). And Christ shows her and gives her as Mother to all Christians of all times (John 19:26-27).

Meaning of "Model" in This Case

The Second Vatican Council described Mary as a type and most excellent exemplar of the Church in the order of faith, charity, and perfect union with Christ (*Constitution on the Church*, no. 63). Indeed, since she is "the first and perfect disciple of Christ" (Paul VI: *Marialis Cultus*, no. 35), Mary can also be proposed as a model to be imitated by all!

However, Mary is not a "model" for Christians in the sense that we should try to imitate her literally in every detail of her life. Rather, Mary is the "pattern" or "archetype" for the whole Church and for every one of the faithful because of the perfection of her personal response of faith, hope, and love to the Lord's call.

By reason of the perfect and unique character of her response to the Lord, Mary is an exemplar for all — in the words of Paul VI, "a permanent and universal exemplary value" (*Marialis Cultus*, no. 33). At the same time, by her Spiritual Motherhood, she also has each of us for her children, who can and should live their filial relationship to her in a personal manner.

Imitation of Mary

The Second Vatican Council also stated: "[True devotion to Mary] proceeds from true faith that leads us to recognize the preeminence of the Mother of God, and inspires us to have a filial love toward our Mother and to imitate her virtues" (*Constitution on the Church*, no. 67).

In doing so, the Council was merely following the exhortation of the Popes of the twentieth century, especially Paul VI, who in his Apostolic Exhortation *Signum Magnum* ("The Great Sign") declared:

"Neither the grace of the Divine Redeemer, nor the powerful intercession of his Mother and our Spiritual Mother, nor yet her sublime sanctity could lead us to the port of salvation if we did not respond to them by our persevering will to honor Jesus Christ and the Holy Virgin with our devout imitation of their sublime virtue. It is therefore the duty of all Christians to imitate, in a reverent spirit, the examples of goodness left to them by their heavenly Mother" (nos. 14-15).

What the Church is telling us to do is to take Mary as our Model, to follow her example. This does not mean that we are to copy externals from her (such as physical posture, speech, or gestures) or to adopt her thoughts, opinions, likes, and dislikes.

Rather, it means that we must imitate Mary *in her virtues*, especially her faith, her charity, her humility, her docility to the Holy Spirit, her love for Jesus, and her union with him.

Hence, exemplarity means yielding our lives to Mary's actions as Mother and teacher, placing ourselves under her direction. We say to her: "Teach us to believe, to love, to be united with Jesus as you were. Form us to resemble your Son."

In doing so, we open ourselves to the Holy Spirit. The more we are united with Mary in our efforts to imitate her, the more we are also disposed to the action of the Spirit upon us. And by him we are made to grow in faith and Divine charity and are filled with the mind of Jesus himself, our first and primary Model.

Model of the Church

As mentioned above, Mary is the archetype of the Church. What this means is that something of Mary's holiness is spread abroad in the Church by the Holy Spirit and is diffused into our hearts so that we may live according to the Gospel and build up the Body of Christ on earth.

Some of the characteristics of Mary's exemplarity toward the Church are as follows.

(1) *Attentive faith.* Mary received the Word of God with faith (Luke 1:26-38). This factor was the basis of all her actions as well as her prerogatives and privileges. The same thing is done by the Church especially in the Liturgy.

With faith, the Church accepts, proclaims, and venerates the Word of God and distributes it to the faithful as the bread of life. Then in the light of that Word, she examines the signs of the times and interprets and lives the events of history.

(2) *Prayer.* Mary prayed during her visit to Elizabeth when she recited the *Magnificat* (Luke 1:46-55), at Cana when she informed her Son of the bridal couple's need of wine (John 2:1-12), and before the coming of the Holy Spirit when she meditated with the Apostles in the Upper Room (Acts 1:14). The Church also prays, day after day, presenting to the Father the needs of her children and praising the Lord unceasingly (*Constitution on the Sacred Liturgy,* no. 83).

(3) *Virgin-Mother.* Mary became a Mother without human help but solely by the power of the Holy Spirit (Luke 1:35). This was a miraculous Motherhood, established by God as the exemplar of the fruitfulness of the Virgin-Church. The Church

herself becomes a mother by the power of God in bringing forth children to the spiritual life through Baptism.

(4) *Gift-offering.* Mary offered Jesus to the Father in the Temple (Luke 2:22-25) and on Calvary (John 19:25). The Church offers the Eucharistic Sacrifice of Christ's Death and Resurrection every day down through the ages.

Model of Christians

The Church is one, the one People of God. But she is also a community of persons, a plurality of individuals. Mary is the Model also of every one of the disciples of Christ her Son.

In this sense, there are many ways to imitate her, depending on the ways in which people differ. And every person is in the final analysis the judge of the validity of the specific ways of imitation he or she follows.

We can, however, identify general areas of this imitation of Mary by individuals.

(1) *Allowing oneself to be loved by God.* Although Christians are all aware of the first commandment cited by Christ — to love God (Matthew 22:37) — they are usually not aware of the reverse side of that commandment — to allow oneself to be loved by God. It flows from the Revelation that God is love (1 John 4:16).

Indeed, to allow oneself to be loved by God is the origin and the foundation of holiness. To let oneself be loved by God in imitation of Mary means to accept his gifts, to entrust oneself to his guidance, to know how to thank him, and to create one's own *Magnificat,* one's own "Alleluia" — offering praise for the great things God has done for us.

(2) *Obeying with intelligence.* Christians are to obey God — but with intelligence, as Mary did. She desired clarification

before giving her consent (Luke 1:30). This way of acting indicates God's respect for the human creature and signals a quality of behavior of human beings toward God.

True obedience entails watchful presence and lucid attention, that is, intelligence. Like Mary, Christians are to aim for a very personal and intelligent obedience.

(3) *Listening with one's whole heart.* Christians are to be people who listen just as Mary is the Virgin who listens. In addition, they must listen with their whole heart, meditating on the words they hear. Such listening entails defense of the word heard, discernment in sifting through messages, patience in incomprehension, and protective silence.

(4) *Persevering in faithfulness.* Like the Servant of the Lord and the disciples of Christ, Mary persevered in the pilgrim journey of faith. Christians are to imitate this perseverance in faith.

This involves a global fidelity: toward God, toward oneself, and toward one's proper role, toward other persons, toward all of creation.

(5) *Serving those who should be served.* Mary calls herself the servant of the Lord. The Gospel idea of service is putting one's talents to use in the service of God and others.

It means recognizing at each moment those who should be served, familiarity with the Spirit, and carrying out the service necessary.

(6) *Remaining close to the Cross.* Mary had her joys in life, but she also had her sorrows, culminating in the sorrow at the foot of the Cross (John 19:25-27). Christians are to stand beneath the infinite crosses on which the Son of Man is suspended in his brothers and sisters.

Application to Us

Mary is not only an exemplar for the whole Church in the exercise of this worship but also a teacher of the spiritual life for all of us. She is an example of the worship that consists in making one's life an offering to God. This is an ancient and ever new doctrine that each of us can hear again by heeding the Church's teaching and by meditating on Mary's "Yes" to God: "Let it be done to me according to your word" (Luke 1:38). For that "Yes" is a lesson of obedience to the Will of the Father, which is the way and means of our sanctification.

In our resolve to live as adherents of God and disciples of Christ, we need not have the slightest hesitation to seek an example in Mary. For she was a woman of her time and social environment, fully engaged in the temporal affairs that fell to her and perfectly ordering them according to God's plan.

From Mary, we can learn or learn better that by carrying out our daily tasks as a "service" committed to us by the Lord, we are already in the process of fulfilling the apostolic mission that is ours in virtue of our Baptism.

We can and should count on Mary for help in making all our activities more Christian and fruitful. Having been assumed into heaven, with her maternal charity, Mary cares for the brothers and sisters of her Son who are still on their earthly pilgrimage before being led into their happy homeland. We should devoutly venerate her and commend our lives and apostolates to her maternal care.

In the final analysis, the Christian life is the life of Christ in us. If we are to adapt to it and let it transform us, we have to begin with the actual circumstances of our existence. To a certain extent, the particular aspect in which we view our Lord or our Lady at any given moment is conditioned by the situation of the moment.

In time of trial or mourning, we can turn to Christ and Mary on Calvary. In time of joy, we can make our own Mary's *Magnificat*. Young people considering their vocation can turn to Mary in her exceptional Motherhood, in her life in the home at Nazareth. Widows can think of Mary's situation after the death of Joseph. The elderly can focus on Mary as she finished her life on earth and looked forward to going home to the Father's house.

Those who are entrusted with apostolic responsibility by canonical life find a marvelous example of openness to God's grace in Mary, who under the guidance of the Holy Spirit dedicated herself completely to the Mystery of the Redemption of human beings.

Those who strive for holiness or are committed to service of others — missionaries, future ministers, priests, religious, and lay people — can draw inspiration from Mary's total and free adherence to God in order to live their own vocation in strict coherence with the faith.

These resemblances between our life and Mary's, however, are always partial. They are not the principal reason that she is the Exemplar for all age groups and all situations. The reason is that in every circumstance we can find help and support in her unlimited goodness — for she is the woman whom God himself was pleased to give us for our Mother.

We might conclude with the words of Cardinal Michele Pellegrino citing St. Augustine:

"How can all the faithful imitate Mary as Mother and Virgin? Again, in the words of St. Augustine: 'Do in the depths of your heart what you marvel at in her flesh. Those who believe with their hearts and are justified conceive Christ; those who confess him with their mouths and are saved give birth to Christ. Let your souls, then, be abundantly fruitful and persevere in virginity.' All the faithful can, like Mary, become mothers of Jesus by doing the Will of his Father."

Exemplar

Prayer to Our Lady, Exemplar of Christians

*Dear Mary,
you are the Exemplar of virtues
for the whole company of the Elect.
Model of sublime love,
teach us love for God and others.
Model of faith and hope,
grant that we may be filled with fervent faith
and strengthened by the hope of future glory.*

*Model of humility,
help us to be what we are in God's sight.
Model of persevering prayer,
enable us to pray with our fellow Christians
in union of mind and heart.
Model of worship in spirit,
teach us to offer ourselves as a holy victim
pleasing in God's eyes.*

6

Handmaid of the Lord

A Title Mary Applied to Herself

The title "Handmaid" or "Servant" is the one Mary applied to herself at the Annunciation: "I am the handmaid of the Lord" (Luke 1:38), and at the Visitation: "He has looked upon his handmaid in her lowliness" (Luke 1:48).

This is also one of the titles that the Second Vatican Council applied to our Lady:

"Thus Mary, the daughter of Adam, consents to the Divine Word and becomes the Mother of Jesus. Embracing the salvific Will of God wholeheartedly and impeded by no sin, she consecrated herself totally as the *Handmaid of the Lord* to the person and work of her Son. In subordination to him and with him, by the grace of Almighty God she served the Mystery of the Redemption" (*Constitution on the Church,* no. 56).

"Servant" in the Old Testament

The Greek term used in the Gospel, *doulé,* is the feminine form of a common Old Testament designation for "slave" or "servant." It expresses a well-defined concept that is rooted in the experience of slavery in Egypt and Babylonia (Exodus 13:3,

14; 14:5; 20:2; Leviticus 25:38; Deuteronomy 15:12ff; Ezra 9: 6ff; Zechariah 10:6-12).

Slavery in Israel, especially in the case of Israelite slaves (Exodus 21:2), was regulated by precise norms. The slave was at the disposal of the master *only for work*, but the slave's personal dignity was safeguarded (Exodus 21:2-11; Leviticus 25:39ff; Deuteronomy 15:12ff).

Those who were "servants" acknowledged the power of the one over them; this acknowledgment extended from the viceroy who was the "servant" of the king to the last of his subjects.

Thus, the term "servant" takes on the aspect of an honorific title and is conferred on eminent personages who have had a decisive role in the common good and have placed themselves at the service of others even though free themselves.

Examples of this type are the titles "servant of God" given to Moses, David, and the Prophets. At the same time, the Psalmist, acknowledging that he has received a gift from God, calls himself the "servant of God."

Hence, between God and his servant an indefinable but real relationship is established. In this way, the concept of submission expressed by the word "servant" loses its connotation of *indignity* and acquires a connotation of *affinity*.

"Servant" in the New Testament

The writers of the New Testament who make use of the word or theme of servant are concerned with a theological teaching more than a social one. They wish to show that the type of slavery from which human beings have been freed by God's revelation in Christ is the root of all slavery.

They envision a *voluntary* servitude-slavery, lived first by Christ and then by those who freely chose to follow him. Thus,

Paul regards himself as an Apostle called in a special way to be the "servant of Christ Jesus" (Romans 1:1; Philippians 1:1; Galatians 1:10), and he applies the same epithet to his coworker Epaphras (Colossians 4:12).

In this case, the meaning of "servant" is close to that of "minister," which has the connotation of testimony rendered to Christ (Colossians 4:7). The common meaning of subordination and dependence is modified somewhat by the introduction of the notions of freedom and love that have determined the choice. Called to Christian freedom so as to give himself to the service of his brothers and sisters (Galatians 5:13), Paul has become the "servant of all" (1 Corinthians 9:19) and servant of the Church out of love for Christ (2 Corinthians 4:5).

The servant par excellence of this type is seen in the Letter to the Philippians (2:7) when Paul exalts the theological notion of service (set forth in the Songs of the Servant of Yahweh — Isaiah 42–53) in its twofold aspect: (1) renunciation on the part of Christ of his equality with God in the work of salvation and (2) his acceptance of solidarity with humankind, the servant of sin, in a position of dependence on the Law (Galatians 4:4; 3:13).

Even though assimilated to the condition of a servant, Christ was uncontaminated by sin and free under both the social and the theological aspect, keeping intact his inner spiritual freedom. Hence, servanthood in this sense stresses the free choice of the service rendered to God and to others.

Mary, Servant of the Lord

Scholars tell us that Luke 1:38 vaguely recalls First Samuel 25:41 where Abigail registers her accessibility to become the spouse of David: "Behold, your maidservant who is ready to serve you and to wash the feet of my master's servants!" It also recalls First Samuel 1:11 where Hannah begs God to take her affliction into consideration: "O Lord ... look with pity upon your servant's misery."

While recalling these two dimensions, the Lucan passage also echoes the great moments of the People of God — those moments when the assemblies of the chosen people ratified the terms of the Covenant offered to them by God (Exodus 24:7; 2 Kings 23:1-3; Ezra 10:12; Nehemiah 10:1, 29ff).

Thus, Mary has a role analogous to that of the People of God, when at the foot of the sacred mountain they receive the tablets of the Law and promise to observe them (Exodus 24:3, 7). Then at Cana Mary re-proposes this scenario by urging the servants to do whatever Jesus tells them (John 2:5).

In her own life, Mary exhibits constant and total openness to whatever God desires of her. It was her desire to do the Will of the Most High in every personal encounter, in every action accomplished, just as it was the desire of the Son who came to do his Father's Will (John 8:29; see Hebrews 10:7).

For the Council, this Marian title conserves the psychological and spiritual characteristic of the "Servant of the Lord" of the Old Testament. Mary, although called and sanctified by God, was not purely passive in the hands of God. She expressed her consent freely and conscientiously to the entire Divine Plan.

That is why St. Bernard of Clairvaux can, as it were, plead with Mary at the moment of the Annunciation to give her consent without delay:

"O happy Virgin, open your heart to faith, open your lips to consent, open your bosom to the Creator. Behold, the Desired of All Nations is standing outside and knocking at your door. Oh, if he should pass on while you delay to open, then you would have to begin once more to seek with sorrow him whom your soul loves. Arise, therefore, and make haste to open to him. Arise by faith, make haste by devotion, open by consent."

Indeed, by her consent Mary committed herself responsibly in a joyous and sorrowful service of the person and work of her Son, consecrating herself totally with him and under him to the service of the Mystery of salvation and redemption. Even more, she lived her mission of service with faith and obedience, thanksgiving and suffering.

Jesus, Servant of the Lord

It is evident that to understand fully the meaning of Mary's title as Handmaid of the Lord, we must read it in the light of the above-mentioned "Songs of the Servant of the Lord" and above all in the light of Jesus as the one who fulfills the figure of the "Servant of the Lord": he "did not come to be served, but to serve, and to give his life as a ransom for the many" (Mark 10:45).

There is little doubt that Jesus saw the Songs as the program of his own mission. However, he introduced an important innovation into the prophecy. He changed the title "Servant of the Lord" to that of "Son of Man."

This enables the future glorious condition of the Servant to be better defined. At the same time, the glory and dominion of the Son of Man shine forth as the fruit of his obedience in love unto death.

Thus, the mission of the Servant is that of Jesus: a master meek and humble of heart (Matthew 11:29) who announces salvation to the poor (Luke 4:18-19). He is in the midst of his disciples as one who serves (Luke 22:27), although he is their Lord and Master (John 13:12-15). Indeed, he goes to the very limits of the demands of his love that inspires this service (John 13:1; 15:13) by giving his life for the redemption of the many (Mark 10:43ff; Matthew 20:26ff).

Treated like a criminal (Luke 22:37), he dies on the Cross

(Mark 14:24; Matthew 27:50), knowing that he will rise again, as it is written of the Servant = Son of Man (Mark 8:31; 9:31; 10:32-34; Luke 24:44-46; see Isaiah 53:10ff).

The figure of the Servant pervades the whole Public Life of Jesus. The very words of the Father at Jesus' Baptism are, so to speak, the public investiture of Jesus with his Messianic title. They are taken from Isaiah 42:1 (with the slight change of Servant to Son), where the mission of the Servant is announced.

The same thing happens when the Baptist announces that Jesus is the Lamb of God who takes away the sin of the world (John 1:29, 36). The word "Lamb" is substituted for Servant, because the latter was akin to "slave" for the Gentiles and seemed degrading to them.

The apostolic preaching applied the title Servant to Jesus in order to proclaim the Mystery of his death (Acts 3:13-14, 18; 4:27-28), which is the source of blessing and light for all the nations (Acts 3:25-26; 26:23). Jesus is a Lamb unjustly slain like the Servant (Acts 8:32-33) who has saved his lost sheep, and the wounds of his body have healed the souls of sinners (1 Peter 2: 21-25).

The Servant Songs are also implicit in other New Testament passages that use their words or conceptions: 1 Corinthians 15: 3-5, concerning the Passion in the Scriptures; 1 Corinthians 11: 23-25, utilizing the words "for you" and "for many" in the formula of the Eucharist; Romans 8:34 and Philippians 2:6-11, indicating that Jesus took the form of a slave or servant; 1 John 2:2; 3:5; 4: 10, concerning his expiation for our sins; and John 10:11, 15, 17, affirming that Jesus lays down his life.

Finally, Philippians 2:5-11 reproduces a hymn that nicely summarizes the Mystery of Christ and his love. It proclaims that Christ has entered into his glory by taking the condition of a Servant and by dying on the Cross in order to carry out his Father's Will.

Mary's Servant Activity

Enlightened by the Angel and fortified with a comprehension of her coming mission, Mary accepts the power given her by authority of the Spirit to collaborate in the realization of God's message. She accepts the task of serving God's plans to the full, and she puts at God's disposal her womanhood so that "he who is to come" might come (Luke 1:38).

During the whole tenor of her mission, she experienced charity toward God and toward human beings, which led her — in the words of St. Augustine — to conceive the Redeemer first in her heart and then in her body; and she experienced, after a brief moment of Messianic joy, all the sufferings undergone by her Son in union with him even to Calvary.

Mary allows herself to be led and placed at the service of Jesus and his Divine Mission, which goes counter to the views of her world. She accepts all as part of her service. Thus, from the moment of the Angel's greeting at the Annunciation to her Assumption into heaven, Mary's whole life is one of loving service.

During her Son's Infancy and Childhood, Mary diligently rears him, watching over him and ensuring that he will grow in wisdom, age, and grace. She also introduces him into the public worship of the Heavenly Father (Luke 2:41-52). In all this she remains the Handmaid of the Lord.

Then during Christ's Public Life Mary maintains a tactful reserve, remaining deliberately inconspicuous. She surfaces at the wedding feast of Cana (John 2:1ff) and in the incident when in company with other relatives she is said to be seeking her Son (Matthew 12:46-50).

Mary is also brought to mind when the woman in the crowd sings the praises of Christ's Mother for having reared him and

Jesus sings his Mother's greater praises by indicating that she was even more to be praised because she not only heard the Word of God but also practiced it (Luke 11:27-28).

Finally, during the Passion and Resurrection, Mary is present beneath the Cross, suffering with her Son and paying the price of her commitment made at the Annunciation: "I am the handmaid of the Lord. Let it be done to me according to your word" (Luke 1:38).

In this regard, St. Francis de Sales has said of Mary: "She went so far as to see her Son and her God die on the wood of the Cross, remaining firm and standing at the foot of it, submitting herself to the Divine Decree by adhering to the Will of the eternal Father.

"Not by compulsion, but by her own free will, she approved and consented to the death of our Lord. She kissed a hundred thousand times the Cross to which he was attached, she embraced it and adored it. O God! What abnegation is this! It is true that the tender loving heart of this Sorrowful Virgin was transpierced by vehement sorrows."

At the same time, Mary is ready to participate in a new birth, that of the Mystical Body of her Son, the Church. This she does, after Christ's Resurrection, in the Upper Room together with the Apostles and disciples at the coming of the Holy Spirit.

Mary — the Poor of Yahweh par Excellence

As already mentioned in Chapter 4, the Prophets spoke of a Remnant of Israel that would remain faithful and that would inherit the promises of Yahweh (Isaiah 6:13; 37:31f; Micah 4:6-7). Gradually this Remnant became fused with the idea of the *anawim*, "the Poor of Yahweh":

> *In the whole land, says the Lord,*
>   *two thirds will be struck down and perish;*
>   *yet one third will remain....*
> *They will call upon my Name,*
>   *and I will answer them.*
> *I will say, 'They are my people,'*
>   *and they will say, 'The Lord [Yahweh] is our God'"*
>   *(Zechariah 13:8-9).*

The Psalmist reinforces this idea when he says, "The Lord loves his people, and he adorns the lowly [i.e., the *anawim*] with victory" (Psalm 149:4). By New Testament times, this Remnant had become purified of sinful interests and completely open to and dependent upon Yahweh.

Mary's servanthood puts her at the head of the New Testament community of the *anawim* that included Zechariah, Elizabeth, the Shepherds at the manger, the afflicted, widows, and orphans as opposed to the haughty and the self-sufficient who trusted in their own strength and showed no need of Yahweh.

The Blessed Virgin immortalized this adventure in faith by her Hymn of the Poor of Yahweh, the *Magnificat* (Luke 1:46-55). As the embodiment of trust in and receptivity to Yahweh (outstanding qualities of the *anawim*), Mary is the link between the Old and the New Testaments, between the hope and promises of the Old Testament and the fulfillment in the Kingdom of God.

Application to Us

This title highlights Mary's role as a model of all Christians. Each of us is called to be the "servant of the Lord" — by humility, poverty, service to Christ, and courage in following the suffering Lord.

The title handmaid "places Mary among the lowly, the poor, and the sick. It places her at our level — indeed, at the lowest place among us.... Her social status was the most modest one, a woman of the people, we might say. She had no external qualities that distinguished her, even though a royal dynasty had come to an end precisely in her person. She belonged to the vast majority.

"'Handmaid' teaches that we came from God and are subject to him: 'He has looked upon the servant in her lowliness,' he has endowed her with favors and brought her to supreme glory" (Pope Paul VI).

From Mary, under the title of "Handmaid of the Lord," we can learn that by performing our daily tasks in a "service" committed to us by the Lord, we are already in the process of fulfilling the apostolic mission that is ours in virtue of our Baptism. For as the Church has stated:

"The perfect example of this kind of spiritual and apostolic life is the most Blessed Virgin Mary.... While leading the life common to all here on earth, one filled with family concerns and labors, she always remained intimately united with her Son and in a completely unique way cooperated in the work of the Savior" (*Decree on the Apostolate of the Laity,* no. 4).

The power set loose by Mary's consent is all-embracing for the history of the world and for our own history, as is indicated by the Augustinian theologian Ansfried Hulsbosch:

"The creative work of God achieves a breakthrough at a decisive point [the Incarnation] only by means of the consenting receptivity of Mary. Each of us must allow the creative work of God to be completed in the whole of his life, through faith and through love in which faith works. The old self in us must make way for the new self that we shall be, but only by our own consent.

"In Mary the whole world is called to arise to its completion in a new world. She is the voice of the universe looking forward to completion. St. Bernard of Clairvaux expresses this splendidly...: 'With justice are the eyes of all creation bent upon you, for in you and through you and out of you the loving hand of the Most High has newly created everything that he created."

Prayer to Our Lady, Handmaid of the Lord

*Blessed are you, O Mary,
Handmaid of the Lord.
You welcomed the Angel's announcement
and became the Mother of the Word.
In the silence of your heart,
you meditated on the heavenly words
and became a disciple of the Divine Master.*

*Open our hearts
to the blessedness of listening.
By the power of the Holy Spirit,
may we too become a holy place
in which the Word of salvation
is fulfilled today.*

7

Help of Christians

A Title Used from Earliest Times

From the very beginning Catholics have called upon Mary, especially in times of adversity, trials, heresies, persecutions, and wars. The reason is not hard to determine and was spelled out by Pope Leo XIII:

"It has always been the habit of Catholics in danger and in arduous times to fly for refuge to Mary and to seek peace in her maternal goodness, which shows that the Catholic Church has always, and with justice, put all her hope and trust in the Mother of God.

"Associated with her Son in the work of the salvation of the human race, our Lady has favor and power with him greater than any other human or angelic creature has ever obtained or can obtain.

"And, as it is Mary's greatest pleasure to grant her help and comfort to those who seek her, it cannot be doubted that she will deign, even anxiously, to receive the aspirations of the Universal Church" (Encyclical *Supremi Apostolatus* ["The Supreme Apostolic Office"], September 1, 1883).

Hence, it was altogether natural for Mary to be given the title "Help of Christians" by the faithful of every century.

Primitive Appeals to Mary's Help

Already in the first generation of Christians we see the singular honor and devotion accorded to Mary. The Angel of the Incarnation greets her with great respect as "full of grace" (Luke 1:28), and her cousin Elizabeth does likewise by the words "Mother of my Lord" (Luke 1:43).

The early Church attests that the model of the Virgin has become most significant for Christian piety. She does so through the profession of faith, which proclaims Christ as Son of God "born of the Virgin Mary" (this is the second-century formula of the baptismal creed found in the various apocryphal works of the New Testament, e.g., the *Protevangelium of James*). The Church also does so in the Roman funeral monuments of the second/third centuries, e.g., the frescoes in the Priscillian cemetery in which Isaiah is shown pointing with his hand to the Mother of God seated with the Child Jesus in her arms.

The *Apostolic Tradition* of Hippolytus, which exerted a huge influence on the Eastern Liturgies, presents the primitive theme of the Virgin in the first part of the Eucharistic Prayer: "Sent from heaven into the bosom of the Virgin, conceived in her womb, he was made flesh and manifested himself as [God's] Son, born from the Spirit and from the Virgin."

Mary thus finds a place in the Church's thanksgiving because of her connection with the Incarnation of the Son. A bit later, the Virgin, already associated with her Son in the economy of salvation, will find a place with him in the Church's thanksgiving. She will be named before the Apostles in the *Communicantes* (Commemoration of the Saints) of the Roman Canon or after the Prophets in the chronological listing of the Eastern Anaphora. Hence, Mary is on the highest level of the heavenly Church and the first one whose memorial the earthly Church (represented by the Eucharistic Assembly) demands be celebrated.

By the third century, the *Sub Tuum* comes into vogue, the first prayer to the Virgin Mother of God. It is a prayer for help in trials and sin. It stresses Mary's Divine Motherhood, her virginity, her holiness, and her powerful intercession in time of adversity.

By the fourth century, we have an illustration of the praying Madonna at the cemetery on the Nomentanian Way, that is, one who intercedes.

We also have the *Prayer to the Mother of God*, which is of patristic derivation: "Hope of all Christians; pacifier of the Divine Wrath; after God, sole refuge, light, strength, riches, and glory of all who come to you; the one who assists her devotees in all their contingencies of soul and body; the one whose intercession with God is all-powerful and is put at the disposal of sinners."

From the Fifth to the Eleventh Centuries

By the fifth century, the Akathist Hymn (or Prayer) has added a rich series of terms witnessing to Mary's help. And by the sixth/seventh centuries the first part of the Hail Mary has been introduced into the Mass of the Annunciation.

In the sixth-century *Antiphonary* of St. Gregory the Great, we find texts derived from the Greek tradition, among which is the Antiphon: "Rejoice, O Virgin Mary; you have vanquished all heresies in the whole world," which is attributed to the Roman Victor the Blind. Allied to this there is the Antiphon that has become part of every Office of our Lady: "Make me worthy of praising you, O holy Virgin; grant me strength against your enemies."

In the seventh century, in a hymn erroneously attributed to St. Ambrose, there is a general invitation to pray to the Blessed

Virgin: "Therefore, let us pray, O people, to the Virgin Mother of God that she may obtain for us peace and freedom."

At the same time, in Sermon II: "On the Birth of St. Mary," composed for the new feast of the Assumption, we find the antiphon that will be repeated in the Office of the Blessed Virgin and at the *Benedictus* of the Marian Office for Saturday: "Holy Mary, succor the miserable, help the weak, comfort the weeping; pray for the people, intervene for the clergy, and intercede for the devoted feminine sex."

Still in the seventh century, we find the first invocations of the Litany of Mary including the simple supplication "Holy Mary, pray for us" as well as the first prayers addressed to Mary by St. Ildephonsus of Toledo, which then become part of the Mozarabic liturgical books.

In the ninth century the great liturgical reformer Alcuin of York composes a Sacramentary for private devotion that includes two votive Masses of the Blessed Virgin that were a prelude to the Office of Mary with prayers to Mary.

In the tenth century, prayers to the Virgin continue to be expressed in litanaic invocations and hymns. One example is the prayer of Odo of Cluny who customarily calls the Blessed Virgin "Mother of mercy." This passes on into the Litany of Loreto and ends up in the primitive text of the *Salve Regina Misericordiae*, "Hail, Queen of Mercy."

In the eleventh century, beautiful prayers spring up such as the prayer of Fulbert of Chartres that begins with the words: "Holy Virgin Mary, Queen of Heaven," as well as the *Salve Regina* ("Hail, Holy Queen") and the *Alma Redemptoris Mater* ("Mother Benign of Our Redeeming Lord"), which call upon Mary's powerful help.

Vanquisher of the Devil

Parallel with the appearance of prayers to Mary was the meditation of the Church (especially through the Fathers) on the text of Genesis 3:15 in its Vulgate form: "I will put enmity between you and the Woman, between your seed and her seed; she shall crush your head, and you shall lie in wait for her heel." The conclusion was that there exists a state of enmity between the devil and the posterity of Adam and Eve, especially Mary and her Son.

After the Fall, God does not abandon humankind but establishes his plan of salvation. Everything comes from him and his goodness, but human beings must participate in the Divine Plan, which is carried out *through* humans and *with* humans. This participation consists in the struggle against the enemy, an enemy of cosmic proportions.

The Fathers were vividly aware of this struggle, which is so capital as to determine the eternal destiny of every person. Even the life of Jesus is characterized by a struggle without quarter against the enemy, with the most acute moments being those in the desert and at the Passion.

The death of Christ indicates the lengths to which the enmity extends. Yet from that death commences the possibility of victory for all.

There is a kind of crescendo involved. The Old Testament provides an outline of this struggle. A people carries God's promise and his saving plan for all humankind. Christ, *born of the Virgin*, is the culmination of the struggle and of the victory, because all history tends toward him and has meaning in him.

Christ is the complete victor by his power. Every victory of humankind is presence and participation in the unique grace that originates from his "exaltation." On Calvary, he is "raised up" to attract all things to himself, while the enemy is cast out forever. With the Resurrection begins the new creature who can now combat the devil with the certainty of victory.

Mary participated *actively* in the Incarnation. From the Fathers to the ecclesiastical writers of the Middle Ages, there is a constant tradition that loves to stress that Mary conceived the Word of God first in her mind and then in her body, according to an expression of St. Augustine.

The Blessed Virgin is a universal architect of the struggle, because *in her* and *through her,* Christ the sole Mediator, became man. And "she consecrated herself totally... to the Person and work of her Son. In subordination to him and with him, by the grace of Almighty God she served the Mystery of the Redemption" (Vatican II: *Constitution on the Church,* no. 56).

Mary is from the posterity of Eve, but she is also among the members of humankind and has carried off the *fullest* victory over Satan, by reason of her holiness of life and her close union with the Victor of the whole struggle against the devil.

Guerric of Igny (d. 1157) puts this theme in perspective for us:

"Recognizing that by virtue of the Mystery of the Incarnation, Mary is the Mother of all Christians, Christ's blessed Mother also shows herself a Mother to them by her care and loving kindness. She never grows hard toward her children, as though they were not her own.

"The womb that once gave birth is not dried up; it continues to bring forth the fruit of her tender compassion. Christ, the blessed fruit of that womb, left his Mother still fraught with inexhaustible love, a love that once came forth from her but remains always within her, inundating her with his gifts.

"It can be seen that the children themselves recognize her as their Mother. A natural instinct, inspired by faith, prompts them to have recourse to her in all dangers and difficulties, invoking her and taking refuge in her arms like little ones running to their mother.

"To this day we dwell in the shelter of Mary's wings. And in the days to come we shall share her glory; we shall know the warmth of her loving embrace. Then there will be one joyful voice proclaiming the praise of our Mother: Holy Mother of God, in you we all find our home!"

Vanquisher of Heresies

Thus, by the twelfth century, the stage was set for a more extensive devotion to *Mary, Help of Christians*. From the earliest times, the title *Vanquisher of Heresies* had been bestowed on Mary.

St. Cyril of Alexandria (d. 444) declared: "Through you [Mary] the Apostles have proclaimed salvation to the nations...; through you the demons have been put to rout and humankind has been summoned back to heaven; through you every *misguided* creature held in the thrall of idols is led to recognize the truth" (*Homily against Nestorius*).

And St. Germanus of Constantinople (d. 733) spoke to Mary thusly: "Hail, Fountain springing forth by God's design, whose rivers flowing over in pure and unsullied waves of orthodoxy *put to flight the hosts of errors*" (*Sermon I on the Mother of God*).

Accordingly, when the Church suffered from the Albigensian heretics, the offspring of the later Manicheans, it was to the Blessed Mother that she turned. Those who held to this heresy filled the south of France and other parts of the Latin world with their pernicious errors and carrying everywhere the terror of their arms strove far and wide to rule by massacre and ruin.

Historians indicate that the term Albigensians does not

describe a particular sect but a whole complex of historical movements that at the end of the twelfth century and the beginning of the thirteenth were widespread in southern France. They taught that Christ was an angel with a phantom body who, consequently, neither suffered nor rose from the dead, and his redemptive work consisted merely in teaching humans the true (that is, Albigensian) doctrine. They were also animated by a fanatical hatred for the Church and constituted a threat to ordered society, too, by their disregard for public authority.

After repeated attempts to root out the heresies by means of preaching, a solemn condemnation had been pronounced at the local Council of Lombers (1165) and at the Fourth Lateran Council (1215). But spiritual penalties had little effect on the heretics and did not mitigate the danger.

It was then that the Church appealed to Mary through St. Dominic and the Rosary. And Mary, Help of Christians, overcame Albigensianism as well. The heresy gradually lost the impetus it had attained, and by the end of the fourteenth century all trace of it had disappeared.

Vanquisher of the Church's Enemies

Leo XIII wrote (in the above-mentioned Encyclical *Supremi Apostolatus*) that "whenever the Church of God has seemed to be endangered ... by the attacks of violent enemies ... ancient and modern history and the most sacred annals of the Church bear witness to public and private supplications addressed to the Mother of God, to the help she has granted in return, and to the peace and tranquillity she has obtained from God....

"In the sixteenth century... the vast forces of the Turks threatened to impose on nearly the whole of Europe the yoke of superstition and barbarism. At that time, the Supreme Pontiff, St.

Help of Christians

Pius V, after arousing among all the Christian princes zeal for the common defense, strove above all with great ardor to obtain for Christendom the favor of the most powerful Mother of God.

"So noble an example offered to heaven and earth in those times rallied around him all the minds and hearts of the age. And thus Christ's faithful warriors, prepared to sacrifice their life and blood for the welfare of their Faith and their country, proceeded undauntedly to meet their foe near the Gulf of Corinth; while those who were unable to join them formed a band of pious supplicants, who called on Mary and as one saluted her again and again in the words of the Rosary, imploring her to grant victory to their companions engaged in battle.

"Our sovereign Lady did grant her aid; for in the naval battle [of 1571] near the Echinades Islands the Christian fleet [led by Don John of Austria] gained with no great loss to itself a magnificent victory in which the enemy was completely routed."

In the wake of that victory Pius V added the invocation "Mary, Help of Christians" to the Litany of Loreto.

Later, at the beginning of the nineteenth century, Pope Pius VII was held a prisoner under Napoleon I after being driven from the See of Peter by force of arms. The whole Church prayed earnestly to God on his behalf through the intercession of the Blessed Virgin. Thereupon the Supreme Pontiff was unexpectedly released and, on returning to Rome, was restored to the papal throne on May 24, 1814.

As a result, Pius VII established a feast in honor of the Virgin Mother under the title of "Help of Christians" to be celebrated in perpetuity on May 24, the anniversary of his safe return to the city of Rome.

Almost all subsequent Popes have called upon Mary, Help of Christians, and have urged all members of the Church to have recourse to our Lady under this glorious title.

Application to Us

The application of this title to us is quite evident. Mary is our helper in all the *spiritual troubles* that may assail us. She is our helper in all the *material difficulties* that may overtake us. Finally, she is our helper on the *journey to heaven*.

Indeed, as Pope Leo XIII stressed, "Nobody knows and comprehends so well as she everything that concerns us: what help we need in life; what dangers, public and private, threaten our welfare; what difficulties and evils surround us; above all, how fierce is the battle we wage with ruthless enemies of our salvation.

"In these and in all other troubles of life, Mary's power is most far-reaching. She has the most ardent desire to bring consolation, strength, and help to every race of children so dear to her" (Encyclical *Magnae Dei Matris* ["Great Mother of God"], September 8, 1892).

Therefore, Pius IX declared that we should "fly with utter confidence to this most sweet Mother of mercy and grace in all dangers, difficulties, needs, doubts, and fears. Under her guidance, under her patronage, under her kindness and protection, nothing is to be feared, nothing is hopeless....

"Standing at the right hand of her only-begotten Son, Jesus Christ our Lord, she presents our petitions in a most efficacious manner. What she asks she obtains. Her pleas can never be unheard" (Encyclical *Ineffabilis Deus* ["Ineffable God"], December 8, 1854).

Father Pedro Arrupe, former worldwide head of the Jesuits, brings these points home to us in a more concrete manner:

"The Virgin Mary stands indissolubly bound with the work for which Christ wished to be born of her. Wherefore, Jesus, when *his hour* had come, that hour expected and dreaded, from the pulpit of the Cross publicly proclaims her 'Woman' — the new Woman and the Mother of us all. From the day the disciple John had her in his home, she is in everybody's home, with a Mother's concern for all our needs and ready to help in our daily struggles.

"All this might sound like a beautiful story and no more than a series of images in our churches or processions, an interesting specimen of folklore for tourists, before which we remain personally indifferent. But this is another word, the third word of Jesus as he is living today, in the century of atomic energy and space travel.

"Mary, the sorrowful Mother, who has suffered like nobody else in the world, thus becoming our Mother in the order of grace, continues standing near us, standing at the foot of the Cross, while a poor innocent man falls, mercilessly mowed down by the intransigence of the powerful, or another dies a slow death of hunger or leprosy on the streets....

"Mary knows what it is to suffer, for she gave us life in pain, with a love surpassed only by God's love. She, as the Second Vatican Council says, 'with her motherly love cares for all the brothers and sisters of her Son who still journey on earth surrounded by dangers and difficulties.' She is, therefore, a sign of hope and comfort in the midst of this desolate world."

Prayer to Mary, Help of Christians

> *Mary, powerful Virgin,*
> *you are the mighty and glorious protector*
> *of the Church.*
> *You are the marvelous help of Christians.*
> *You are awe-inspiring as an army in battle array.*
> *You eliminated heresy in the world.*

*Amid our anguish, struggle, and distress,
defend us from the power of the enemy,
and at the hour of our death
receive our soul in heaven.*

        St. John Bosco (d. 1888)

8

Immaculate Conception

The Name Mary Gave Herself at Lourdes

The phrase "Immaculate Conception" constitutes one of the most popular Marian titles. Indeed, it is the name that the Blessed Mother called herself when she appeared to St. Bernadette in 1858 to establish the shrine at Lourdes.

Briefly, this phrase means that Mary was never bound by any guilt of original sin. She was not even for a moment deprived of God's grace and friendship and subjected to the power of the devil.

Despite the fact that the doctrine of the Immaculate Conception was only formalized by the dogmatic definition of Blessed Pius IX in 1854, this teaching has been part of the Christian message in some form from the very beginning.

A Doctrine of the "Sense of the Faithful"

It was the "sense of the faithful," the religious sensitivity of the people, that recognized the Immaculate Conception right from the beginning. The strongest manifestations of this important tradition are found in the liturgical cult of the Immaculata, in the teachings of the Fathers of the Church, and in the acts of the

Popes. The latter favored the cult of the Immaculata, explained its meaning and doctrinal content, and prohibited any public teaching against it.

The Christian people from the first knew of the *Protoevangelium* found in Genesis 3:15, the first announcement of salvation, sometimes called the "Gospel before the Gospel." Our forebears, Adam and Eve, had sinned. God punishes them and casts them out of the Garden of Eden.

However, they do not leave without hope because God makes a promise to them that is in fact the first announcement of the Redemption: there will appear a Woman who will be the enemy of Satan, to whom they have yielded. She will be the Mother of a Son who will vanquish the devil.

Aware of this promise, the early Christians, guided by the Holy Spirit, intuited that Mary, the enemy of Satan, had never been subject to him by any stain of sin. They therefore gave Mary the ancient name: "the All-Holy One."

"You Are All-Beautiful, O Mary"

In the Liturgy, the Church sings of Mary's Beauty and applies to her the words that exalt the beauty of the spouse in the Song of Songs (4:7): "You are all-beautiful, O Mary, and there is no stain in you." This is true, of course, of her beauty of soul. But what about her physical appearance? The Bible tells us nothing about that — and for that matter about the physical appearance of Jesus. The Shroud of Turin gives us a hint about the latter, and it is an imposing physical presence.

One day Pius XI distributed pictures of the Shroud and remarked: "Since I am unable to give you a photograph of Mary, I give you one of the countenance that was most like hers."

In the Office of Readings for Holy Thursday we read a

very ancient homily of Melito of Sardis (d. 190) in which Mary is termed the "beautiful lamb." Gregory of Palamas (d. 1359) writes: "Wishing to create an image of absolute beauty, God truly made Mary all-beautiful."

Paul VI urged Mariologists not to overlook "the way of beauty"; he saw in Mary "a masterpiece of human beauty, not sought only in the formal model but realized in the intrinsic and unsurpassable capacity to express the Spirit in the flesh, the Divine likeness in human countenance, the invisible Beauty in bodily nature" (December 8, 1975).

Therefore, our Lady's real beauty is eternal. But there are virtues (e.g., serenity, peace, equilibrium) that also have external repercussions and confer a profound beauty. This is why Mary is the enchantment of the Saints, the model of every Christian — her virtues.

Mary's Physical Beauty

In a Discourse to Catholic Youths on December 8, 1953, Pope Pius XII touched upon Mary's physical beauty:

"In contemplating the Immaculate Virgin, we have as guide the Sacred Liturgy, which does not tire of calling her 'fair as the moon, bright as the sun, awesome as an army set in battle array.'

"Above all, look at Mary 'fair as the moon.' It is a way of expressing her exalted beauty.

"How beautiful the Blessed Virgin must be! How often have we been struck by the beauty of an angelic countenance, by the charm of an infant's smile, by the fascination of a pure glance! Surely in his own Mother's countenance God has gathered together all the splendors of his Divine artistry.

"Mary's glance! Mary's smile! Mary's sweetness! The majesty of Mary, Queen of heaven and earth! As the moon shines resplendent in the dark heavens, so is Mary's beauty set apart from all other beauties, which are but shadows beside her. *Mary is the most beautiful of all God's creatures....*

"Her countenance reveals more than mere natural beauty. God by a miracle of his almighty power has poured into her soul the fullness of his riches; he has made pass into Mary's glance something of his own supernatural and Divine dignity.

"A ray of beauty from God shines in his Mother's eyes.

"Do you not think that Jesus' countenance, that countenance that the Angels adore, must have reproduced in some way the lines of Mary's countenance? For every son's countenance mirrors his mother's....

"But the Church does not compare Mary solely to the moon; again making use of Sacred Scripture, she uses a more vivid figure when exclaiming 'O Mary, you are bright as the sun.'

"Sunlight is far different from moonlight; it is light that warms and vivifies.

"The moon shines upon the Polar icefields, but the icefields remain compact and barren just as darkness and frost endure on moonlit winter nights. Moonlight does not give warmth nor bring life.

"The sun is the source of light, warmth, and life. Now Mary, beautiful as the moon, shines brightly as the sun and irradiates life-giving warmth.

"Whenever we speak of her, or speak to her, let us not forget that she is really our Mother, for through her we received Divine life. She gave us Jesus, himself the source of grace. Mary is the Mediatrix and Dispenser of graces.

"Under the sun's light and warmth, plants grow on the earth and bear fruit; under the influence and with the help of the sun that is Mary, good thoughts fructify in souls."

A Spiritual Portrait of Mary

The following portrait of Mary is taken from a Homily on her Birth by St. John Damascene (d. 749), who composed many hymns for different feasts of the year and Marian Homilies that often contained prayers to our Lady. Replete with Biblical allusions, it constitutes a unique portrait of Mary and a beautiful legacy left us by the last Father of the Church in the East.

> *Today the root of Jesse has produced its shoot:*
> *she will bring forth a divine flower for the world....*
> *Today the Creator of all things, God the Word, composes a new book:*
> *a book issuing from the heart of his Father*
> *and written by the Holy Spirit,*
> *who is the tongue of God....*
>
> *O daughter of King David and Mother of God, the universal King;*
> *O Divine and living object whose beauty has charmed God the Creator;*
> *your whole soul is completely open to God's action*
> *and attentive to God alone.*
> *All your desires are centered only on*
> *what merits to be sought and is worthy of love.*
> *You will have a life superior to nature*
> *— but not for your own sake.*
> *For it has not been created for you*
> *but has been entirely consecrated to God,*
> *who has introduced you into the world*
> *to help bring about our salvation in fulfillment of his plan*
> *— the Incarnation of his Son*
> *and the Divinization of the human race.*
>
> *Your heart will find nourishment in the words of God:*
> *they will make you fruitful*
> *like the fertile olive tree in the house of God,*
> *like the tree planted near the living waters of the Spirit,*

like the tree of life that has yielded its fruit in due time
— the incarnate God who is the life of all things.

Your eyes will be ever turned toward the Lord,
toward the eternal and inaccessible light.
Your ears will be ever attentive to the Divine words
and the sounds of the harp of the Spirit,
through whom the Word has come to take on our flesh....
Your nostrils will inhale the fragrance of the Bridegroom,
the Divine fragrance with which he scented his humanity.

Your lips will savor the words of God
and will rejoice in their Divine sweetness.
Your most pure heart, free from all stain,
will ever see the God of all purity
and will experience ardent desire for him.
Your womb will be the abode
of the One whom no place can hold.
Your milk will provide nourishment for God,
in the little Infant Jesus....

Your hands will carry God,
and your knees will serve as a throne for him
that is more noble than the throne of the Cherubim....

Your feet, led by the light of the Divine Law,
will follow him along an undeviating course
and guide you to the possession of the Beloved.

You are the temple of the Holy Spirit,
the city of the living God,
made joyous by abundant flowers,
the sacred flowers of Divine grace.
You are all-beautiful and very close to God,
above the Cherubim and higher than the Seraphim,
right near God himself.

Lourdes and the Immaculate Conception

In 1858, four years after the definition of the Dogma of the Immaculate Conception, Mary as it were placed her stamp of approval on it by appearing to a 13-year-old unlettered child of France, St. Bernadette Soubirous, telling her: "I am the Immaculate Conception."

The child had never heard that expression and was completely unaware of what it meant. Nonetheless, by her life and work, she made it possible for the whole world to know the Immaculate Conception in the future.

Out of the seven appearances to the Saint grew the world-famous shrine of Lourdes — a paean of praise to the Virgin Mary. It would be safe to say that Lourdes is the best-known shrine of Mary, drawing millions of pilgrims annually.

Implied in Sacred Scripture

Usually, a teaching that is defined as dogma is contained in Sacred Scripture in some way. However, not all doctrines are contained in Scripture with equal clarity. Some are there only in implicit fashion. Such is the case with the doctrine of the Immaculate Conception.

As the Second Vatican Council declares: "[Mary] is already prophetically foreshadowed in the promise of victory over the serpent that was given to our first parents after their fall into sin (see Genesis 3:15). Similarly, she is the Virgin who will conceive and bear a Son, whose name will be called Emmanuel (see Isaiah 7:14)" (*Constitution on the Church*, no. 55).

Mary is "full of grace" because of that blessing with which God the Father has filled us "in the heavenly places with Christ" (Ephesians 1:3).

It is a spiritual blessing that is meant for all people and that bears in itself fullness and universality. It flows from the love that, in the Holy Spirit, unites the consubstantial Son to the Father. At the same time, it is a blessing poured out through Jesus Christ upon human history until the end of time: upon all people.

This blessing, however, refers to Mary in a special and exceptional degree: for she was greeted by Elizabeth as "blessed among women" (Luke 1:42). In the soul of this Daughter of Zion, there is manifested, in a sense, all the glory of grace, that grace which the Father has given us in his beloved Son.

In the language of the Bible, grace means a special gift, which according to the New Testament has its source precisely in the Trinitarian life of God himself, God who is love (see 1 John 4:8). The fruit of this love is the "election" spoken of in Ephesians 1:4-6. On the part of God, this election is the eternal desire to save humankind through a sharing in his own life (see 2 Peter 1:4): it is a salvation through a sharing in supernatural life.

Hence, as the already mentioned citation from the Song of Songs indicates, Mary is all-beautiful and there is no stain in her.

The Fathers and the Teaching

The early Church writers, such as St. Justin Martyr and St. Irenaeus in the second century, laid the bases for Mary's singular privilege by holding up her beauty in the Eve-Mary parallel. Eve listened to the serpent, turned away from God, and moved toward sin. Mary listened to the Angel, turned toward God, and moved away from sin.

To this, later Fathers added the fact of Mary's fullness of grace. In the fourth century, St. Ephrem declared that the

Immaculate Conception

Cherubim are not the equal of Mary in holiness, the Seraphim yield to her in loveliness, and the legions of Angels are inferior to her in purity.

And he sums up his thought by the words: "Indeed you [Christ] and your Mother are beautiful in every respect. In you, Lord, there is no stain; and in your Mother, there is no spot."

In the same century, St. Ambrose shows that Mary's freedom from sin was a belief current in the early Church: "Receive me, Lord, not from Sarah but from Mary. For [Mary] is a Virgin not only uncorrupted but also a Virgin uncorrupted by any stain of sin."

A feast of Mary's birth was celebrated in the East in the sixth century, and in the seventh century a feast of Mary's Conception.

In the ninth century, St. Theodore the Studite of the Eastern Church wrote the following beautiful words about Mary's holiness:

"No creature was ever so holy as the blessed and most admirable Virgin Mary. What is purer than she? What more faultless? So greatly was she loved by God, the supreme and most pure light, that by the coming of the Holy Spirit he united his own substance with hers and came forth from her as a perfect man, although in his own nature there was no alteration or mingling.

"How marvelous that in his great love for us God was not ashamed to take his own maidservant as his Mother! What condescension! He who is supremely good did not refuse to be called the child of his own nature, for he loved her who was manifestly the fairest of all creatures and took as his own her who was worthier than the powers of heaven.

"It is of Mary that the admirable Zechariah speaks when he says: 'Sing and rejoice, daughter of Zion, for I am coming to dwell in the midst of you, says the Lord' (2:14). And it seems to me that the blessed Joel is referring to her when he cries out: 'Do not be afraid, O land; be glad and rejoice, for the Lord has done great things for you' (2:21)."

The Medieval Theologians and the Teaching

In the tenth century, St. Paschasius Radbertus wrote that the veneration of Mary's birth throughout the whole Church showed that she was immune from sin.

In the eleventh century, St. Anselm wrote that "a purity greater than which cannot be found outside God" should shine in the Virgin, for to the Virgin God decreed to give his only Son whom, begotten from himself as his equal, he heartily loved as himself.

From the thirteenth to the fifteenth centuries theologians debated concerning the Immaculate Conception. Because of their emphasis on the universal need for salvation, some of the greatest theologians of the Church (e.g., St. Bernard, St. Thomas Aquinas, and St. Bonaventure) were held back from asserting the Immaculate Conception.

St. Thomas, for example, who was greatly devoted to our Lady, took refuge in the idea of an immediate sanctification of Mary after she had incurred original sin.

These theologians reasoned that if Mary was conceived without original sin, she had no need of Christ's Redemption. In that case, she was not a creature like us, born in a fallen state. Furthermore, if we take away from Mary the fruits of the Redemption, we do not make her a privileged creature but a person deprived of the Divine adoption worked by Christ.

It was left for the Franciscan theologian Blessed Duns Scotus to find a solution. He pointed out that, rather than detracting from the Redemption, the privilege of a total immunization, preserving Mary from all sin, even original, would represent the most glorious result of Christ's work.

The modern theologian Xavier Le Bachelet has nicely summarized the argument of Scotus:

"There are two kinds of ransom: one is ransom paid for an individual already prisoner, redemption by *liberation*; the other is ransom paid even before the acquired right of servitude is exercised, redemption by *preservation*.

"In making an anticipated application of his merits to his Mother to preserve her from the taint of original sin, which as a daughter of Adam she had naturally to incur, Jesus Christ became more fully her Redeemer.

"Far from being diminished, the excellence of the Redemption is enhanced by Mary's privilege."

The Popes and the Teaching

The Popes of the later Middle Ages loved this teaching and helped keep it before the people. In 1477, Pope Sixtus IV approved a Mass and Office in honor of the Conception of Mary, and in 1482 the same Pontiff declared that belief in the Immaculate Conception was not heretical (as some theologians had claimed).

In 1546, the Council of Trent excluded the Blessed Virgin from the doctrine of the universality of original sin.

In 1617, Pope Paul V forbade denial of the Immaculate Conception in public sermons and writings. And in 1622, Pope Gregory XV extended the prohibition to conversation and writing.

In 1661, Pope Alexander VII affirmed the traditional belief in the Immaculate Conception. In 1708, Pope Clement XI made the Feast of the Immaculate Conception a Holy Day of Obligation.

In 1846, Mary was officially declared the Patroness of the Church in the United States under her title of Immaculate Conception.

In 1849, Blessed Pius IX asked the bishops of the world for their views on the definability of the Dogma of the Immaculate Conception. Receiving a positive feedback, he solemnly defined the Dogma of the Immaculate Conception in 1854.

Application to Us

In the doctrine of the Immaculate Conception there is an aspect that might be termed a *pure principle* because of Mary's great mission to become the Mother of the Lord. In the face of this aspect, we can only praise the marvels worked by the Lord.

There is, however, another aspect that is of concern to us: the fact that Mary never committed the slightest fault even though she was a human being like us, intelligent and free.

It is here that we, as it were, put our finger on how Mary is to be imitated. Her holiness can draw us and enable us to discover the original beauty of human nature, pervaded by God's grace. And it can inspire us to tend toward that beauty — with the help of baptismal grace, actual graces, and the constant struggle against sin.

By meditating on the Immaculate Conception, we become truly aware of what we need: the strength to overcome sin that is all around us and the power to renounce Satan, who can do nothing against those who refuse to yield to his temptations.

Immaculate Conception

Mary reminds us that we too have been redeemed by the grace of Christ and we are stronger than we think; we can and we must overcome every assault of the Evil One.

In this way, Mary is not some absent and distant ideal to be merely contemplated. She is by our side to help us and to make us as like to herself as possible — in the same way that she herself has succeeded in becoming as like to Christ as possible.

A constant aid in this respect — and one that is at everyone's fingertips — is the indulgenced invocation to the Immaculate Conception that has become the favorite of Catholics: "O Mary conceived without sin, pray for us who have recourse to you."

Prayer to the Immaculate Conception

Mary, Virgin most pure,
your greatness began
at the first instant of your existence
with the privilege of your Immaculate Conception.
It was fitting that you should be adorned
with the greatest purity ever possible to a creature.
You are the Immaculate Virgin
to whom God the Father decreed
to give his only Son.
You are the Immaculate Virgin
whom God the Son himself chose to make his Mother.
You are the Immaculate Virgin
whom the Holy Spirit willed to make his Bride
and in whom he would work the tremendous miracle
of the Incarnation.

Help me to imitate your sinlessness
by keeping my soul free from willful sin

through the faithful observance of God's commandments.
Let me imitate your fullness of grace
by frequent reception of Communion
and assiduous prayer —
which will make my soul holy
and give me the grace and need to practice virtue.
Transform me into a living image of Jesus
just as you were.

9
Mary the Virgin

The Name of Mary in Scripture

This title, "Mary the Virgin," is also rendered as "St. Mary the Virgin" and "The Virgin Mary." Offshoots of it are "The Virgin" and "The Blessed Virgin" — the latter of which has already been mentioned in passing, so to speak, in the Introduction (in the section "The Most Frequently Used Title"). In any case, the title comprises two parts: "Mary" and "Virgin." We will discuss first the name itself and then "Virgin."

The name *Mary* has the form *Myriam* in the Hebrew Old Testament and *Maryam* in the Aramaic, *Miriam* in the Greek translation of the Old Testament, and *Maria* in the Greek New Testament. It is the name held by eight other persons in the Bible besides the Mother of Jesus.

In the Old Testament, this name is held by two people: (1) the sister of Moses, usually called Miriam, who sang a song of praise after the crossing of the Red Sea (Exodus 15:20-21) and who was later punished for opposing Moses (Numbers 12); (2) a woman descendant of Judah (1 Chronicles 4:17 — although the text could also be referring to a male descendant of Ezra with that name).

In the New Testament, the name Mary is held by six women: (3) Mary Magdalene, the woman "from whom seven devils had gone out" (Luke 8:2); (4) Mary, the sister of Lazarus and Martha, who is portrayed as a devoted listener of Christ (Luke 10:38-42); (5) Mary, the mother of James and John, one of the witnesses of Jesus' crucifixion and of the empty tomb (Mark 15:40-47); (6) Mary, wife of Clopas (John 19:25), whom some identify with the woman in number 5; (7) Mary, the mother of John Mark, in whose house Peter takes refuge after being freed from prison in Jerusalem (Acts 12:12); (8) a Christian at Rome who is greeted and praised by Paul in the Letter to the Romans: "My greetings to Mary, who has worked hard for you" (16:6).

Meaning of the Name Mary

Over the years, more than seventy meanings have been attached to the name *Mary* — most based on devotion rather than philology. Two such explanations have given rise to titles of Mary that are favorites among Catholics.

The first is the explanation of St. Jerome based on the Hebrew term for "sea" (*yam*), which produced the Latin *stilla maris*, meaning "drop of the sea" — i.e., of the sea that is God. A copyist's error turned the phrase into *stella maris* meaning "Star of the Sea." It became a favorite name for Mary and part of the Marian literature through the Hymn *Ave Maris Stella* ("Hail, Star of the Sea").

The second explanation also comes from St. Jerome. He proposed an alternative meaning based on the Aramaic *mar*, which means "lord," although, scholars point out, the form should have been *marta*. This interpretation enjoyed wide acceptance and became the usual title applied to Mary in modern languages and meaning "lady": "My Lady" (Madonna) in Italian and "Our Lady" (Notre Dame) in French.

Modern philology has been able to indicate three meanings

of Mary as more probable (though not yet certain). The first connects the name with the Egyptian *mara* meaning "satiated, fat, or corpulent" — hence, in accord with Oriental feminine aesthetic, beautiful. The second relates the name to the Egyptian *mari* meaning "loved." The third relates it to the language of the inhabitants of Palestine, the Canaanites, which is akin to Hebrew.

Archeological expeditions that took place in Ugarit (Ras Shamra in Syria) in 1929 have made this language better understood today. These unearthed the Ugaritic idiom that was spoken and written in those regions. In the tablets that have been found, the name *myrm* is well attested. It derives from the verb *rwm* and has the meaning of "high" or "lofty," hence "exalted" or "august." Therefore, our Lady would be "The Exalted One" or "The Sublime One." This last meaning for Mary seems to be the most probable — and it fits our Lady very well.

Feast of the Name of Mary

The liturgical feast of the Holy Name of Mary originated in Spain and was approved by the Holy See in 1513. Innocent XI extended its observance to the whole Church in 1683 in thanksgiving for the victory of John Sobieski, King of Poland, over the Turks, who were besieging Vienna and threatening the West. The feast was assigned to September 12, the date of the victory, which occurred only four days after the Feast of the Nativity of Mary.

The feast remained in the Roman Calendar as a lesser Feast of Mary until the publication of the new Roman Missal, revised in accord with the principles of the Second Vatican Council in 1970. It was then dropped from the universal calendar because it was thought to be a duplicate of the Feast of the Nativity of Mary (the same fate overtook the Feast of the Holy Name of Jesus, which was thought to be a duplicate of the Nativity of Jesus).

However, the 1975 edition of the Roman Missal added a Votive Mass of the Name of Mary that could be celebrated on open days. Then in 1987, the new liturgical book *Collection of Masses of the Blessed Virgin Mary* was published by the Church, and among its 46 Masses that can be celebrated on open liturgical days is "The Holy Name of the Blessed Virgin Mary" (no. 21).

The Mass teaches that God the Father is glorified first of all on account of the Name of Jesus, i.e., on account of the Person of his Son, his power and saving mission — in no other name is there salvation.

The Father is then glorified on account of the Name of Mary, i.e., on account of the person of Christ's Mother and her mission in the History of Salvation.

The Name of Mary is celebrated as (1) a name of honor, for God has so exalted her name that human lips will never cease to praise her; (2) a holy name, for it marks out the woman who was entirely full of grace and found favor with God and gave birth to the Son of God; (3) a maternal name, for the Lord Jesus dying on the altar of the Cross gave her to us as our Mother so that we might call upon her and be strengthened in our needs; and (4) a name responsive to need, for the faithful on whose lips her Name echoes turn to her with confidence as their Star of hope and their Mother in time of danger.

The new edition of the Roman Missal issued under Pope John Paul II in 2002 has restored the Feast of the Holy Name of Mary to September 12 as an Optional Memorial.

Mary the Virgin

Mary's Virginal Conception of Jesus

Mary conceived Jesus without "knowing man," remaining a Virgin. Two of the Gospels testify to this, and the oldest professions of faith declare it: "I believe … in Jesus Christ … who was conceived by the Holy Spirit, born of the Virgin Mary, and became man." The virginal conception of Jesus is very closely linked with the Mystery of the Incarnation.

The Gospels of Matthew and Luke both say the same thing. The conception of Jesus is the work of the Holy Spirit. Joseph is only the legal (adoptive) father of Jesus. The conception takes place while Mary and Joseph are only promised in marriage, but at the moment of birth they are living together in marriage in accord with the custom of that time.

Scholars tell us that, on the historical level, the exegete can certify the existence of belief in such a virginal conception, not only in the communities of Matthew and Luke but also in an earlier tradition, source of their common documentation. It is probable that the theme first circulated among Judeo-Christian groups, like the Church of Matthew itself.

Our belief in the reality of the virginal conception, based on the testimony of the Gospels, is of the same order as our belief in the Resurrection of Jesus. A purely symbolic interpretation overthrows all the objective reality of the testimony received by the original Church and all the radical newness of the Mystery of Jesus the Savior (see 1 Corinthians 15:14: "If Christ has not been raised, our preaching is valueless and so is your faith").

Salvation comes from God alone and not from human powers. The very Name of Jesus indicates this, for it means "God saves." In this regard, the virginity of Mary is a sign of the radical human poverty before God, who saves by his grace (see Luke 18:26-27). Poverty of the heart is the secret of hope.

The virginal conception was for Mary and for Joseph

— and remains for us — the sign that makes it possible with our human understanding to grasp something of the Mystery of God the Son.

Mary Ever Virgin

In calling Mary "ever Virgin," Tradition is saying that after conceiving Jesus in virginity Mary always remained a virgin, abstaining from all conjugal relations. This also implies that the birth of Jesus left intact the virginity of his Mother.

The Gospels furnish no argument against this teaching: Luke says: "Mary gave birth to her firstborn Son" (2:7). This alludes to the legal prescriptions concerning the first male child of a family, even if there were no other children.

Matthew declares: "Joseph had no relations with [Mary] until she bore a Son" (1:25). The Semitic locution "before" or "until" makes no judgment about the future. Thus: "Michal was childless until the day of her death" (2 Samuel 6:23).

On several occasions, the Gospels speak of "brothers of Jesus," e.g., James and Joseph (Matthew 13:55). But these are sons of another Mary, expressly named "the mother of James and Joseph" (Matthew 27:56), who cannot be identified with the Mother of Jesus and who is always named after Mary Magdalene.

In addition, in the Semitic world the name "brothers" was often given to relatives and confederates: Abraham says to Lot — who was his nephew — "We are brothers" (Genesis 13:8).

The Church's Tradition has always maintained that Mary was ever Virgin. The *Protevangelium of James*, a legendary account of the second century, relates that when Joseph became the husband of Mary he was old and a widower with several children. This shows that belief in Mary's perpetual virginity was already widespread and attempts were being made to counter the objection of "brothers of Jesus."

Mary the Virgin

In the third century, Origen (d. 253) vigorously defends the virginity of Mary before and after the birth of Jesus. For him, Jesus is the beginning of chastity for men, and Mary of chastity for women.

In the fourth century (350-375), Zeno of Verona expresses the belief of the Church: "How great a Mystery! The Virgin Mary conceived inviolate. After the conception a virgin gave birth. After the birth, a virgin she remained."

In 384, the Ecumenical Council of Constantinople, stated: "And he was made incarnate by the Holy Spirit and the Virgin Mary." The person of Mary is grammatically and doctrinally united with the Holy Spirit as the human co-principle of the Incarnation and the humanization of the Son of God for the salvation of human beings.

Extremely important is the term "Virgin" linked to the person of Mary as a noun in apposition rather than as an adjective or an attribute. Indeed, syntactically, the Greek text says: "Mary the Virgin," and indicates doctrinally the essential characteristic, the significant element, of the human contribution to the Incarnation.

Following the *Catechism of the Catholic Church*, we know that the eyes of faith can discover in the context of the whole of Revelation the mysterious reasons why God in his saving plan wanted his Son to be born of a Virgin. These reasons touch on the Person of Christ and his redemptive mission as well as on the welcome Mary gave that mission on behalf of all human beings.

(1) Mary's virginity manifests God's absolute initiative in the Incarnation. Jesus has only God as Father: He was never estranged from the Father because of the human nature that he assumed. He is naturally Son of the Father as to his Divinity and naturally Son of his Mother as to his Humanity, but properly Son of the Father in both natures.

(2) Jesus is conceived by the Holy Spirit in the Virgin

Mary's womb because he is the New Adam, who inaugurates the new creation.

(3) By his virginal conception, Jesus, the New Adam, ushers in the new birth of children adopted in the Holy Spirit through faith. Participation in the Divine life arises not from blood nor from the will of the flesh nor from the will of humans but from God. The acceptance of this life is virginal because it is entirely the Spirit's gift to human beings. The spousal character of the human vocation in relation to God is fulfilled perfectly in Mary's virginal Motherhood.

Mary is a Virgin because her virginity is the sign of her faith unadulterated by any doubt and of her undivided gift of herself to God's Will. It is her faith that enables her to become the Mother of the Savior.

At once Virgin and Mother, Mary is the symbol and the most perfect realization of the Church: "The Church, contemplating Mary's mysterious holiness, imitating her charity, and faithfully fulfilling the Will of God, becomes herself a mother by accepting the Word of God in faith. By means of her preaching and Baptism, she brings forth to a new and immortal life children who are conceived as the work of the Holy Spirit and born of God.

"The Church is also a virgin who preserves whole and pure the fidelity she has pledged to her Spouse" (*Constitution on the Church*, no. 64).

St. Bede the Venerable (d. 735) gives the argument from fittingness for Mary's virginity: "It is indeed fitting in every respect that when God decided to become incarnate for the sake of the whole human race none but a virgin should be his Mother, and that, since a virgin was privileged to bring him into the world, she should bear no other son but God.

"'Behold, a virgin will conceive and bear a Son, and he will be called Emmanuel' (Isaiah 7:14), 'a name that means God-is-with-us' (Matthew 1:23). And so Mary gave birth to her firstborn Son, the Child of her own flesh and blood. She brought forth the God who had been born of God before creation began, and who, in his created Humanity, rightly surpassed the whole of creation.

"As Scripture says, 'She named him Jesus' (Luke 2:21). Jesus, then, is the name of the Virgin's Son. According to the Angel's explanation, it means one who is to save his people from their sins (see Matthew 1:21)."

A Teaching of the Church

The Church has always taught this doctrine. St. Leo the Great (d. 461) wrote: "Mary brought [Christ] forth with her virginity untouched, just as she had conceived him with her virginity untouched."

Pope Hormisdas (d. 523) stated: "Christ did not open his Mother's womb in birth; by the power of the Deity he did not undo his Mother's virginity."

The First Lateran Council (1123) stated: "[Mary], in the fullness of time and without male seed, conceived by the Holy Spirit God the Word himself — who before all time was begotten of God the Father — and incorruptibly brought him forth, and after his birth preserved her virginity inviolate."

Although this was not an Ecumenical Council, Pope Martin I supported it. Hence, theologians maintain that this fact rendered the statement a Dogma of Faith. In 1555, Paul IV issued a Bull condemning those who denied the virginal conception and who taught that Joseph was the father of Jesus. He affirmed that Mary was a Virgin "before birth, in birth, and perpetually after birth."

In conclusion, if there was any doubt about Mary's virginity being a Dogma of Faith, it is swept away by the fact that the Second Vatican Council refers to Mary as Virgin, Virgin Mother, and ever Virgin over thirty times in its decrees, as indicated by the Marian scholar Father Michael O'Carroll of the Congregation of the Holy Spirit.

Application to Us

We can apply this title to ourselves no matter to what state we have been led by God — the married state or the single state. Our task, like Mary's, is to make purity the sign of our faith unadulterated by any doubt and of our undivided gift of ourselves to God's Will.

And the best way to do so is by calling upon the Name of Mary and following her example. We can take a page out of the fifty-first chapter of the Book of Sirach and say: "I will glorify your Name ... because you have freed my body from perdition. By your Name you have liberated me from the many tribulations I was enduring and from the very depths of the netherworld. I will always praise your Name: do not abandon me in the day of distress and desolation. I will always praise your Name and sing hymns to you in thanksgiving!"

The words of the great Marian Doctor St. Bernard (d. 1153) will also help us in this regard:

"The evangelist Luke says, 'And the Virgin's Name was Mary.'

"Let us make a few observations about this Name, which signifies 'Star of the Sea' and is wondrously fitting for the Virgin Mother.

"She is rightly likened to a star because just as a star sends forth its rays without suffering loss, so the Virgin has brought

Mary the Virgin

forth her Son without diminishing her integrity. A ray takes nothing away from the light of the star, and the Son took nothing away from the Mother's virginity.

"Mary is the noble star from Jacob, whose ray illumines the whole universe, whose splendor shines out for all to see in heaven, reaches even unto hell, spreads out over the earth, and by warming souls more than bodies increases virtues and puts an end to vices.

"Mary is the shining star that glitters over this immense sea of darkness and is resplendent with merits and all aglow with examples for our imitation.

"You who find yourself in the turbulence of this sea, cast about between the billowing waves and tempests without finding land on which to set your feet, do not take your eyes away from the refulgence of this Star unless you want to be drowned by the waves.

"If you are immersed in the winds of temptation or hurled against the reefs of tribulations, look at the Star and call upon Mary. If you are overcome by the waves of pride, ambition, slander, and hatred, look at the Star and call upon Mary. When wrath, or avarice, or the enticements of the senses are shaking the ship of your soul, look at the Star and call upon Mary.

"In danger, anguish, or doubt, think of Mary and call upon her. Let the Name of Mary never be far from your lips or heart. And to obtain the fruit of her prayers, do not forget the example of her life.

"Following Mary, you will never lose your way. Praying to her, you will never sink into despair. Contemplating Mary, you will never go wrong. With Mary's support, you will never fall. Beneath her protection, you will never fear.

"Under her guidance, you will never grow weary. And with her help, you will reach your heavenly goal."

Prayer to Mary the Virgin

> O Virgin Mary,
> who are flooded with the purest joy
> in the presence of the Divine Word made Man
> from your most pure flesh
> and nourished in your virginal womb,
> grant that we may imitate on earth
> your purity that was resplendent
> in the Mystery of the Annunciation
> and your love of the newly born Jesus.
>
> Like you, may we make it our increasing aim
> ever to seek Jesus during life
> so that we may love God
> with all our heart, soul, and strength
> and be completely dedicated to him
> both in this world and in the next.

10

Mediatrix

Mediatrix in Three Ways

According to world-renowned Mariologist J.B. Carol, O.F.M., "a mediator or mediatrix is one who stands between two persons or groups of persons either to facilitate an exchange of favors or to reconcile parties at variance [with one another]." The universal mediation of Mary, i.e., her maternal function in the acquisition, impetration, and distribution of graces, is certainly one of the most interesting and actual aspects of the entire Mystery of Mary in the History of Salvation.

Carol goes on to say that "our Lady may be styled 'mediatrix' either (a) because, as worthy Mother of God and full of grace, she occupies a middle position between God and his creatures; or (b) because, together with Christ and under him, she cooperated in the reconciliation of God and humankind while she was still on earth; or (c) because she distributes the graces that God bestows on his children.

"No matter in which of these three meanings it may be taken, Mary's mediation must always be understood as secondary to, and dependent on, Christ's primary and self-sufficient mediatorial role....

"For some theologians, the title 'Co-Redemptrix' refers to Mary's cooperation in the Redemption in the sense that she knowingly and willingly gave birth to the Redeemer (technically: indirect, remote cooperation) and that she dispenses to us the fruits (graces) of the Redemption already accomplished by Christ alone (i.e., cooperation in the subjective Redemption).

"The majority [of theologians], however, believes that, besides the two types of cooperation just mentioned, Mary also contributed to the Redemption itself, i.e., to the redemptive action of Christ that was consummated on Calvary (called objective Redemption). Specifically: Together with Christ (though in total subordination to him and in virtue of his power), Mary atoned or satisfied for our sins, merited every grace necessary for salvation, and joined the Savior's sacrifice on Calvary to appease the wrath of God."

As a result of this joint operation of Jesus and his Mother, God canceled the debt of the human race and took its members back into his friendship that had been broken by sin.

Pope St. Pius X, in his 1904 Encyclical *Ad Diem Illum Laetissimum* ("On That Joyful Day"), indicated that Mary conceives and gives birth to us as Mother of the Redeemer:

"The Blessed Virgin did not conceive the eternal Son of God merely in order that he might be made man, taking his human nature from her, but also in order that by means of the nature assumed from her he might be the Redeemer of man....

"Accordingly, in the same holy bosom of his most chaste Mother, Christ took to himself flesh and united to himself the spiritual Body formed by those who were to believe in him. Hence, Mary, carrying the Savior within her, may be said to have also carried all those whose life was contained in the life of the Savior....

"Thus, in a spiritual and mystical fashion, we are all children of Mary, and she is Mother of us all."

Mary also gave spiritual birth to humankind at the foot of the Cross. Like a Mother suffering the pangs of childbirth, she stood by the Cross and in union with and subordinate to Christ gave spiritual birth to the members of the Mystical Body. This point is brought out by the words of Father Pierre Benoit, a world-renowned Scripture scholar:

"In the birth pangs of the Church, in the agony of the Cross, Jesus was not alone. As man, sensitive and suffering, he needed a helper and his Mother stood beside the Cross. She helped to accept and offer everything to God; like a Mother, she shared in the birth of the Church.

"In my opinion it is incorrect to speak of Mary as 'Virgin Priest'; she is not a priest. Jesus is the one and only priest and all other priests are his sacramental representatives. But Mary is the Mother of that priest and she alone can fill that role. She helped her Son to consummate his sacrifice.

"Thus all the graces that come to us from Jesus — and they come from him alone since he is the one source of salvation — come through the hands of Mary. Mary, in glory beside her Son, collaborates with him in distributing these graces, just as in her role of Mother, a role at once humble and exalted, she had collaborated with him in the winning of grace."

History of the Title

The whole history of the Church demonstrates the existence of recourse to Mary to obtain her intercession in every circumstance of life. We have seen this in Chapter 7: "Help of Christians."

At the same time, the Fathers of the Church consistently made statements that indicated Mary's great power of mediation.

In the third century, St. Irenaeus wrote: "Mary, espoused but yet a virgin, became by her obedience a cause of salvation for herself and the whole human race" (*Against Heresies*, III, 22).

In the fourth century, St. Jerome stated: "Death came through Eve, but life through Mary" (*Epistle* 22, 21).

At the Council of Ephesus in the fifth century, St. Cyril of Alexandria pronounced the greatest Marian sermon of antiquity, relating Mary's mediation to her office as Mother of God and her relationship with the Blessed Trinity.

With Basil of Seleucia in the fifth century, the word Mediatrix itself appeared in the context of the Annunciation: "Hail, full of grace: set up as a Mediatrix of God and human beings, so that the walls of enmity should be torn down and heavenly and earthly things come together as one" (*On the Annunciation*).

Thus, from the fifth through the sixteenth centuries, Fathers, Doctors, preachers, and hymnologists explained or assumed Mary's mediation without contradiction. In the Middle Ages, it was mainly through the influence of St. Bernard of Clairvaux (d. 1153) that the doctrine of Mary's mediation became familiar to the Catholic faithful — through such sayings as the following: "God has willed that we should have nothing that did not pass through the hands of Mary."

St. Thomas Aquinas (d. 1274) made use of the term Mediatrix in reference to Mary in his commentary on the Gospel of John. Later, St. Bernardine of Siena (d. 1444) applied to Mary the mediatorship of all graces: "I do not hesitate to say that [Mary] has received a certain jurisdiction over all graces.... They are administered through her hands to whom she pleases, when she pleases, and as much as she pleases."

Beginning with the seventeenth century to 1921, a huge output of material was published concerning this doctrine. The two most popular books on our Lady during this time — *True Devotion to Mary* by St. Louis Grignion de Montfort (d. 1716) and *The Glories of Mary* by St. Alphonsus Liguori (d. 1787) — both were composed on the theme of Mary's universal mediation.

1921 to the Present

As a result of the growing clamor on all sides for the definition of a Dogma about Mary's mediation of all graces, Cardinal Mercier, Archbishop of Malines, Belgium, petitioned Pope Benedict XV in 1921 for such an act. He received permission to have a Mass and Office of "Mary, Mediatrix of All Graces" celebrated in all dioceses of Belgium and saw the establishment of three commissions by Pope Pius XI to study the question. But no definition was forthcoming.

In the preparatory phase for the Second Vatican Council, which ended in the spring of 1960, almost 500 bishops and other prelates requested that Mary's universal mediation be defined. However, this did not come to pass because of the decision that Vatican II should not define any new Dogmas and because of the fear of setting back the ecumenical effort. Pope John Paul II reiterated the same point in 1999 when he declined to define a Dogma of Mary as Mediatrix of All Grace.

In this connection, an interesting point was made in 1984, when Cardinal Confalonieri, in the name of the Chapter of St. Mary Major in Rome, asked for the definition of Mary's universal mediation. The future Benedict XVI, Cardinal Joseph Ratzinger of the Congregation for the Doctrine of the Faith, replied that such a solemn pronouncement was not needed. The reason he adduced for this view is most enlightening: "The doctrine of Mary's universal mediation is already adequately set forth in the various documents of the Church." The Cardinal so much as said that it is a secure doctrine, already officially taught.

The truth of this declaration can be seen in the writings of the latest Popes as well as Vatican II and the Liturgy.

The Doctrine and the Magisterium

Perhaps Blessed Pope Pius IX in his 1854 Apostolic Constitution *Ineffabilis Deus* ("Ineffable God") containing the solemn definition of the Dogma of the Immaculate Conception paved the way for this title with his words:

"Let all the children of the Catholic Church, who are most dear to us, hear our words. With even more ardent zeal for piety, religion, and love, let them continue to venerate, invoke, and pray to the Blessed Virgin Mary, Mother of God, conceived without original sin. Let them with utter confidence have recourse to this sweetest Mother of mercy and grace in all dangers, difficulties, necessities, doubts, and fears.

"Under her guidance, patronage, kindness, and protection, nothing is to be feared and nothing is hopeless. For, while bearing toward us a truly motherly affection and having in her care the work of our salvation, she is solicitous about the whole human race.

"And since she has been appointed by God to be the Queen of heaven and earth, and is exalted above all the choirs of Angels and Saints, and even stands at the right hand of her only-begotten Son, Jesus Christ our Lord, she presents our petitions in a most efficacious manner. What she asks she obtains. Her pleas can never be unheard."

In the wake of those words, papal documents have often portrayed Mary as Mediatrix of all graces. Pope Leo XIII, for example, in his 1891 Encyclical *Octobri Mense* ("The Month of October"), stated: "It may be affirmed with ... truth and precision that, by the Will of God, absolutely no part of that immense treasure of every grace that the Lord amasses ... is bestowed on us except through Mary."

The same doctrine was taught by Pope St. Pius X in his Encyclical *Ad Diem Illum Laetissimum* ("On That Joyful Day"),

Pope Pius XI in his 1928 Encyclical *Miserentissimus* ("Most Merciful"), and Pope Pius XII in his May 13, 1946, radio message. St. Bernard's dictum that God wills us to have everything through Mary is found in the writings of Blessed Pius IX, Leo XIII, St. Pius X, Pius XII, and Blessed John XXIII.

Paul VI solemnly promulgated this teaching, as it is included in the *Constitution on the Church*. And in his 1968 Apostolic Exhortation *Signum Magnum* ("The Great Sign"), he changed the Council wording to make it stronger. *"She makes herself* their Advocate, Auxiliatrix, Aid-Giver, and Mediatrix."

Vatican II, after a lengthy argumentation for and against the doctrine, adopted the following neutral text: "Therefore, the Blessed Virgin is invoked in the Church under the titles of Advocate, Helper, Benefactress, and Mediatrix" (*Constitution on the Church*, no. 62).

It also stressed that the titles just mentioned "are to be so understood that they neither take away nor add anything to the dignity and efficacy of Christ the one Mediator." Indeed, "the unique mediation of the Redeemer does not exclude but rather gives rise among creatures to a manifold cooperation that is but a sharing in this unique source" (Ibid.).

The *Catechism of the Catholic Church* (nos. 968-970) sets forth this same doctrine on Mary's universal mediation with quotes from Vatican II: "She cooperated by her obedience, faith, hope, and burning charity in the Savior's work of restoring supernatural life to souls.... By her manifold intercession [she] continues to bring us the gifts of eternal salvation."

Mass of "Mary, Mother and Mediatrix of Grace"

In 1971, the Congregation for Divine Worship approved a Mass of "The Blessed Virgin Mary, Mother and Mediatrix of Grace." This Mass, faithfully following the teaching of the Second Vatican Council, commemorates both the maternal role of our Lady and her function of mediation and is currently celebrated in many places on May 8.

In 1987, this Mass was included in the new *Collection of Masses of the Blessed Virgin Mary* — 46 Masses that can be celebrated on open days, especially Saturdays.

The Mass gives pride of place to Christ, "truly God and truly human ... the one Mediator ... always living to make intercession for us" (Preface). It also commemorates our Lady as "Mother of the Author of grace," for God the Father, in his eternal wisdom and love, chose her as the Mother and companion of the Redeemer.

The Mass text goes on to make the following points:

(1) The Virgin Mary is Mother of grace, for in her chaste womb she carried him who is "truly God and truly human" (Entrance Antiphon), and brought forth for us "the Author of all grace" (Opening Prayer).

(2) The Virgin Mary is the Mediatrix of grace, for she was the handmaid of Christ in gaining for us the greatest of all graces: redemption and salvation, the Divine life and unending glory.

(3) Our Lady's mediation is interpreted as "the love that she bestows as a mother: [a love] of intercession and pardon, of prayer and grace, of reconciliation and peace" (Preface).

Christ: The One Mediator

There is no doubt that Jesus is the one Mediator between God and human beings: "No one comes to the Father except through me" (John 14:6). He is the Mediator in an absolute, original, and exclusive sense. When we apply the term Mediatrix to Mary, we use it in a relative and subordinate sense as a participation in the unique Mediation of Christ.

Thus, the Apostles of Jesus were also mediators, as are missionaries and those who proclaim the Gospel down the ages. So also are pastors and parents who educate children in the Faith. Indeed, all baptized persons who bear witness to Christ by their lives are mediators.

Every form of the Christian apostolate is a mediation. But it is clear that we are talking about one that is subordinate to and dependent upon that of Christ, who remains the sole Mediator. Neither does he lose this prerogative when others participate in it.

Even if Christ shares this prerogative of mediation with creatures, Mary's participation in it has an extension and importance that are unique: it is proportionate to her role as Mother of God (what greater participation could there be than consenting to the Incarnation of the Word, through which consent Christ was born of her?), as our Mother, as collaborator with Christ in the whole work of the Redemption.

Saints and theologians affirm that through Mary we have received Christ, fount of every grace; hence, even all the graces that come to us through him. The Divine Motherhood is thus the principal source of Mary's mediation.

The expressions of Vatican II render fully legitimate the title of Mediatrix of All Graces attributed to Mary. It merely needs to be explained more fully. She is a Mediatrix dependent on the unique Mediation of Christ and is called upon to apply the Redemption to all souls.

The word grace is used here in its broadest sense and includes whatever produces, conserves, increases, and perfects the Christ-life in us. It includes sanctifying grace, the infused virtues, the gifts of the Holy Spirit, all actual graces, the charisms, and material goods that aid the attainment of heaven.

All human beings are affected by the Mediatrix. Those

who lived before her received their graces in view of her future effectiveness as the universal Mother. Those who come after her receive their graces from the actual exercise of her function as Mediatrix.

Leo XIII stated in his 1894 Encyclical *Iucunda Semper Expectatione* ("An Ever Joyful Expectation") that every grace communicated to human beings has three stages: by God it is communicated to Christ; from Christ it passes to Mary; and from Mary it descends to us. This is how God wills to dispense grace.

Furthermore, Mary distributes grace to all, not just to those who pray to her. She reinforces all prayer, whether it is immediately referred to God or passes by the intercession of the other Saints. Anyone who receives any grace whatever receives it through and from Mary.

A Decree issued by the Sacred Congregation of Rites for the 1947 canonization of St. Louis de Montfort, the great Marian Apostle, and approved by Pius XII, nicely sums up this Catholic belief historically and doctrinally:

"Gathering together the tradition of the Fathers, St. Bernard teaches that God wants us to have everything through Mary. This pious and salutary doctrine all theologians hold in common accord [as of 1947].

"We call it a pious and salutary doctrine because Mary is the most loving Mother not only of Christ but of all of us, and she exercises her power given her from above for the good of human beings in bestowing Divine graces in abundance."

Application to Us

This title of Mary as Mediatrix is of great importance to us. It means that we are assured of receiving all the graces we need from the hands of our loving Mother in heaven. We should, then, frequently call upon her to dispense graces to us as needed.

However, there is another aspect to this title, which is nicely borne out by Pope John Paul II:

"In effect, Mary's mediation *is intimately linked with her motherhood*. It possesses a specifically maternal character, which distinguishes it from the mediation of other creatures who in various and always subordinate ways share in the one mediation of Christ, although her own mediation is also a shared mediation.

"In fact, while it is true that 'no creature could ever be classed with the Incarnate Word and Redeemer,' at the same time 'the unique mediation of the Redeemer does not exclude but rather gives rise among creatures to *a manifold cooperation* which is but a sharing in this unique source.' And thus 'the one goodness of God is in reality communicated diversely to his creatures' (*Constitution on the Church*, no. 62)" (Encyclical *Redemptoris Mater* ["Mother of the Redeemer"], no. 38).

Hence, this Marian title tells us that we too have an obligation to actively participate in the mediation of Mary and her Son. We have to make sure to utilize all our forces to advance the salvation won for the world by Christ. Whatever we can do in this regard is of immense importance.

In this sense, we are, in the words of St. Paul, "filling up what is lacking in the sufferings of Christ" (Colossians 1:24).

What is more, we should realize that if we do not carry out the saving work intended to be done by us, it will go undone.

Prayer to Our Lady, Mediatrix of Graces

> *Most holy Mary,*
> *great Queen of heaven,*
> *the very treasure of life*
> *and ever-flowing channel of Divine grace!*

*By the ineffable virtues
infused into your soul
at your Immaculate Conception,
you were so pleasing in God's sight
that you were privileged
to conceive in your virginal womb
the very Author of life and grace,
Jesus Christ, our Lord.*

*By becoming the Mother of the God-Man,
you also became the Mother of redeemed humankind.*

*Mother of grace and life,
of mercy and forgiveness,
turn to me your kind face.
Behold my many miseries of soul and body.
Raise me up to a state of perfect friendship
with God.
Obtain for me
the grace of final perseverance.*

11

Mother of the Church

Championed by Pope Paul VI

On November 21, 1964, Pope Paul VI gave a closing homily for the third session of the Second Vatican Council in which he proclaimed Mary "Mother of the Church." Like all the homilies opening and closing conciliar sessions, this too is closely connected with the acts of the Council.

Indeed, it has even more importance inasmuch as it expresses the intention of Paul VI to clarify and combine the Papal Magisterium (i.e., Teaching Office) and the Conciliar Magisterium, the latter of which had on that very day approved the *Dogmatic Constitution on the Church*.

In that Constitution, Chapter 8 — dedicated to Mary Most Holy in the Mystery of Christ and the Church — was the fruit of a lengthy and painstaking elaboration. During the elaboration, Paul VI had on various occasions pointed to the opportunity to speak of Mary as the Mother of the Church.

The Council Fathers had accepted the papal invitation but had made only an equivalent affirmation in this regard. They had hesitated to use the papal phrase verbatim because of their ecumenical preoccupation — the desire not to disturb the Separated Brethren.

However, the Pope — because of personal conviction

and devotion as well as the requests of theologians and pastors — believed the time was ripe to solemnly attribute to the Blessed Virgin the title Mother of the Church and to ask that she be venerated by the Christian people hereinafter under this title.

Obviously, this was not a formal definition ("ex cathedra") of a Dogma. Rather it was an act of great prominence of the Papal Magisterium, analogous to that of Pius XII with the proclamation of the Queenship of Mary.

In fact, it was even more binding than the latter because it took place in an Ecumenical Council with the obvious intention of completing the declarations of the Council Fathers. It also included the explicit assertion that the new title "expresses in an admirable synthesis this Council's recognition of the privileged place that the Blessed Virgin has in the Mystery of Christ and the Church" and that the Conciliar *Constitution on the Church* is, as it were, "sealed by the proclamation of Mary as Mother of the Church."

Paul VI stated: "For the glory of the Blessed Virgin and our consolation, we declare most holy Mary Mother of the Church, that is, of the whole Christian people, both faithful and pastors, who call her a most loving Mother. And we decree that henceforth the whole Christian people should, by this most sweet name, give still greater honor to the Mother of God and address prayers to her."

As can be seen, the Pope's justification for the title is based on the Divine Motherhood of Mary, through whom the Word became flesh and united to himself as Head his Mystical Body, which is the Church. The Supreme Pontiff especially emphasized the logical link between Mary's Divine Motherhood and her relationship to the Church:

"Mary is the Mother of Christ who, immediately upon becoming incarnate in her virginal womb, took to himself as Head his Mystical Body, which is the Church. Mary, therefore, as Mother of Christ is to be regarded as Mother also of all the faithful and pastors, that is, of the Church."

History of the Title

The Fathers of the Church wrote little directly related to this title. St. Augustine (d. 430) in a text quoted by Vatican II has the closest text to the title itself: "[Mary] is truly the Mother of the members [of Christ], which is what we are, because she cooperated by charity that the faithful should be born in the Church who would be members of that Head, she herself being truly in the Body Mother of the Head himself" (see *Constitution on the Church*, no. 53).

This teaching is also echoed in the works of the Fathers and ecclesiastical writers. Clement of Alexandria (d. after 211), speaking of Mary says: "I love to call her Church." St. Epiphanius (d. 403) calls Mary the "Mother of the living." He thus not only makes her the New Eve but also inserts in her Divine Motherhood all the living in Christ.

This idea continues in Severian of Gabala (d. after 408) for whom our Lady is the "Mother of salvation," in Theodotus of Ancyra (d. 446) for whom she is the "Mother of the Economy of Salvation," and in St. Proclus of Constantinople (d. 446) for whom Mary has indeed "generated the Mystery."

Finally, Isaac of Stella (d. 1178) expresses a parallelism whereby even the Church by means of the same bridehood and motherhood that are proper to Mary "brings forth the total Christ."

In the Middle Ages, Mary is called "Mother of the Nations" and "Mother of the Christian People." St. Peter Damian (d. 1072) speaks of the Church coming from Mary, Rupert of Deutz (d. 1130) calls Mary "Mother of the Churches," and St. Bonaventure

(d. 1274) says that the Church took her origin from Mary.

The first to use the title itself seems to have been Berengaud (d. twelfth century): "Mary is the Mother of the Church because she brought forth him who is the Head of the Church." In the thirteenth century, an English Cistercian also states: "Mary seems to be Mother of the Church, for since she is certainly Mother of the Head, not unfittingly she is understood to be Mother also of the Body. The Church is, therefore, Mother of Mary, and Mary is Mother of the Church."

From then on more and more material is available about the maternal role of Mary toward the Church.

The Ecclesiastical Magisterium had also substantially and faithfully anticipated this teaching of Paul VI. Benedict XIV in 1748 stated: "The Catholic Church, taught by the Holy Spirit, has always venerated Mary with expressions of filial homage and devotion as a most loving Mother," and these words were used by Vatican II in the *Constitution on the Church* (no. 53).

Leo XIII, in his 1895 Encyclical *Adiutricem Populi* ("Helper of the People") stated: "[Mary] was in very truth the Mother of the Church, the Teacher and Queen of the Apostles." St. Pius X, in his 1904 Encyclical *Ad Diem Illum Laetissimum* ("On That Joyful Day") recalled the union of the faithful with Christ, their Head, in the womb of the Virgin Mary.

Pius XII stated that Mary bestowed on the Mystical Body of Christ that same motherly care and fervent love that she bestowed on the Infant Jesus. Blessed John XXIII used the title five times, and Paul VI also used it several times before the proclamation.

Mother of the Church

The Title in Scripture

There is little doubt that the two principal texts on which this title rests are those of the Annunciation of the Word (Luke 1:26-38) and the third word of Christ from the Cross directed to Mary and the Apostle John: "Behold your son.... Behold your Mother" (John 19:25-27).

In the first text, Christ who has Mary as Mother is the Head in whom the whole Mystical Body, the Church, is also included. In the second text, John who is given Mary as his Mother stands for all the followers of Christ.

Other texts brought to bear on this title are Genesis 3:15 and Revelation 12:1-8. In the former, Mary is the Mother of Christ and his associate in the victory over the devil. In the latter, she is the Mother of "the rest of his descendants." These who are given life by Christ are therefore all children of Mary.

There are also the "signs" that prefigure Mary and the Church in the Old Testament. Although these can be applied to both, they especially illustrate the Motherhood of Mary.

They are: the New Eve, Paradise of God, Ark of the Covenant, Jacob's Ladder, City of God, Tabernacle of the Most High, Strong Woman, and New Creature. Possibly the richest figure Biblically speaking is the "Daughter of Zion," which was also implicitly recalled regarding Mary in the Angel's salutation at the Annunciation.

We might sum up by saying that Mary was intimately involved in four key events in the History of Salvation.

(1) At the Incarnation of the Word, she received the Son of God in the purity of her heart and, conceiving him in her virgin womb, gave birth to our Savior and so nurtured the Church at her very beginning.

(2) At the Passion of Christ, she commiserated completely

with her Son as he hung on the Cross, and he appointed her as the Mother of all human beings.

(3) At the Descent of the Holy Spirit, Mary joined her prayers to those of the Apostles and so became the pattern of the Church at prayer.

(4) By her Assumption into heavenly glory, Mary cares for the pilgrim Church with a Mother's love, following the Church's progress homeward until the day of the Lord dawns in splendor.

Meaning of the Title

Some may object by asking how one who is a member of the Church can also be the Mother of the Church. But in truth there is no contradiction. We must merely recall that words are used in different senses.

Dante had already hinted at such a thing in his beautiful Prayer to Mary, when he addressed our Lady as "the Daughter of your Son." He was using the words analogically, i.e., in different senses.

In this phrase the term "Daughter" is used analogically. Mary is not the natural daughter of Jesus (only his spiritual daughter). But the term "Son" in the phrase is used with its ordinary meaning: Jesus is truly Mary's Son.

The same type of thinking is involved in saying that Mary is the Mother of the Church. Mary is a member or daughter of the Church in one sense and Mother of the Church in another sense — without any contradiction between the two senses.

She is a member of the Church insofar as she pertains to the people of the New Covenant, she too needed the Redemption of Christ, and she is our sister.

She is the Mother of the Church insofar as the Church was

already present in seed at the Incarnation; then the Church was entrusted to Mary by Christ hanging on the Cross, and Mary continues to exercise that spiritual Motherhood that was activated by her cooperation in the work of the Redemption so that salvation may be applied to the whole People of God.

At the same time, Mary is also the Model (or Image) of the Church: "In her the Church admires and exalts the most excellent effect of the Redemption and joyfully contemplates, as in a flawless image, that which the Church herself desires and hopes to be" (Vatican II: *Constitution on the Sacred Liturgy*, no. 103).

Mary is the disciple who is perfect in the following of Christ. With eyes fixed on Mary, the Church strives to follow closely in the footsteps of her Son and be fashioned more and more in that image of Christ which she admires and praises in his glorious Mother.

Mary is a Virgin unsurpassed in purity of faith. The Church always tries to imitate her in this respect, for the Church is herself a virgin who keeps whole and unsullied the faith she has given to her Bridegroom.

Mary is a bride joined to Christ in an unbreakable bond of love and united with him in suffering. As the Church contemplates Mary in the light of the Word truly made flesh, she reverently enters more deeply into the surpassing Mystery of the Incarnation and takes on more and more the image of the Bridegroom.

Mary is a Mother by the overshadowing of the Holy Spirit, and filled with loving concern for all her children. The Church — by imitating Mary's love and faithfully carrying out the Divine Will and through the Word of God she has received — herself becomes a mother. For by preaching and Baptism the Church brings forth to new and immortal life children conceived by the Holy Spirit and born of God.

Mary is a Queen adorned with jewels, sharing eternally in

the glory of the Lord. As the Church looks upon Mary, she sees the perfect image of the Church's future glory.

Thus, the renowned theologian Pierre Grelot can say: "It would be insufficient to call Mary the figure of the Church if the word figure is given the same meaning it has for the personages and realities of the Old Testament. She is something greater and better than a figure.

"Next to Christ, in her humble position, she in some way personifies the Church, and it is not unintentional that the fourth Gospel depicts her at the foot of the Cross becoming by the will of Christ the Mother of the beloved Disciple who represents all Christians.

"Because she is the Mother of Christ, because her maternal suffering associated her with the Passion of her Son, by virtue of the will of Christ she concretely personifies and signifies the maternity of the Church as its source, which is precisely the fruit of the Cross. In a word, in Mary the Mystery of the Church is positively revealed in its most perfect form."

A Teacher of the Spiritual Life

In his classic Apostolic Exhortation *Marialis Cultus* ("Marian Devotion"), Pope Paul VI indicated that flowing from her title "Mother of the Church" is the fact that Mary is a model of the spiritual attitude with which the Church celebrates and lives the Divine Mysteries. Thus, "Mary is also a teacher of the spiritual life for individual Christians" (no. 21).

The Pope also declares: "Mary is above all the example of the worship that consists in making one's life an offering to God. This is an ancient and new doctrine that each individual can hear again by heeding the Church's teaching, but also by heeding the very voice of the Virgin as she, anticipating in herself the wonderful petition of the Lord's Prayer — 'Your will be done' (Matthew 6:10) — replied to God's messenger: 'I am the handmaid of the Lord. Let what you have said be done to me' (Luke 1:38).

"And Mary's 'yes' is for all Christians a lesson and example of obedience to the Will of the Father, which is the way and means of one's salvation" (no. 21).

Thus, Mary is the Mother of the Church because she is her model, because she shows to whoever wants to become a disciple of Christ — and hence a member of the Church — what are the elements that pertain to this choice, how they should and can be the followers of Christ.

Mary is "the attentive Virgin," who receives the Word of God with faith and adheres to it so completely that the word "is made flesh" in her flesh and sanctifies her fully. The Church, too, is attentive to the Word of God so that she may transmit it incorrupt throughout the centuries and offer it to human beings of all times and all places.

The disciple cannot but let himself be guided by the Church in the duty to listen in order to be conformed to that word, which unveils the truth.

Mary is "the Virgin in prayer": her song before Elizabeth becomes a model of and an invitation to the praise of God, the glorious and grateful narrative of the "great things" that God works in history.

The Church narrates for the people the action of salvation that God accomplishes in time, overcoming the egoism, falsehood, and death that dominate the world and helps Christians to know how to read a mysterious presence of God that accompanies the journey of his creatures.

Mary is "the Virgin presenting offerings" who presents Jesus in the Temple and thus enters the Mystery of Jesus who offers himself to the Father as a victim of expiation for the sin of the world.

On Calvary, beneath the Cross of Jesus, Mary is present and while offering the suffering of a mother, "unites herself with a maternal heart to his sacrifice and lovingly consents to the immolation of this victim which she herself had brought forth."

The Church continuously offers the sacrifice of Jesus as the redemption of the world and through her children lives human suffering as the participation in the Passion of Jesus, thus turning every sorrow into an occasion for salvation.

When we call Mary "Mother of the Church," we are all recalled to this Mystery of love and sorrow that is consumed on Calvary and that is perpetuated in the Church through the Sacraments and principally the Eucharist. Hence, to invoke Mary under this title renews fidelity to the Church and summons everyone to more lively and personal participation in the Christian community from which and in which faith is born and grows.

In this way, Christians discover every day the immense gift of belonging to the Church and they are led to question themselves as to the best way to carry out this responsibility.

Application to Us

The *Constitution on the Church* states: "However, while in the person of the Blessed Virgin the Church has already reached that perfection by which she exists without spot or wrinkle (see Ephesians 5:27), the faithful are still striving to conquer sin and grow in holiness. That is why they raise their eyes to Mary, who shines forth as the model of virtues before the whole community of the Elect" (no. 65).

The title "Mother of the Church" can help us in our striving for holiness. It presents our Lady to us as the model of various virtues for us to imitate.

Model of sublime love, Mary reminds us that the Church

must stand before all peoples as the sacrament of God's love, and since we are a part of the Church we should constantly strive to bear witness to God's love.

Model of profound humility, Mary urges us to emulate that forgotten virtue in a world gone mad with self-aggrandizement.

Model of persevering prayer in oneness of mind and heart, Mary encourages us to pray always and to join with others in prayer in a spirit of self-giving.

Model of worship in spirit, Mary exhorts us to help bring about true worship for God's Church by offering ourselves as a holy victim, pleasing in God's eyes.

Model of liturgical worship, Mary summons us to listen, to pray, and to offer as we celebrate the Divine Mysteries while awaiting the coming of her Son.

This title also reminds us of the great regard Christ and his Mother have for the Church. It should lead us to "think with the Church," to have the same mind as the Church, to love the Church, and to be faithful to that Church until death.

At the same time, it also brings to mind that the Church includes not only those who are its active members but also all those who are potential members — all those whom Christ died to save.

Prayer to the Mother of the Church

> O Mary,
> look upon the Church...
> gathered about you to thank you
> and to celebrate you as their Mystical Mother....
> We ask you now
> that we may be made worthy of honoring you

*because of who you are
and because of what you do
in the wondrous and loving plan of salvation.
Grant that we may praise you,
O holy Virgin!*

*May your most human voice,
O most beautiful of virgins,
O most worthy of mothers,
O blessed among women,
invite the world to turn its eyes
toward the life that is the light of human beings,
toward you who are the precursor-lamp of Christ,
who is the sole and the highest Light of the world.*

Paul VI

12
Mother of God

The Fundamental Title

The title "Mother of God" is the fundamental title of the Blessed Virgin Mary and the one that gives rise to all her other titles. It celebrates the wonderful and inexpressible Mystery by which the Father of mercies sent his Son from heaven into the womb of the Blessed Virgin to be his saving Word and our Book of Life.

At the same time, the title lays the basis for the preeminence of Mary, Mother of God, in the consciousness of Christians. It enables the Marian Mystery to be formulated in the successive ages both theologically and linguistically by dwelling on both the Person and the work of the Redeemer.

In the words of the eminent theologian Karl Rahner, "The Word was made flesh because a maiden of our race knelt down at the Angel's message and in the freedom of her heart and with the total unconditional gift of herself said: 'Be it done to me according to your word' (Luke 1:38).

"God willed this freely given love of his creature as the means by which the eternal Word of the Father should enter the world to take this world up into his own life. That was the way he willed to come into this world. As a consequence, Mary, of the same race as ourselves, is the portal of eternal mercy, the gate of heaven, through which we are in fact saved and redeemed and taken up into the life of God.

"The Divine Motherhood of the Blessed Virgin is therefore God's grace alone, and her own act, inseparably. It is not simply a physical motherhood, it is her grace and her deed, placing her whole self, body and soul, at the service of God and his redemptive mercy to humankind.

"And since this Divine Motherhood — as an act of faith personally made — belongs intrinsically to the history of Redemption which [Mary] has decisively influenced, she has a place in our creed and our piety."

Thus, this title also protects the reality of the Incarnation and the unity of Christ — the fact that he was true God and true Man, two natures but one Person. Indeed, it flows from the Dogma of the Divine Motherhood of Mary.

Perhaps Cardinal John Henry Newman (d. 1890) best described this fact in a way to let us see all the aspects it involves:

"Now, as you know, it has been held from the first, and defined from an early age, that Mary is the Mother of God. She is not merely the Mother of our Lord's manhood, or of our Lord's body, but she is to be considered the Mother of the Lord himself, the Word incarnate.

"God, in the person of the Word, the Second Person of the All-glorious Trinity, took the substance of his human flesh from her, and clothed in it he lay within her; and he bore it about with him after birth, as a sort of badge and witness that he, though God, was hers.

"He was nursed and tended by her; he was suckled by her; he lay in her arms. As time went on, he ministered to her, and obeyed her. He lived with her for thirty years, in one house, with an uninterrupted intercourse, and with only the saintly Joseph to share it with him.

"She was the witness of his growth, of his joys, of his sorrows, of his prayers; she was blest with his smile, with the touch of his hand, with the whisper of his affection, with the expression of his thoughts and his feelings for that length of time."

Based on the Scriptures

Mary's Divine Motherhood is based on the Scriptures. These bear witness that Mary is the Mother of the Son of God because the fruit of her womb is a Divine Person.

In Galatians 4:4-6, Paul writes: "When the fullness of time had come, God sent his Son born of a woman, born under the Law, to redeem those who were under the Law, that they might receive the adoption of children. And that you are children is shown by the fact that God has sent into our hearts the Spirit of his Son who cries out: 'Abba, Father!'"

In order to come into this world, the Son of God chose the medium of a woman. He wished to have a mother like all of us. Although this passage does not explicitly name the Blessed Virgin, it is clear that she is the one in question. The Son of God will be "the Son of Mary" (Mark 6:3; see Matthew 13:55; John 6:42).

In Matthew 1:18-25, we are told that the child conceived by the Virgin Mary will be Divine. He will save his people from their sins as the Emmanuel — God-with-us. If in the Old Covenant the people was exclusively the people of Yahweh, under the New Covenant this people belongs at the same time to both the Father and the Son.

The new Emmanuel has received all power in heaven and on earth (Matthew 28:19). Therefore, he also has his people (Matthew 1:21), who is the people of Yahweh (see Matthew 2:6).

Concerning this new people that he has acquired, Jesus

will say: "On this rock I will build *my Church*" (Matthew 16:18), and "Go and announce *to my brothers...*" (Matthew 28:10), and "Behold, I am *with you*" (Matthew 28:20).

Hence, it is clear that even for Matthew the One to be born of Mary has an absolutely unique nature: He is a Divine Being.

In the first chapter of Luke, Mary is greeted as Mother of the Son of God with allusions to her as the new Ark of the Covenant (1:35: new tent; 1:39-44, 56: new Ark) as well as with the explicit profession of Elizabeth (1:43: "the Mother of my *Lord*").

Elizabeth is here using a term ("Lord") that meant God to Hellenistic Jews — as is implied by the verses that follow: "What was spoken to her from the *Lord*" (45) and "My soul magnifies the *Lord*" (46).

In John, we learn that the evangelist wrote his Gospel "that you may believe that Jesus is the Messiah, the Son of God and that believing you may have life in his Name" (20:31). And John also, though never using the name of Mary, calls her the "Mother" of the Son of God (2:1; 19:25).

The Title and the Magisterium

The first known mention of the title "Mother of God" concerning Mary is found in St. Hippolytus of Rome (d. 236). It is also found a bit later in the third century in the prayer *Sub Tuum* ("Under Your Patronage, O Holy Mother of God...").

During the fifth century this title was attacked by Nestorius, Patriarch of Constantinople (428), because of his views on Christology. He saw two Persons in Christ — not one. Hence for him, the Son of God was one thing, the son of Mary another.

In 431, the Council of Ephesus defended the true teaching of one Person with two natures in Christ and approved the title of Mother of God in reference to Mary.

In 451, the Council of Chalcedon officially promulgated the normative decision set forth at Ephesus. It spoke of "one and the same Son, our Lord Jesus Christ, the same perfect in Godhead and the same perfect in human nature, true God and true Man, the same with a rational soul and body, consubstantial with the Father according to the Divine Nature, consubstantial with us according to the human nature, 'like us unto all things except sin' (Hebrews 4:15).

"He was born of the Father before all ages according to the Divinity, but in these last days was born of the Virgin Mary, Mother of God according to the humanity."

In 553, the Second Council of Constantinople condemned an erroneous interpretation of Chalcedon and reiterated that Mary is the Mother of God because God the Word, "born of the Father before the ages, was made flesh of her in the last days."

In 681, the Third Council of Constantinople stated that Jesus Christ was born of the Holy Spirit and the Virgin Mary, rightly and truly the Mother of God according to his humanity.

Throughout the centuries this teaching has been constant in Church documents. It was taught in the sixteenth century by Paul IV and in the twentieth century by Pius XI in 1931, the fifteenth centenary of the Council of Ephesus.

Pius XII also referred to it frequently as the source of all the privileges and graces of Mary, e.g., "The Woman, whose Son is the Son of the Most High who 'will reign in the house of Jacob forever (Luke 1:32),' 'the Prince of Peace (Isaiah 9:6),' 'the King of kings and Lord of lords (Revelation 19:16),' this Woman has received from God singular privileges of grace above all other creatures."

The Second Vatican Council called Mary "Mother of God" twelve times in chapter 8 of the *Constitution on the Church* and recalled the Divine Motherhood in three other documents: *Constitution on the Liturgy* (no. 103), the *Decree on Ecumenism* (no. 15), and the *Decree on the Eastern Churches* (no. 30).

The following are two of the most relevant citations of the Council in this regard:

"At the announcement of the Angel, the Virgin Mary received the Word of God both in her heart and in her body and gave Life to the world. Hence, she is acknowledged and honored as the true Mother of God and of the Redeemer" (*Constitution on the Church*, no. 53).

"The Christians of the East render high praise, in very beautiful hymns, to Mary, ever Virgin, whom the Ecumenical Council of Ephesus solemnly proclaimed to be God's most holy Mother so that Christ may be truly and properly acknowledged as Son of God and Son of Man, in accord with the Scriptures" (*Decree on Ecumenism*, no. 15).

Finally, the *Catechism of the Catholic Church* (no. 495) summarizes Mary's Divine Motherhood in this way: "Called in the Gospels 'the Mother of Jesus,' Mary is acclaimed by Elizabeth, at the prompting of the Spirit and even before the birth of her Son, as 'the Mother of my Lord.' In fact, the One whom she conceived as man by the Holy Spirit, who truly became her Son according to the flesh, was none other than the Father's eternal Son, the second Person of the Holy Trinity. Hence, the Church confesses that Mary is truly 'Mother of God.'"

The Title and the Liturgy

In his Apostolic Exhortation on Devotion to the Blessed Virgin Mary (*Marialis Cultus*), Pope Paul VI stated that "the Christmas Season is a prolonged commemoration of the Divine, virginal, and salvific Motherhood of her whose 'inviolate virginity brought the Savior into the world.'... In the revised ordering of the Christmas period it seems to us that the attention of all should be directed toward the restored Solemnity of Mary the Holy Mother of God.

"This celebration, placed on January 1 in conformity with the ancient indication of the Liturgy of the City of Rome, is meant to commemorate the part played by Mary in this Mystery of Salvation. It is meant also to exalt the singular dignity that this Mystery brings to the 'holy Mother' ... through whom we were found worthy to receive the Author of life" (no. 5).

Indeed, scholars have shown that even before the four Marian Feasts of Eastern origin (i.e., Birth of Mary, Annunciation, Purification, and Assumption) entered the Roman Rite in the seventh century, the Octave Day of Christmas was already celebrated at Rome as a day of commemoration of Mary and her maternal role in the Incarnation.

Later, under the influence of the Gallican Rite, the Octave of Christmas took on the character of the Feast of the Circumcision of the Lord. This passed on into the Roman Missal of St. Pius V in the sixteenth century even though the proper texts of the day retained a clearly Marian tone.

In the eighteenth century, a movement arose in Portugal to obtain a special feast of the Divine Motherhood of Mary, bypassing the celebration of January 1 and putting the accent on the mystical reality celebrated in the abstract Marian title. So in 1751, Benedict XIV granted this feast to the dioceses of Portugal to be celebrated on the first Sunday of May with proper texts composed by the Pontiff himself.

Later the feast of the Divine Motherhood of the Virgin was extended to other dioceses and religious orders, and from 1914 on it was assigned to October 11. In 1931, on the fifteenth centenary of the Council of Ephesus, Pius XI extended this feast to the whole Latin Church on October 11.

In the wake of the renewal of Vatican II, the 1969 Roman Calendar returned the feast once again to January 1, its original date. Hence, in keeping with the many traditional texts of the Roman Liturgy for the Octave of Christmas that exalted the virginal Motherhood of Mary on this day, the date of January 1 allows us to celebrate this fundamental Marian privilege precisely in Christmastime, i.e., in its rightful place at the heart of the celebrations of the Incarnation.

Meaning of the Title

The title "Mother of God" tells us the manner in which Christ came among us. Pope Paul VI brought this out very well in an allocution on April 4, 1970:

"Did [Christ] come among us of himself? Did he come without any relation, without any cooperation on the part of humanity? Can he be known, understood, and contemplated prescinding from the real, historical, and existential relationships that his appearance in the world necessarily entails?

"It is clear that the answer is No. The Mystery of Christ is inserted in the Divine Plan of human participation. He came among us in accord with the medium of human generation. He willed to have a Mother; he willed to become incarnate through the vital mystery of a woman, blessed among all women....

"It is from Mary that we have Christ, in our very first relationship with him. He is a human being as we are; he is our brother through the maternal ministry of Mary. If we wish to be Christians, we must be Marianists, i.e., we must recognize the essential, vital, and providential rapport that unites our Lady to Jesus and that opens to us the way that leads to him."

Mary has been chosen by God so that the Son of God might become a human being. This is the reason why Mary is in the plan of salvation. Conceiving, forming, bringing forth, and rearing this Child who is God, Mary became the Mother of God.

Mary formed her Son's humanity, not only his body. Like all other mothers, she awakened the psychology of her Son and in this way humanized him.

As A. Delesalle has said: "Mary conceives and brings forth, in his human nature, One who is God from all eternity. Jesus is not God by the fact that he is conceived or born of Mary (this would not be a Mystery but an absurdity because it would make Mary Mother of the Divine Nature).

"Mary is Mother of God because from her own flesh she gives to the Word a human nature like hers. And just as in ordinary human generation the terminus of the parents' generative action is not the human nature produced but the person subsisting in this nature, so in the case of Mary: her maternal action reaches to the Person of the Word, who by this very fact is truly her Son."

By means of this "folly" of God, we can grasp his love for us and his plan of salvation. He takes on all of human existence but without diminishing his transcendence, without altering his Divine existence as such.

Mary is in no way a goddess. She represents all of humanity, and, through her, God takes on human nature. Even though God had all things, for the work of salvation he willed to receive human fragility, the capacity to act, to suffer, and to die as a human being in solidarity with all human beings so as to save them.

Yet we must be careful to stress that this does not mean God had need of a mother or that Mary transmitted to Jesus his Divinity. At the same time, Mary is a poor creature like us, needful of redemption. She is the Mother of God because her Son is Divine, not because she is a goddess.

The Dutch theologian Eduard Schillebeeckx has nicely

summarized some aspects of the human side of Mary's maternity:

"Mary was Jesus' Mother. That means that Jesus, as a man, was brought up by Mary and Joseph. This is, of course, a great Mystery and difficult for the human mind to grasp. Nonetheless, we must affirm the Dogma that Christ was a true human being and, as such, had to be brought up and educated, in the strictest sense of the word, by his Mother.

"His human qualities and character were formed and influenced by his Mother's virtues. And when we read in Scripture that Christ went around in the land of Palestine doing good, and realize that the human goodness was God's love, we are bound to acknowledge too that Mary had a maternal share in this Christian interpretation of God's love.

"It is common human experience that the mother's features are recognizable in the child, and this was true in the case of Mary and Jesus. Mary's function in the Incarnation was not completed when Jesus was born. It was a continuous task, involving the human formation of the young man, as he grew up from infancy to childhood and from childhood to adulthood. How this was accomplished is hidden from us."

Application to Us

The title "Mother of God" has special meaning for Catholics. It tells us that Mary has much influence with her Divine Son — just as every mother does with her child. Therefore, it encourages us to have frequent recourse to her in our difficulties as well as in our joys.

At the same time, this title also has another meaning for us. Mary was Christ's Mother more by her faith than by her physical bearing and rearing of him. Only of her is it said that she "pondered all these things and kept them in her heart" (Luke 2:19).

The Fathers stated with complete justification that "Mary conceived her Son first in her heart and then in her body." Herein lies the greatness of Mary's Divine Motherhood.

Her singularity stems from her spiritual attitude of conscientious and hence meritorious fidelity to the Divine mission rather than her condition of fortunate Mother of the promised Messiah.

In this image of the Virgin's Divine Motherhood can be included all those who like her believe. For it is faith that causes God to be born in the heart of the believer.

Indeed, when a woman shouted out to Jesus the praises of the Mother who bore him in her womb and nourished him at her breast, he quickly answered: "Rather, blessed are those who hear the Word of God and put it into practice" (Luke 11:27-28). He even likened such people to a mother, sister, and brother to him (Luke 8:21).

In the words of the nineteenth-century theologian M.J. Scheeben, "The personal distinguishing mark of Mary is, as a rule, determined by the fact that she is called Mother of God or, for our point of view here, she who bears God.

"The element that in the Divine Motherhood forms the distinguishing mark of the person and the grace of the Divine Motherhood is the following: a supernatural, spiritual union of the person of Mary with that of her Son. This union, brought about by the Will of God, underlies her maternal activity as contrasted with the humanity of her Son and completes and perfects her bodily union with him."

As a consequence of this teaching, it follows that we can all be parents and brothers and sisters of Christ by faith. We can give birth to him in the hearts of those who do not know him.

Prayer to Mary, Mother of God

O Blessed Lady,
you are the Mother of Justification
and those who are justified;
the Mother of Reconciliation
and those who are reconciled;
the Mother of Salvation
and those who are saved.

What a blessed trust, and what a secure refuge!
The Mother of God is our Mother.
The Mother of the One in whom alone we hope
and whom alone we fear
is our Mother....

The One who partook of our nature
and by restoring us to life
made us children of his Mother
invites us by this to proclaim
that we are his brothers and sisters.

Therefore, our Judge is also our Brother.
The Savior of the world is our Brother.
Our God has become — through Mary — our Brother!

St. Anselm of Canterbury

13

Mother of Mercy

Mercy — Compassion for the Misery of Others

The History of Salvation is, in the final analysis, identified with the history of human misery that is perennially intertwined with the history of the Divine Mercy.

In the History of Salvation, the protagonists on the human side are Adam and Eve together with all their descendants. On the Divine side, the protagonists are Christ, who is Mercy, and Mary, who is the "Mother of Mercy."

Mercy consists in feeling compassion for the misery of others and in acting to alleviate it. Misery may refer to any evil, whether physical or moral. Thus, we have the traditional corporal and spiritual works of mercy.

The corporal (or material) works of mercy are: (1) To feed the hungry. (2) To give drink to the thirsty. (3) To clothe the naked. (4) To visit the imprisoned. (5) To shelter the homeless. (6) To visit the sick. (7) To bury the dead.

The spiritual works of mercy are: (1) To admonish the sinner. (2) To instruct the ignorant. (3) To counsel the doubtful. (4) To comfort the sorrowful. (5) To bear wrongs patiently. (6) To forgive all injuries. (7) To pray for the living and the dead.

Over this whole ocean of corporal or physical miseries shines forth the maternal mercy of Mary, greeted by the Church with the very consoling title of Mother of Mercy, which sometimes becomes Queen of Mercy.

History of the Title

The title is generally attributed to St. Odo of Cluny (880-942). However, even before his time there are references — both in the Eastern and in the Western Church — to Mary's mercy toward all her suffering children, although a full-scale devotion to the Mother of Mercy did not yet exist.

Thus, in the third century we find a reference to this title in a reconstructed text of the *Sub Tuum* (the oldest known prayer to our Lady), which says: "We take refuge beneath your mercies, O Mother of God."

In the fourth century, St. Ephrem (d. 378) called Mary "the inexhaustible fount of mercy." About that same time, the Akathist Hymn came into use with the line "Let every hymn yield that seeks to match your infinite mercy."

In the fifth century, Jacob of Sarug (d. 521) spoke of Mary as the "Mother of Mercy" in a sermon: "How many terrors did not the Mother of Mercy experience when you [Jesus] were buried and the guards of the sepulcher barred her way so that she could not draw near to you?"

In the seventh century, St. Sophronius of Jerusalem (d. 639) called Mary "the abyss of mercy," and in the next century St. Germanus of Constantinople (d. 733) declared: "No one without you [Mary] will be granted the gift of mercy."

In the eighth century, Bishop David of Benevento gave Mary the name "Most Merciful," and Ambrose Autpert (d. 784) invoked Mary's mercy in these words: "Come to the relief of those enmeshed in misery.... Have compassion on the afflicted."

Finally, in the tenth century, St. Odo popularized the title and the devotion to the Mother of Mercy. On a Christmas Eve, he prayed to Mary as follows:

"Dear Lady, on this night you gave the Savior to the world; be my intercessor. I have recourse to your glorious and singular giving birth, O most devout Lady, and ask you to incline the ears of your mercy to my prayers.

"I am greatly afraid that my life is displeasing to your Son. Therefore, since it was through you that he manifested himself to the world, I pray that through you he will also have mercy on me."

The title and devotion to the Mother of Mercy spread rapidly after that. By the eleventh century, people were urged to have recourse to the Mother of Mercy. It became part of a series of miraculous occurrences in the lives of Christans that were attributed to the Mother of Mercy.

The title also became part of litanies that were circulated before the advent of the official Litany of the Saints and Litany of Loreto. In these early litanies, the invocation "Holy Mother of Mercy" was placed after the invocations to the Blessed Trinity.

In addition, the title was utilized in the ancient forms of the liturgical Office of our Lady, which contained "Blessings" asked of Mary. One such Blessing was: "May the Mother of Mercy come to our aid this day. Amen."

Finally, the title appeared more and more in the sermons of preachers and in the prayers of the people. It entered into the Marian vocabulary and teaching of the Church.

Basis in Scripture

Although there is no specific Scripture text naming Mary as "Mother of Mercy," there are several texts that form the basis for this title.

The first text is that of the Annunciation (Luke 1:26-38), which gives Mary's gracious consent to become the Mother of the Son of God, who will save his people from their sins. Once she knows all the pertinent information, Mary does not hesitate to agree to help save her suffering people.

Her decision is based on a host of reasons, but among them is unquestionably her compassion for the world, so aptly brought out by St. Bernard (d. 1153):

"[Mary,] we also await a word of compassion, we who are miserably oppressed by a sentence of damnation. You are offered the cost of our salvation; if you consent, we shall be quickly set free.

"The whole world prostrate before you awaits your answer. On a word of your lips depends the consolation of the miserable, the redemption of prisoners, the liberation of the condemned, and the salvation of... the whole human race."

The second text is that of the Visitation (Luke 1:39-45), which sets forth Mary's visit to her cousin Elizabeth immediately after the Annunciation. Although aware that she herself is with child, Mary does not hesitate to go to the aid of Elizabeth, her aged cousin. She immediately undertakes the journey from Nazareth to Elizabeth's house in the hill country — which scholars estimate took several days.

Undoubtedly, the reason for Mary's haste is her compassion and love for her cousin in her time of difficulty and her desire to be of help.

Thus, for three months, she remains with Elizabeth, aiding and comforting her. Then, only after the birth of the child John, does she return to Bethlehem to prepare for her own childbearing.

The third text with an example of Mary's great compassion is that of the Marriage Feast at Cana (John 2:1-11). Jesus goes with his disciples to a marriage feast, and Mary is also there.

During the festivities, which in keeping with custom continue for some time, Mary becomes aware that the wine has run out and the feast will be spoiled for the bride and groom. With Pope John Paul II, we can see in this happening "a sign of all the other risks to which the beginning love of the bride and groom was to undergo successive exposure."

Mary takes compassion on the couple and immediately brings the lack of wine to her Son's attention. Jesus replies that his time has not yet come. But Mary knows her Son and serenely continues her act of intercession to remedy the situation. She instructs the waiters to do whatever Jesus tells them.

In the natural course of things, Jesus accedes to his Mother's urgent request and changes water into the best of wines. The festivities continue and Mary's compassion is vindicated.

The fourth text is that of the Crucifixion, which states that Mary is standing valiantly near the Cross on which her Son is dying a slow and extremely painful death (John 19:1).

Mary's love and compassion have committed her to stand by her beloved Son through this darkest of valleys. And she offers herself in union with him for the life of the world.

The fifth and last text is that of the Descent of the Holy Spirit (Acts 1:14; 2:1-4). After the Ascension of her Son into heaven, Mary's compassion for the disciples in this time of fear and dread in the absence of their Master leads her to remain in continuous prayer with them. She comforts and counsels these souls who have lost their leader and are at sea as to what to do.

Then Mary is in their midst when the power of the Holy Spirit descends on them and gives new strength and direction to their lives. Exiting from the Upper Room, they spread throughout the world, proclaiming the Good News with unflinching courage and ultimately giving their lives for their Master.

It is this compassion of Mary that led Christians to call her the "Mother of Mercy" — and with complete justification. For wherever there is someone in difficulty, there is Mary to apply consolation, help, and mercy.

Meaning of the Title

The title "Mother of Mercy" is capable of two meanings. The first is that Mary is the Mother of the Merciful One, i.e., Christ, the Son of God. The second (a kind of corollary of the first) is that Mary is a merciful Mother toward all her children in the world. And it is this second one that is primarily intended by the Church and her members when they utilize the title.

St. Thomas Aquinas (d. 1274) says: "When the Blessed Virgin conceived the Eternal Word in her womb and gave him birth, she obtained half the Kingdom of God. She became Queen of *Mercy* and her Son remained King of *Justice*." Christ arranged that all mercies dispensed to human beings should pass through her hands and be disposed as she pleases.

Thus, the title really embodies two titles, both of which speak of our Lady's graciousness and are much loved by the faithful: *Queen of Mercy* and *Mother of Mercy.*

The title "Queen of Mercy" celebrates the kindness, the generosity, and the dignity of the Blessed Virgin, who from her place in heaven fulfills the role of Queen Esther (Esther 4:17). She never ceases praying to her Son for the salvation of her people as they confidently fly to her for refuge in their trials and dangers.

The Blessed Virgin is thus the gracious and compassionate Queen who has herself uniquely known God's loving kindness and stretches out her arms to embrace all who take refuge in her. Hence, she is rightly addressed as solace of the repentant and hope of the distressed.

Mother of Mercy

St. Albert the Great (d. 1280) says: "Mary was the only one to whom the privilege of sharing in the Passion of Christ was given. To be able to reward her for it, her Son wished her to share also in the merits of the Passion.

"And to make her a sharer in the benefit of the Redemption, he wished her to be his partner also in the suffering of the Passion, in order that she, as she was his helpmate in the Redemption, might also be Mother of all by reparation. And as the whole world is indebted to God for his Passion, so all would be indebted to their Queen for her *Compassion*."

The title "Mother of Mercy" is a fitting one both because our Lady brought forth for us Jesus Christ, the visible manifestation of the mercy of the invisible God, and because she is the Spiritual Mother of the faithful, full of grace and mercy.

In the words of St. Lawrence of Brindisi (d. 1619), "the Blessed Virgin is called 'Mother of Mercy,' i.e., the most merciful, the most compassionate Mother, the most tender Mother, the most loving Mother." For from her place in heaven, she points out the needs of the faithful to her Son, with whom she interceded on earth in behalf of the bridegroom and bride of Cana.

St. Bernard (d. 1153) says: "Kings and Queens, because they are invested with majesty do inspire awe and make their people fear to come near them. But how can any persons fear to approach this Queen of Mercy? She inspires no terror, shows no severity to anyone, but is so tender and agreeable."

In a vision, St. Bridget of Sweden (d. 1373) is said to have heard Mary say: "I am the Queen of Heaven and the Mother of Mercy. I am the joy of the righteous and the door through which sinners come to God. I am called by all the Mother of Mercy. It is my Son's mercy toward human beings that has made me merciful too."

Thus, as St. Alphonsus Liguori (d. 1787) says, "Mary is not

called the Mother of Mercy. She *is* the Mother of Mercy. And she proves herself to be such by the loving tenderness with which she helps us all."

Referring to our Lady's great concern for sinners, St. Bernard calls Mary the Promised Land flowing with milk and honey. And St. Leo the Great (d. 461) says that when he looks at her, he no longer sees God's justice but only his mercy, for Mary is full of the mercy of God.

Benedict XV (d. 1922) says that Mary moves the Divine Mercy: "The sight of her reminds God of his Covenant and causes him to be mindful of his mercy. Mary is that heavenly stream that brings to the hearts of wretched mortals all God's gifts and graces."

Leo XIII (d. 1903) says that Mary is the realization of the Divine Mercy. And St. Pius X (d. 1914) adds that she is the sign of the Divine Mercy.

John Paul II (d. 2005) declares: "Mary is the one who 'knows most the Mystery of the Divine Mercy.' She knows what it cost and how great it is. In this sense, we call her also the 'Mother of Mercy....'

"These express the particular preparation of her soul, of her whole personality, for knowing how to discern — in the complex events of the first Israel and of every person and then the whole of humanity — that mercy in which 'from age to age' (Luke 1: 50) all share in accord with the eternal plan of the Blessed Trinity" (*Dives in Misericordia*, no. 9).

The Pact or Covenant of Mercy

We might bring home more concretely what this title means by taking a look at the Ethiopian Church's "Pact or Covenant of Mercy," which is an integral part of its devotion toward our

Lady. By this Pact, Jesus is said to have promised Mary that she would deliver from every trial those who would invoke her name and celebrate her memory.

For the Ethiopian Church, this Pact is akin to a "third Testament" of the Divine Economy for the salvation of human beings. It is said to have been concluded between Christ and his Mother on Calvary where, according to tradition, after the Death of the Lord, Mary was accustomed to retire to pray. One day, Jesus appeared to her surrounded by legions of Angels and bestowed upon her this singular privilege in favor of her devoted followers.

This Church has woven around the incident a hymn of forty-two stanzas that invoke Mary and say among other things: "This Pact of mercy is the name of our Lady, the holy and doubly Virgin Mother of God. When she is invoked, trembling overtakes the firmament of the heavens and the depths of the earth to the very foundations of the netherworld. Moreover, the wings of Angels are overwhelmed with fear like leaves shaken by the wind.

"When this name is invoked, besides the fear of creatures, even our Lord and Savior, her Son, who holds omnipotence in his hands, when he summons the sinner into his presence to pronounce the punitive sentence, is affected upon hearing invoked the Virgin's name that is written like a pact on the forehead of sinners. He leaves the hall of justice with clemency and does not carry out the sentence."

All the above follows from what John Paul II says about Mary in the Encyclical *Dives in Misericordia*: "Through her hidden and at the same time incomparable sharing in the Messianic Mission of her Son, [Mary] was called in a special way to bring close to people that love which he had come to reveal: the love that finds its most concrete expression vis-à-vis the suffering, the poor, those deprived of their own freedom, the blind, the oppressed, and sinners, just as Christ spoke of them in the words of the prophecy of Isaiah, first in the synagogue at Nazareth (see Luke 4:18) and then in response to the question of the messengers of John the Baptist (see Luke 7:22).

"It was precisely this 'merciful' love, which is manifested above all in contact with moral and physical evil that the heart of her who was the Mother of the Crucified and Risen One shared in singularly and exceptionally."

Application to Us

In recent years, the Church has included a Mass entitled "Holy Mary, Queen and Mother of Mercy" in the Collection of Masses of the Blessed Virgin Mary, which can be celebrated on open days in the Liturgical Year. The formula of that Mass nicely summarizes what the title Mother of Mercy can mean for us.

First, Mary is a prophet extolling the mercy of God. In her *Magnificat* (Luke 1:46-55) she twice praises God's mercy: "He has mercy on those who fear him in every generation"; "He has come to the help of his servant Israel, for he has remembered his promise of mercy" (Luke 1:50, 54).

Therefore, this title is a great reminder for us always to praise God's mercy in union with Mary.

Mary is also a woman who has uniquely experienced God's mercy. She is thus well aware of the great graces that flow from that mercy and desires that we take advantage of it. As Bernardine of Bustis (d. 1513) declares, Mary is more eager to grant us graces than we are to receive them. Therefore, no matter when we go to her, we find her hands filled with generous mercies.

As St. Peter Canisius (d. 1597) exclaimed, "Happy the day when the humble handmaid of the Lord had risen so high that she had become the Queen of heaven and of the world, so high that she could go no higher! Arrived at the royal throne itself, she is seated there in glory, next to Christ! Indeed, happy and holy is that day when a Queen and Mother was established in the Kingdom of God, who was at the same time both powerful and good.

"While remaining Mother of our Judge, she is a Mother to us, full of mercy. She constitutes our protection; she keeps us close to Christ, and she faithfully takes the matter of our salvation into her charge."

It is very clear that we should make use of this title of Mary and continually pray to her to obtain mercy for us in all the difficulties of life. At the same time, we should never forget that the mercy she dispenses is from God, and thus we should praise the Triune God for his overflowing goodness to us in our miseries.

In return, we should strive to show compassion and mercy to others while living in this world. In this age of the all-present media, we can find many people who are suffering and need our help.

Above all, we should be ever mindful that our Mother of Mercy is "the hope of those who have no hope." Therefore, we should never succumb to despair but instead call upon Mary in the words of St. Bernard:

> *O Lady,*
> *who can lack confidence in you,*
> *since you help even those who are in despair?*
> *And I have not the least doubt that,*
> *when we run to you,*
> *we shall obtain all we desire.*
> *Let those who have no hope, hope in you.*

Prayer to Mary, Mother of Mercy

Blessed Virgin Mary,
who can worthily repay you with praise and thanks
for having rescued a fallen world
by your generous consent!
Receive our gratitude
and by your prayers obtain the pardon of our sins.
Take our prayers into the sanctuary of heaven
and enable them to make our peace with God.
Holy Mary,
help the miserable,
strengthen the discouraged,
comfort the sorrowful,
pray for your people,
plead for the clergy,
intercede for all women consecrated to God.
May all who venerate you
feel now your help and protection.

Be ready to help us when we pray,
and bring back to us the answers to our prayers.
Make it your continual concern
to pray for the people of God,
for you were blessed by God
and were made worthy
to bear the Redeemer of the world,
who lives and reigns forever.

Attributed to St. Augustine of Hippo

14

Mother of the Savior

Centrality of the Paschal Mystery

According to the *Catechism of the Catholic Church* (no. 571), the Paschal Mystery of Christ's Cross and Resurrection stands at the center of the Good News that the Apostles — and the Church following them — are to proclaim to the world. God's saving plan was accomplished "once for all" (Hebrews 9:26) by the redemptive Death of his Son Jesus Christ.

The Scriptures had foretold this Divine Plan of salvation through the putting to death of the righteous one, "[the Lord's] Servant" (Isaiah 53:11) as a Mystery of universal redemption, i.e., as the ransom that would free human beings from the slavery of sin.

Jesus' redemptive Death fulfills Isaiah's prophecy of the Suffering Servant. Jesus himself explained the meaning of his Life and Death in the light of God's Suffering Servant (Matthew 20:28; Luke 24:25-27).

The idea of the Redemption in virtue of which God frees or ransoms also includes the idea of acquisition in virtue of which he "purchases" a people as his own. As the Letter to Titus (2: 13f) indicates, Jesus is "Savior" insofar as he "sets us free from all iniquity" and "makes us a pure people marked out for his own."

Furthermore, the term Redemption, like the majority of

Messianic terms derived from the Old Testament, can be applied either to the first or to the second coming of Christ. It serves not only to designate the work performed by Christ on Calvary but also to indicate what he will accomplish at the end of time. In both cases there is question of a deliverance, a liberation, but even more of an acquisition, a taking possession by God.

Finally, this work of Redemption is a completely free act of Christ. By embracing in his human heart the Father's love for people, Jesus "loved them to the end" (John 13:1), for "greater love no man has than this, that a man lay down his life for his friends" (John 15:13).

Out of love for his Father and for human beings, whom the Father wants to save, Jesus freely accepted his Passion and Death: "No one takes my life from me, but I lay it down of my own accord" (John 10:18).

The Center of the History of Salvation

It is interesting to point out that the theme for 1997 in keeping with the preparation for the Great Jubilee of 2000 at the beginning of the Third Millennium was "Christ the Redeemer, the one Savior of the world."

The Incarnation of Jesus Christ represents the center of the History of Salvation. With his coming, "the one Mediator between God and human beings" (1 Timothy 2:4-6), a new era is inaugurated, the era foretold by the Lord through the Prophets, the Messianic Age.

During his Life, Christ brings to fulfillment the salvific plans of God; he is the Physician who comes to heal the wounds of humankind (see Mark 2:17), the Shepherd who comes to gather together his dispersed flock (see John 10; Matthew 15:24), the One who confirms with his own Blood the New Covenant between God and humankind and institutes a new People, the true People of God (see Matthew 16:18; Mark 14:58).

The Incarnation of the Word represents the center of the sacramental economy in which is inserted the Church, prolongation of Christ, who is the Head, Principle, Fount of Life, Mediator, and Final Goal of the world of nature and grace: of the former as Creator and of the latter as Redeemer. His Incarnation and Redemption thus assume a universal scope and have a beneficial effect on the whole cosmos.

A Title Emphasized by Vatican II

Although the title "Mother of the Savior" had been known in the Church, it was Vatican II that highlighted it for our time:

"The Sacred Scriptures of the Old and New Testaments as well as ancient Tradition cast more and more light on the role of the *Mother of the Savior* in the Economy of Salvation and, as it were, propose it for our consideration.

"The Books of the Old Testament describe the History of Salvation and the gradual preparation for the coming of Christ into the world. These primitive documents, as they are read in the Church and understood in the light of further and fuller Revelation, bring the figure of a Woman, *Mother of the Redeemer,* into a gradually clearer light" (*Constitution on the Church,* no. 55).

It is true that the Cross is the unique sacrifice of Christ, the one Mediator between God and human beings. However, as the Council indicates, because in his incarnate Divine Person he has in some way united himself to every person, the possibility of being made partners — in a way known to God — in the Paschal Mystery is offered to all human beings.

"Christians are bound by both the need and the duty to battle against evil through many tribulations and even to suffer death. But as those who have been linked with the Paschal Mystery and patterned on the dying Christ, they will hasten forward to resurrection in the strength that comes from hope.

"All this holds true not only for Christians but for all people of goodwill in whose hearts grace works in an unseen fashion. For, since Christ died for all, and since the ultimate vocation of all is in fact one, and Divine, we must believe that the Holy Spirit in a manner known only to God offers to all the possibility of being associated with this Paschal Mystery" (*Constitution on the Church in the Modern World*, no. 22).

This is achieved supremely in the case of his Mother who was associated more intimately than any other person in the Mystery of Christ's redemptive suffering. The union of the Mother with the Son in the work of salvation was manifested from the time of Christ's virginal conception up to his Death.

"By a disposition of Divine Providence, [the Blessed Virgin] was on earth the loving Mother of the Divine Redeemer and above everyone else and in a unique fashion the generous associate and humble handmaid of the Lord.

"Mary conceived, brought forth, and nourished Christ. She presented him to the Father in the Temple and was united with him in suffering as he died on the Cross. In this completely special manner, she cooperated in the Savior's work by her obedience, faith, hope, and ardent love in restoring supernatural life to souls" (*Constitution on the Church*, no. 61).

Pope St. Pius X, in his 1904 Encyclical *Ad Diem Illum Laetissimum* ("On That Most Joyful Day") had already elaborated on this theme:

"Jesus, who is the Word made flesh, is also the Savior of the human race. Now, as God-Man he acquired, just as others, an individual body. But as restorer of our race, he acquired a spiritual and Mystical Body — the society of those who believe in Christ. 'So we, being many, are one Body in Christ' (Romans 12:5).

"Now, the Virgin conceived the eternal Son of God not only that he might by assuming human nature from her become a man, but that he might through the nature assumed from her become as well the Savior of mortals. For this reason the Angel announced to the shepherds: 'Today there is born to you a Savior, who is Christ the Lord' (Luke 2:11).

"Thus, in one and the same bosom of his most chaste Mother, Christ, at one and the same time, assumed flesh and united to himself a spiritual Body that is joined together from those who were to believe in him.

"In this way, Mary, by bearing the Savior in her womb, can be said to have borne all those whose life was contained in the life of the Savior. All of us, therefore, who are united with Christ and are, as the Apostle says, 'members of his Body, made from his flesh and bones' (Ephesians 5:30), have come forth from the womb of Mary, after the manner of a Body that is joined to its Head.

"Hence, in a spiritual and mystical sense we are called the children of Mary, and she is Mother of us all.... If, then, the most Blessed Virgin is at once the Mother of God and the Mother of human beings, can anyone doubt that she makes every effort to ensure that Christ, 'the Head of his Body, the Church' (Colossians 1:18), should infuse into us, his members, the gifts that are his, in order that we may above all come to know him and to live by him!"

A Title Based on Scripture

In Israel, the king was the elect of God who communicated to his elect a Divine power and wisdom (see 1 Kings 3:28). Among other things, he offered services such as armed protection, justice, and accountability. The key to the function of these services was not only the king himself but also his household.

In this connection, the role of the queen-mother was essential. As *wife*, the queen can be a source of embarrassment to the security of the kingdom: she can be a principle of dissension in the prevailing polygamy.

As *mother*, however, she is the principle of stability. Often she is the one responsible for obtaining the throne for her son through her political sense and astuteness. She also frequently acts as the king's regent (in the case of kings who were too young to rule).

She knows the king through and through and can speak to him in ways that no one else can. And the king is willing to listen to her without qualms because he knows she is interested only in him alone.

The Bible thus sets forth the role of the women who have been designated as "figures of Mary." Under the inspiration of the Lord of Israel, they prepared for the election and the coming of the Messiah or Savior, the Son of David: Eve, Sarah, Rebekah, Rachel, Leah, Zipporah, and Bathsheba. And throughout the Books of Kings the name of the king's mother is carefully preserved.

The Prophets too dwell on the Mother of the Messiah. In the faith of Israel, the Messianic hope continues to be bound to texts that associate the saving mission of the Messiah with a Divine action upon his Mother (Isaiah 7:4-9; Micah 5:2; Jeremiah 13:18; 22:26; Ezekiel 19:14).

The Sages also set forth this idea. By her intelligent activity, the *ideal wife* becomes the glory of her husband and the happiness of his household (Proverbs 31). It is the timid Esther who has the courage to stand up to King Xerxes for the salvation of her people and the devout Judith who makes the daring decision that leads to the liberation of her city.

At the same time, the Sages also state that the true royal heir, "by whom kings reign," is a Wisdom born of God before all ages (Proverbs 8:1-36). This eternal Wisdom was planted by the Most High in the land of Israel (Sirach 24:12) and has her seat in the holy tent ("Temple," verse 10), from which she derives growth and efflorescence prior to calling all nations.

These figures all enter into the faithful Jew's image of the Mother of the Messiah, bearer of total and definitive salvation. The Evangelists presuppose that such figures are known whenever they speak of Mary as simply the Mother of Jesus Christ.

The sacred writers show that Mary is the Mother of the Savior (Matthew 1:18-23; Luke 1:28-32), who liberates not only Israel but also all the nations (Luke 2:30-32). And Mary becomes associated with the drama of the Savior from the moment that a sword pierces her soul (Luke 2:35) as evidenced from her collaboration in Christ's first miracle at Cana (John 2:1-11).

History of the Title

There is little in the Fathers of the Church with respect to this title of Mary. Scholars believe that the reason for this lack is that the Fathers included the Redemption in the Incarnation. Hence, they did not treat Mary's participation in the work of her Son.

St. Irenaeus (d. 202), in speaking about the New Eve, states: "Eve was disobedient; although she was still a virgin, she did not obey ... and became a cause of death to herself and to all humankind.

"So Mary, having a predestined husband but being still a Virgin, was obedient and became a cause of salvation to herself and to the whole human race."

When we add another line from Irenaeus, "The Son of God was born of the Virgin," we can say why Irenaeus can be put on the side of "Mother of the Savior."

Another one of the Fathers who can be said to foreshadow this title is St. Ambrose (d. 397): "Alone Mary has worked the salvation of the world and conceived the redemption of all human beings."

He also said: "Mary gave birth to the Victor and defeated the devil." These two quotations taken together also lead to the title.

The first writer to mention Mary's part in the Redemption seems to have been John the Geometer (d. tenth century): "You [Christ] have given not only yourself as a ransom for us but also your Mother after yourself as a ransom at every moment. Thus, you have indeed died for us once, but she has died a thousand times in her will, with her heart pierced for you as well as for those for whom she, like the Father, had given her own Son and knew him to be delivered to death."

Sts. Peter Damian (d. 1072) and Anselm of Canterbury (d. 1099) reflected upon Mary's sufferings at the death of Jesus, and Arnold of Bonneval (d. after 1056) showed their redemptive effect: "The Mother's affection cooperated greatly in her own manner to render God propitious, since the charity of Christ brought to the Father both his own desires and those of his Mother so that what the Mother requested the Son approved and the Father granted."

Mary obtained a common effect with Christ in the salvation of the world as a result of the Incarnation from the moment when she was told "The Lord is with you" (Luke 1:28) and her presence on Calvary: "There was then only one will between Christ and Mary, and both together offered only one burnt offering, she in the blood of her heart and he in the blood of his flesh."

Beginning in the thirteenth century, theologians began to mention a partnership between Jesus and Mary, a helper or associate for Christ in the world's redemption. St. Bonaventure

(d. 1274) insisted on the unicity of Christ's Redemption yet still spoke of Mary paying the price of the ransom of the human race. She did so by "her veneration for God, her compassion with Christ, and her pity for the world, especially for the Christian people."

The Spanish theologian Quirino de Salazar (d. 1646) continued this way of thinking by stating that Mary was not given to Christ as his Mother only, but as "helper and companion to redeem the human race." Indeed, every grace bestowed on the Virgin, even the very benefit of her first creation, is a grace of redemption and expiation that is ordered to wiping out sins, not her own but those of others, i.e., all the transgressions of the human race.

Finally, taking us up to the nineteenth century, M.J. Scheeben capped the argument for Mary's participation in the work of Redemption: "[The four reasons given by him] obviously demand Mary's cooperation, not in order to achieve or complete the intrinsic power of the redeeming work but only to perfect its beauty and loveliness in all respects, especially its organic connection with humankind to be redeemed, whereby the perfect completion of its application and applicability was conditioned."

The twentieth century history has been mentioned above in the section "A Title Emphasized by Vatican II."

Meaning of the Title

The meaning of this title of our Lady tells us that Mary is completely associated with the Redemption. Just as Christ is responsible both for the objective Redemption and the subjective Redemption, so is Mary — through her Son.

The term *objective Redemption* refers to the fact that Jesus achieved the redemption of the whole world and everyone in it. The term *subjective Redemption* refers to the actual acceptance of that redemption by each individual.

Thus, just as Jesus merited the graces by which each person can be moved to take hold of the redemption offered, Mary also is involved in obtaining help for every person to partake of the redemption offered.

In other words, Mary is so intimately connected with the Redemption worked by Christ that she is actively involved in it until the end of the world.

In addition, nowadays this title is also given a meaning that is more in keeping with the current thinking of Catholics in the wake of Vatican II. In this respect, Christ the Savior refers not only to spiritual liberation but to material well-being as well.

Christ came to make the whole life of his people better both spiritually and materially. And it is this that the Church continually labors for in all parts of the world.

Since Mary is the Mother of the Savior, she too is intensely involved in the complete lives of people today. And her magna carta is the *Magnificat*, which tells us of the wondrous works God has wrought for his people, the Remnant. These benefits apply to us who are his people of the New Covenant.

Thus, just as Christ is the sole and definitive liberator, Mary — by reason of her whole being and her practice of total openness to the action of God and to the intimate communication with the incarnate Son of God — is the redeemed person beyond compare. And through her maternal intercession and through her singular example she continually indicates to contemporary human beings the concrete way to full human and Christian realization. If Christ is the Redeemer, Mary is the model of the new person redeemed in Christ.

Application to Us

The Church tells us that the eternal love of the Father manifested in the history of humankind through the gift of his Son to the world (John 3:16) comes to human beings through Mary, Mother of God, Mother of the Savior, and Mother of all human beings.

Accordingly, all those who belong to the Church, Body of Christ, in whom is revealed the Mystery of salvation willed by the Father and accomplished by the Son, must feel her maternal function. We thus should have confident recourse to Mary and seek in her faith the sustenance of our own faith.

Mary will then enable us to renew the commitment made at our Baptism and renewed during our lifetime. She will remind us that at Baptism we all died with Christ to sin and in him rose to a new life, the life of the Spirit.

Our Lady will keep before us the fact that the Holy Spirit in Baptism rendered us conformed to Christ. This total assimilation to Christ belongs to the very essence of a Christian but must also be translated into the actions of Christians, into our very lives.

The Mother of the Savior will enable us to rediscover the greatness and the requirements of our baptismal vocation and show us how to live in the new life in Christ.

Above all, she will obtain for us the power to take hold of the redemption in our real life situation with all the problems of our time. She will see to it that we become more human (in the best sense) and more Christian.

Prayer to Mary, Mother of the Savior

Hail (or Rejoice), Mother of the Lamb and the Shepherd.
Hail (or Rejoice), sheepfold of the spiritual flocks.
Hail (or Rejoice), shelter against invisible enemies.
Hail (or Rejoice), entrance to the gates of paradise.
Hail (or Rejoice), because heaven embraces earth.
Hail (or Rejoice), because earth sings together with heaven.
Hail (or Rejoice), perennial voice of the Apostles.
Hail (or Rejoice), unshakable courage of the Martyrs.
Hail (or Rejoice), solid bulwark of the Faith.
Hail (or Rejoice), radiant sign of grace.
Hail (or Rejoice), you through whom hell was rendered armorless.
Hail (or Rejoice), you through whom we were reinvested with glory.
Hail (or Rejoice), O immaculate Bride.

15

New Eve — New Woman

A Title Used by Vatican II and Pope Paul VI

The term "New Eve" ("New Woman") was highlighted by the Second Vatican Council:

"The holy Fathers see Mary as not merely a passive instrument in the hands of God but as cooperating in the salvation of human beings with free faith and obedience.

"Indeed, as St. Irenaeus says, 'By obedience she became the cause of salvation for herself and the whole human race.'

"Thus, not a few of the early Fathers joyfully assert with him: 'The knot of Eve's disobedience was untied by Mary's obedience. What the virgin Eve bound through her unbelief Mary loosened by her faith.'

"Comparing Mary with Eve, they call her the 'Mother of the living,' and still more often they say: 'Death through Eve, life through Mary'" (*Constitution on the Church*, no. 56).

Pope Paul VI also dealt with this theme in two of his Apostolic Exhortations. The first was his *Signum Magnum* ("Great Sign") in 1967: "If then we contemplate the humble Virgin of Nazareth in the glory of her prerogatives and her virtues, we will see her shine forth before our eyes as the 'New Eve,' the exalted Daughter of Zion, the zenith of the Old Testament and the dawn of the New, in which the 'fullness of time' is actuated."

The second is his *Marialis Cultus* ("Devotion to the Blessed Virgin Mary") in 1974: "With regard to Mary, the [Eastern and Western] liturgies celebrate [the Incarnation] as a feast of the New Eve, the obedient and faithful Virgin. With a generous 'fiat' ['let it be'] (see Luke 1:38), she became through the working of the Spirit the Mother of God, but also the true Mother of the living. In addition, by receiving into her womb the one Mediator (see 1 Timothy 2:5), she became the Ark of the Covenant and the true Temple of God" (no. 6).

Mary, the New Eve

The Bible shows us Eve as taken from Adam's rib to be a "helper [for him] like unto himself" (Genesis 2:18) and she is called the "mother of all the living" (Genesis 3:20). The first Adam, with Eve by his side, brought sin and death into the world. The Second Adam, Christ, brought light and grace (see Ephesians 4:24; Romans 5:17-19), and the New Eve was by his side.

The clearest testimony to this teaching of the Church is found in St. Justin Martyr (d. 165) and especially St. Irenaeus of Lyons (d. 202): "It was right and necessary that Adam be restored in Christ ... that Eve be restored in Mary so that a Virgin, become advocate of a virgin [Eve], might erase and abolish the disobedience of a virgin by her obedience as a Virgin."

Tertullian (d. 230) instituted the symbolism of Christ falling into a deep sleep on the Cross, and during that sleep of the New Adam there was born from his side the Church, the New Eve, Mother of the living.

This symbolism was later taken up by other Fathers, among whom are Sts. Ambrose, Jerome, and Augustine, and in the Middle Ages "Mother of the living" came to be applied to Mary as well as the Church.

Hence, although the first Eve let herself be enslaved by the devil, the New Eve experienced the freedom of soul given by the Spirit to those who are open to him. She responded to God with complete acceptance. She gave free and full consent to the event of the ages, which with the advent of the Divine Son, the New Adam, ushered in the New Creation.

The New Woman

Mary is also the New Woman, the one promised in the Proto-Gospel (Genesis 3:15), and greeted by Elizabeth as blessed among all women (Luke 1:42), from whom the Son of God became truly human (Galatians 4:4). She is the New Woman anticipating the mysterious "hour" of Jesus at the wedding feast of Cana (John 2:4), representing and personifying the Messianic people.

Mary is the New Woman standing at the foot of the Cross (John 19:25-27) as the New Eve, Mother of the living, who, in a quasi-spousal relationship with the New Adam, contributed to the birth of the New People of God in the Spirit. Finally, she is the New Woman resplendent in heaven as the Woman clothed with the sun and crowned with stars (Revelation 12:1).

Pope John Paul II has beautifully summarized this teaching: "According to the prophecy of Genesis 3:15, the Woman was destined to be an ally of God in the struggle against the devil. She was to be the Mother of the One who would crush the head of the enemy. Nevertheless, in the prophetic perspective of the Old Testament, this offspring of the Woman who was to conquer the spirit of evil seemed to be necessarily a man.

"Herein intervenes the wondrous reality of the Incarnation. The offspring of the Woman who fulfills the prophecy is not a simple man. He is indeed fully human, thanks to the

Woman whose Son he is, but at the same time he is true God. The Covenant established at the beginnings between God and the Woman takes on a new dimension. Mary enters into the Covenant as the Mother of God.

"In order to respond to the image of the woman who had committed the sin, God gives rise to an image of a perfect Woman, who receives a Divine Motherhood. The New Covenant goes far beyond the exigencies of a simple reconciliation. It raises the Woman to a height that no one could have imagined" (January 4, 1984).

The Ideal Human Instrument

Father Ronald Knox, the great Scripture scholar, had some splendid words to say about the Woman chosen by God to aid the Redeemer:

"Our Lady is the culmination of that long process of selection, of choosing here and rejecting there a human instrument suited to his purpose, which is so characteristic of God's dealings with this ancient people.

"I think we can observe, throughout the whole of that process, two principles at work. One is that God chooses, every now and again, the unlikely candidate, the one we should not have chosen; chooses the younger son rather than the elder, the despised character rather than the prominent character.

"You see, he will show us that grace is free; that his choice falls on this human instrument or that without any antecedent merits on their part to account for it. And at the same time, he proves that this choice was justified; as the history of their dealings unfolds itself, we realize that the unlikely candidate was the right candidate, corresponds with the grace given and, not under compulsion but with free election of the will, seconds God's purposes and proves a ready accomplice for his salutary designs.

"God's grace and man's free will corresponding with it — that ancient mystery is illustrated at every turn of the Old Testament story, until at last we turn over the page into the New Testament and find its ideal illustration in the life of our Lady herself.

"In her, as nowhere else, God had found the human instrument suited to his purpose: the worthy receptacle of a grace that had not dwelt on earth since Adam lost his paradise. The work of selection is consummated; mankind stands ready for its Redeemer."

Teaching of the Church

Pope Pius XII brought together the two traditions — Mary as the New Eve and as the Woman in Genesis 3:15 — in three important doctrinal works.

"Free from all sin, original and personal, and always most intimately united with her Son, Mary offered [Jesus] on Golgotha to the eternal Father together with the [burnt offering] of her maternal rights and her motherly love, like a New Eve, for all the children of Adam contaminated through his unhappy fall" (Encyclical *Mystici Corporis* ["Mystical Body"]).

"We must remember especially that, since the second century the Virgin Mary has been designated by the holy Fathers as the New Eve, who although subject to the New Adam, is most intimately associated with him in that struggle against the infernal foe which, as foretold in the Proto-gospel, would finally result in that most complete victory over sin and death which are always mentioned together in the writings of the Apostle of the Gentiles" (Apostolic Constitution *Munificentissimus Deus* ["Most Munificent God"] defining the Dogma of the Assumption).

"Mary, in the work of Redemption, was by God's Will joined with Jesus Christ, the cause of salvation, in much the same way as Eve was joined with Adam, the cause of death.... The Blessed Virgin is Queen not only because she is the Mother of God but also because she was associated as the second Eve with the New Adam" (Encyclical *Ad Caeli Reginam* ["On the Queenship of Mary"] instituting the Feast of Mary's Queenship).

The "Mass of Holy Mary, the New Eve," found in the Collection of Masses of the Blessed Virgin Mary issued by the Church in 1987, describes Mary this way: conceived without stain and enriched by gifts of grace, Mary is indeed the New Woman, Mother and Companion of Christ, Author of the New Covenant.

It also sets forth the many aspects of this teaching. Mary is celebrated as:

(1) the firstfruits of the New Creation; (2) the new earth, where from the moment of her Immaculate Conception justice dwells; (3) the firstfruits of the New People of God; (4) the first Disciple of the New Law; (e) the second Eve given a new heart in keeping with the prophecy of Ezekiel 1:9; (5) a Woman preparing the new wine for the Church; (g) a faithful Virgin who made a complete self-giving to the sacrifice of the New Law; and (6) the new Jerusalem, the holy city, the dwelling-place of God in keeping with Revelation 21:1-5a.

Mary and the Modern Woman

In a splendid 1973 Pastoral Letter entitled *Behold Your Mother*, the Bishops of the United States dealt with Mary in various aspects of the life of Christians today. They held her out as the model of all real feminine freedom and stressed her part in the emancipation of womanhood and in foreshadowing the role of Christian women in contemporary Church and society:

New Eve — New Woman

"According to the Gospels, Christ showed an enlightened attitude toward women: in his conversation with the Samaritan Woman at the well; in his friendship with Martha and Mary, especially in defense of Mary's preference to listen to his words rather than wait upon him; in his behavior toward the Syro-Phoenician woman with the sick daughter (Mk 7:29); in his appearance as risen Lord to Mary Magdalene, whom he sends to announce the Good News to his Apostles. These incidents, interpreted in their cultural context, give us a basis for a genuine emancipation and liberation of womanhood.

"The dignity that Christ's Redemption won for all women was fulfilled uniquely in Mary as the model of all real feminine freedom. The Mother of Jesus is portrayed in the Gospels as *intelligent* (the Annunciation, 'How can this be?'); *apostolic* (the visit to Elizabeth); *inquiring and contemplative* (the Child lost in the Temple); *responsive and creative* (at Cana); *compassionate and courageous* (at Calvary); a woman of *great faith*. These implications in the lives of Jesus and Mary need to be elaborated into a sound theology on the role of women in the contemporary Church and society" (nos. 141-142).

Pope Paul VI sketched such a Marian theology in the above-mentioned *Marialis Cultus*. He set forth the role of Mary and modern women: she is a mirror of the expectations of the women of our day (no. 37).

(1) The modern woman is anxious to participate with decision-making power in the affairs of the community. She can thus contemplate with intimate joy Mary, "who, taken into dialogue with God, gives her active and responsible consent, not to the solution of a contingent problem, but to that event of world importance which is the Incarnation."

(2) The modern woman lives in a world that extols the value of marriage but looks down upon virginity as counterproductive. By realizing that Mary's choice of the state of virginity in God's

plan prepared her for the Mystery of the Incarnation, she can thus "appreciate that Mary's choice was not a rejection of the values of the married state but a courageous choice that she made in order to consecrate herself totally to the love of God."

(3) The modern woman lives in a world where self-assurance is important. She can thus note with pleasant surprise "that Mary of Nazareth, while completely devoted to the Will of God, was far from being a timidly submissive woman or one whose piety was repellent to others. On the contrary, she was a woman who did not hesitate to proclaim that God vindicates the humble and the oppressed and removes the powerful people of this world from their privileged positions (see Luke 1:51-53)."

(4) The modern woman wishes to support the liberating energies of people and of society. She can thus recognize in Mary, "who stands out among the poor and the humble of the Lord, a woman of strength, who experienced poverty and suffering, flight and exile (see Matthew 2:13-23)."

Revealer of the Transforming Design of the Christian Economy

Pope Paul VI, elsewhere, also points out the power of devotion to Mary, who reveals to us the transforming design of the Christian Economy:

"How sweet, how consoling it is for us who wish to walk in the footsteps of the Lord to have before us Mary, her image, her remembrance, her kindness, her humility and purity, her greatness. How close to us the Gospel is in the power that Mary personifies and radiates with human and superhuman splendor!

"And any fear that we would have is dissipated — fear that in marking our spirituality with devotion to Mary, our religious sense, our vision of life, and our moral energy would become soft, weak, and almost infantile — when we draw close to her, the poetess and prophetess of the Redemption.

"She it is who reveals the transforming design of the Christian Economy, the historical and social result that still draws its origin and strength from Christianity: 'God,' she sings, 'has scattered the proud in the imagination of their hearts; he has put down the mighty from their thrones and exalted those of low degree' (Luke 1:51-52).

"And at this point the second way is opened for us by our Lady, so that we may reach our salvation in the Lord Christ: it is her protection. She is our ally, our advocate. She is the confidence of the poor, of the lowly, of the suffering. She is even the 'refuge of sinners.' She has a mission of pity, goodness, and intercession for all."

Application to Us

This Marian title calls us to imitate Mary in her modernity, so to speak, i.e., the aspects mentioned above. It tells us that in imitating her we should never give up living as people of our day or our state of life.

What should happen when we strive to imitate Mary is that we yield our lives to her action as Mother and Teacher. We place ourselves under her direction.

We ask to learn from Mary — the first and perfect disciple — how to live as children of the Father, as disciples of Christ, in docility to the Holy Spirit, each according to our personal vocation, even as she lived according to hers, every moment of her life.

Far from being a literal copying, our imitation of our Lady should lead us to discover and take hold of what constitutes our own fidelity day by day — just as she did during her life on earth.

At the same time, we can remain confident that in every circumstance we will find help and support in the unbounded goodness of the Woman whom the Lord himself was pleased to give us for our Mother.

We might well conclude with the splendid words of Pope Paul VI: "The figure of the Blessed Virgin does not disillusion any of the profound expectations of the men and women of our time but offers them the perfect model of the disciple of the Lord: the disciple who builds up the earthly and temporal city while being a diligent pilgrim toward the heavenly and eternal city, the disciple who works for that justice which sets free the oppressed and for that charity which builds up Christ in people's hearts" (*Marialis Cultus*, no. 37).

Prayer to Our Lady, the New Woman

Blessed are you, O Mary,
the New Woman.
Conceived without stain of sin
and enriched by gifts of grace,
you are the New Eve,
associated with Jesus, the New Adam,
as his Mother and Companion.
By your faith and obedience,
you undid the loss inflicted on humankind
by the unfaithfulness and disobedience
of the first Eve.

Help us to emulate
the active and responsible consent
that you gave in dialogue with God.
Teach us to make courageous choices
as you did in choosing the state of virginity.
Give us a love for the poor and lowly
in accord with your life and sentiments
as expressed in the **Magnificat** *prayer.*

16

Our Lady of the Blessed Sacrament

Mary, "Woman of the Eucharist"

In addition to "Our Lady of the Blessed Sacrament," this title could also be phrased as "Our Lady of the Eucharist." In both forms this title refers to the Sacrament of the Eucharist and to the Sacrifice of the Mass.

In his 2003 Encyclical *Ecclesia de Eucharistia* ("The Church of the Eucharist"), Pope John Paul II wrote:

"Mary can guide us toward this most holy Sacrament because she herself has a profound relationship with it.

"At first glance, the Gospel is silent on this subject. The account of the institution of the Eucharist on the night of Holy Thursday makes no mention of Mary. Yet we know that she was present among the Apostles who prayed 'with one accord' (Acts 1:14) *in the first community that gathered after the Ascension in expectation of Pentecost.* Certainly Mary must have been present at the Eucharistic celebrations of the first generation of Christians, who were devoted to 'the breaking of the bread' (Acts 2:42).

"But in addition to her sharing in the Eucharistic Banquet, an indirect picture of Mary's relationship with the Eucharist can be had, beginning with her interior disposition. *Mary is a 'woman of the Eucharist' in her whole life....*

"If the Eucharist is a Mystery of Faith that so greatly transcends our understanding as to call for sheer abandonment to the Word of God, then there can be no one like Mary to act as our support and guide in acquiring this disposition. In repeating what Christ did at the Last Supper in obedience to his command: 'Do this in memory of me!' we also accept Mary's invitation to obey him without hesitation: 'Do whatever he tells you' (John 2:5).

"With the same maternal concern which she showed at the wedding feast of Cana, Mary seems to say to us: 'Do not waver; trust in the words of my Son. If he was able to change water into wine, he can also turn bread and wine into his Body and Blood, and through this Mystery bestow on believers the living memorial of his Passover, thus becoming the "bread of life".'

"In a certain sense Mary lived her *Eucharistic faith* even before the institution of the Eucharist, by the very fact that *she offered her virginal womb for the Incarnation of God's Word*. The Eucharist, while commemorating the Passion and Resurrection, is also in continuity with the Incarnation.

"At the Annunciation Mary conceived the Son of God in the physical reality of his Body and Blood, thus anticipating within herself what to some degree happens sacramentally in every believer who receives, under the signs of bread and wine, the Lord's Body and Blood.

"As a result, there is a profound analogy between the *Fiat* ['Let it be done'] which Mary said in reply to the Angel, and the *Amen* which every believer says when receiving the Body of the Lord. Mary was asked to believe that the One whom she conceived 'through the Holy Spirit' was 'the Son of God' (Luke 1:30-35).

"In continuity with the Virgin's faith in the Eucharistic Mystery we are asked to believe that the same Jesus Christ, Son of God and Son of Mary, becomes present in his full Humanity and Divinity under the signs of bread and wine" (no. 53).

Our Lady of the Blessed Sacrament

Presence of Mary in the Eucharist

Mary cooperated in a singular way in the Savior's work of restoring supernatural grace to souls — she is a Mother to us in the order of grace. By reason of this close connection with Christ and us, Mary could not be absent from our celebration of the Eucharist.

However, we must not see her presence there as the presence of Christ. The Consecration effects the Real Presence of the Christ of Glory in the act of his sacrifice under the appearances of bread and wine, with his Body and Blood, Soul and Divinity. Nothing of the kind is true in Mary's humanity. Yet the presence of Jesus brings with it in some way the presence of his Mother.

The Christ who becomes present on the altar is the same Christ who took from Mary his Body and Blood of the Eucharistic Sacrifice that are given as nourishment to us. The reality of the Word made flesh can be perceived only in its twofold relation of Son: the one according to which he is eternally engendered by the Father and the one according to which he was begotten in time by Mary.

Hence, our faith in the Eucharistic Christ includes a background reference to his Mother according to the flesh: *Ave verum Corpus natum de Maria Virgine* — Hail true Body born of the Virgin Mary!

In addition, the real action that Christ exercises in the Eucharist brings with it the presence of those on whom his action is exercised, and whom he gathers together through it. This action, which transcends the limits of time and space, concerns in the first place Mary.

Inasmuch as she is the beneficiary, the first fruit of the Redemption, the first and perfect Christian, Mary lives in the glory of the life of her Son, because she does not cease to receive it from him. This is in virtue of the unique and ever active offering by which he has "forever perfected those who are being sanctified" (Hebrews 10:14). Wherever Christ's Sacrifice is, there too is Mary, like the stream that cannot be cut off from its source.

Associated with the work of salvation, Mary retains her special place in God's plan of redemption. Her presence at the Cross is the guarantee of an ever active presence in the Eucharist of her Son. She can only exercise her mediation "interiorly" to the salvific action of Jesus, but wherever this action is, there too is the action of Mary!

Accordingly, in his Encyclical *Redemptoris Mater* ("The Mother of the Redeemer"), Pope John Paul II declares: "The piety of the Christian people has always very rightly sensed a *profound link* between devotion to the Blessed Virgin and worship of the Eucharist; this is a fact that can be seen in the Liturgy of both the West and the East, in the traditions of the Religious Families, in the modern movements of spirituality, including those for youth, and in the pastoral practice of the Marian Shrines. *Mary guides the faithful to the Eucharist*" (no. 44).

Thus, at every liturgical celebration, Mary the Mother of God is with us as our Model, our Intercessor, and our Mother. And she is even more each of these things in the Marian celebrations. We should have frequent recourse to her and increase our devotion to her.

Each Marian liturgical celebration is also intended to give us a better understanding of Mary's part in our salvation, a true catechesis of Mary.

As the Liturgy honors Mary over the course of a year, the Mysteries of Christ become present to us in their relationship with her.

Our Lady of the Blessed Sacrament

The Church's Reason for Honoring Mary

The Church honors Mary because of her singular dignity as Mother of the Son of God and, therefore, beloved Daughter of the Father and Temple of the Holy Spirit.

When Mary is honored, her Son is duly acknowledged, loved, and glorified, and his commandments are observed. To venerate Mary correctly means to acknowledge her Son, for she is the Mother of God. To love her means to love Jesus, for she is always the Mother of Jesus.

When we pray to our Lady, we do not substitute her for Christ; rather, we glorify her Son, who desires us to have loving confidence in his Saints, especially his Mother. To imitate the "faithful Virgin" means to keep her Son's commandments.

As Christ summed up his life by the words: "Not my will but yours be done" (Luke 22:42), so Mary could say: "Let it be done to me according to your word" (Luke 1:38). And as Jesus described his task on earth with the words: "The Son of Man did not come to be served but to serve" (Matthew 20:28), so Mary could say: "I am the handmaid of the Lord" (Luke 1:38).

That is why we rejoice to honor her. We pay homage to her and promise to imitate her Son. She encourages us and reminds us how like her we can and must be united to the sacrificial will of Jesus, in which is all our holiness.

Devotion to Mary in the Eucharist

The Church renders devotion to our Lady in the Eucharist because Mary is joined by an inseparable bond to the saving work of her Son, which is made present in the Eucharist.

The Liturgy makes present Christ's Paschal Mystery (his Life, Death, and Resurrection) enabling us to render fitting worship to God and to obtain the graces Christ gained for all human beings. This is only right since she is inescapably joined to the saving work being re-presented.

Mary brings a very human complementary note to the worship we render to the Father through Christ in the Holy Spirit — a note of loving contemplation, interior silence, joyous giving, and spiritual promptitude.

As Pope John Paul II has put it, "Mary is present in the *memorial* because she was present in the *event!*... She is continuously united both with Christ the High Priest and with the Church, the worshiping community, in the saving event and in the liturgical memorial."

Consequently, she does not have a different cult but occupies a special place in the unique "Christian" cult, capable of making the Church community relive mysteriously in the present the historical past of the saving actions of Christ and (because of this) not dissociate the united action of Christ and his Mother even in its cultural-ritual-liturgical re-evocation. This enables the Church to celebrate the memorial of the Blessed Virgin not in her own special liturgical cycle but in the unique liturgical cycle of the Mysteries of Christ.

Therefore, we pay honor to the eminent dignity of Mary and the unique character of her maternal mission in God's plan. We have recourse to her intercession and invoke her as the "woman who in a hidden manner and in a spirit of service watches over the Church and carefully looks after her until the glorious day of the Lord" (Paul VI: *Marialis Cultus* ["On Devotion to the Blessed Virgin Mary"], Introduction).

Liturgical devotion to Mary also leads to imitation of Mary: "The perfect model of the disciple of the Lord: the disciple who builds up the earthly and temporal city while being a diligent pilgrim toward the heavenly and eternal city, the disciple who works for that justice which sets free the oppressed and for that charity which assists the needy; but above all the disciple who is the active witness of that love which builds up Christ in people's hearts" (Ibid., no. 37).

An Intrinsic Element of Christian Worship

Since Marian devotion is firmly rooted in the revealed Word of God and has solid dogmatic foundations, it is an intrinsic element of Christian worship.

This devotion is based on (1) the singular dignity of Mary, Mother of the Son of God, and therefore beloved Daughter of the Father and Temple of the Holy Spirit; (2) the part she played at decisive moments in the History of Salvation that her Son accomplished; (3) her holiness, already full at her Immaculate Conception yet increasing all the time as she obeyed the Father's Will and accepted the path of suffering; (4) her mission and the special position she holds within the People of God as preeminent member, shining exemplar, and loving Mother; (5) her necessary and efficacious intervention for those who call upon her; and (6) her glory that ennobles the whole of humankind.

According to St. Louis de Montfort, devotion to Mary is the ardor to serve her in order to serve God better. It must be (a) *interior*, more in the heart than in practices; (b) *steadfast*, based on faith and not fluctuating with moods and feelings; (c) *disinterested*, more intent on God than on the graces to be obtained (although the prayers of petition and thanksgiving are important elements in the general devotion that moves us to serve God); (d) *oriented toward Christ*, in whom we are brought to the Father; and (e) *confident and heartfelt*, since in us the spiritual is fleshly, i.e., communicates through the flesh.

Mary in the Eucharistic Celebration

Mary is prominently mentioned every day in the Ordinary of the Mass in the Introductory Rites at the Confiteor, in the Liturgy of the Word at the Nicene Creed, and in the Eucharistic Prayer.

The Roman Rite offers a valid synthesis of all the possible links between the celebration of the Eucharistic Mystery and the Blessed Virgin. The Preface of Eucharistic Prayer II recalls the Incarnation of the Word through the power of the Holy Spirit in the Virgin Mary: it is an ancient, universal, and essential mention because it unites the Eucharistic Mystery with the moment of the Incarnation, of which the Eucharist is also a recapitulation.

The same remembrance is found in Eucharistic Prayer IV after the Sanctus. Eucharistic Prayer I solemnly expresses the union with Mary in the *Communicantes* in which her title of perpetual Virgin and her essential role as Mother are also recalled.

In a similar way, Eucharistic Prayer III expresses with intense supplication the desire of those praying to share with the Mother the inheritance of the children: "May he make us an everlasting gift to you [the Father] and enable us to share in the inheritance of the Saints with Mary, the Virgin Mother of God." Mary is also mentioned in each of the other six approved Eucharistic Prayers.

Liturgical Marian Celebrations in the United States

In the annual calendar for the United States, there are fifteen liturgical celebrations of the Blessed Virgin Mary plus Masses.

Three celebrations are of highest rank known as *Solemnities*: Mary, Mother of God (January 1), Assumption (August 15), and Immaculate Conception (December 8).

Three celebrations are of high rank known as *Feasts*: Visitation (May 31), Birth of Mary (September 8), and Our Lady of Guadalupe (December 12).

Five celebrations are of moderate rank known as *Obligatory Memorials*: Immaculate Heart of Mary (Saturday after the Solemnity of the Sacred Heart of Jesus), Queenship of Mary (August 22), Our Lady of Sorrows (September 15), Our Lady of the Rosary (October 7), and Presentation of Mary (November 21).

Four celebrations are of lesser rank known as *Optional Memorials*: Our Lady of Lourdes (February 11), Our Lady of Mount Carmel (July 16), Dedication of Saint Mary Major (August 5), and The Most Holy Name of Mary (September 12).

There are also Masses of the Blessed Virgin Mary on Saturday that may be celebrated during Ordinary Time (outside Advent, Christmastime, Lent, and Eastertime).

Celebrations of Mary outside the Proper Calendar

Outside the proper liturgical calendar of the United States, there are 46 Masses of the Blessed Virgin that may be celebrated under certain circumstances throughout the year.

Most of the texts of these Masses are from local churches, religious institutes, or already in the *Sacramentary*. They are intended primarily for the Marian shrines where Masses in our Lady's honor are celebrated frequently, but also for all Church communities, especially on Saturdays.

The Masses are distributed over the seasons of the Liturgical Year: three in Advent, six in Christmastime, five in Lent, and four in Eastertime — all honor Mary under titles that accord with the theme of the season. There are twenty-eight Masses in Ordinary Time subdivided into three sections: (1) 11 Masses honor her under *titles derived from Scripture*; (2) nine Masses honor her under *titles that indicate her cooperation in fostering the spiritual life of the faithful*; and (3) eight Masses celebrate her under *titles that indicate her compassionate interceding on behalf of the faithful*.

Our Model in the Celebration of the Mysteries

In addition to the aspect of the indissoluble union between Christ and Mary in the Economy of Salvation and in its sacramental realization, there is another aspect. Mary is united in the Mystery of the Church as her model in the celebrations of the Mysteries.

First of all, Mary is the *attentive Virgin* with respect to the Word of God; she thus appears as the model of the Church who meditates, is attentive to, accepts, lives, and proclaims the Word that became incarnate in Mary.

Secondly, Mary is the *Virgin in prayer*, because of her prayerful attitude as well as the sentiments that the Holy Spirit infused into her heart and that coincided with the grand divisions of ecclesial prayer, which has its roots in the Eucharistic Prayer: the *praise* and *thanksgiving* found in the *Magnificat*, the *intercession* at Cana, and the *petition* for the coming of the Spirit in the Upper Room.

Thirdly, Mary is the *Virgin presenting gifts* in the Temple of Jerusalem and on Calvary. This experience both in its active aspect (*Mary offers*) and in its passive aspect (*Mary is offered*) becomes the exemplar for the Church in her sacrificial offering of the Eucharist and prayer.

Fourthly, Mary is the *Virgin-Mother*. As such she is the model of that active collaboration with which the Church also labors, through preaching and the Sacraments (especially Baptism,

Confirmation, and the Eucharist) to transmit the new life of the Spirit to human beings.

In this sense, every official liturgical celebration must be *implicitly Marian,* insofar as it must be celebrated by the Church with the very sentiments that were in Mary. The Marian note characterizes every celebration of the sacred Mysteries and makes liturgical spirituality an authentically Marian spirituality in the best sense of the word.

The Magnificat *in a Eucharistic Key*

Pope John Paul II, in his Encyclical *Ecclesia de Eucharistia* (no. 58) also says:

"In the Eucharist the Church is completely united to Christ and his sacrifice, and makes her own the spirit of Mary. This truth can be understood more deeply by *rereading the Magnificat in a Eucharistic key.* The Eucharist, like the Canticle of Mary, is first and foremost praise and thanksgiving.

"When Mary exclaims: 'My soul magnifies the Lord and my spirit rejoices in God my Savior,' she already bears Jesus in her womb. She praises God 'through' Jesus, but she also praises him 'in' Jesus and 'with' Jesus. This is itself the true 'Eucharistic attitude.'

"At the same time Mary recalls the wonders worked by God in Salvation History in fulfillment of the promise once made to the fathers (see Luke 1:55), and proclaims the wonder that surpasses them all, the redemptive Incarnation. Lastly, the *Magnificat* reflects the eschatological tension of the Eucharist.

"Every time the Son of God comes again to us in the 'poverty' of the sacramental signs of bread and wine, the seeds of that new history wherein the mighty are 'put down from their thrones' and 'those of low degree are exalted' (Luke 1:52) take root in the world. Mary sings of the 'new heavens' and the 'new earth' which find in the Eucharist their anticipation and in some sense their program and plan.

"The *Magnificat* expresses Mary's spirituality, and there is nothing greater than this spirituality for helping us to experience the Mystery of the Eucharist. The Eucharist has been given to us so that our life, like that of Mary, may become completely a *Magnificat*!"

Devotion to Mary in Private Prayer

The Eucharist is the greatest prayer — public worship and prayer. However, we can also show devotion to Mary by our private prayers. Catholics have done so since the Apostles prayed with the Mother of Jesus in the Upper Room while awaiting the coming of the Spirit promised by him. Then in union with Mary they received the Spirit of the Lord and encountered Jesus himself in a new way.

Mary has always been a sure guide for Catholics in prayer. Indeed, true devotion to Mary takes its origin from Christ, finds its complete expression in Christ, and leads through Christ in the Spirit to the Father. This devotion necessarily reflects God's plan of redemption, in which a special form of veneration is appropriate to the singular place that Mary holds in that plan.

Devotion is rendered to Mary because she is the chosen Daughter of God the Father, the faithful Spouse of God the Holy Spirit, and the devoted Mother of God the Son. Her prerogatives flow from these qualities and make her the loving Mother of the Church as well as the closest imitator of Christ and the model of the faithful.

It follows that praying with Mary is beneficial to all who

practice it. Indeed, praying with no one less than Jesus can assure such benefit to us as Mary can.

Mary and Prayer

Prayer was Mary's constant companion. She lived it all her life. During her childhood in the Temple, she meditated on the Sacred Scriptures and recited the Psalms, remaining in continuous touch with her God.

At the Annunciation, she made her "Yes" a prayer of acceptance of God's holy Will. Then at the end of her visit to her cousin Elizabeth, which took place immediately afterward, she broke out in a magnificent prayer of praise and thanksgiving — the *Magnificat.*

Throughout Christ's childhood, Mary's prayer remained unobtrusive. We see touches of it, however, in some of the later words of her Son in his parables: the woman who gives all she has to God (Luke 21:1-4), the woman who sweeps the floor religiously looking for a lost coin (Luke 15:8-9), the woman who beats the yeast (Luke 13:21), the woman who importunes the wicked judge (Luke 18:3-5) — all qualities of Mary's life and prayer.

During Christ's Public Life, we get more glimpses of Mary's life of prayer. At the wedding feast of Cana (John 2:1-11), she insists that Jesus help the couple although his time has not yet come. This stance demands a close prayer union with the Father whose plan Jesus was implementing.

Again, when a woman praises his Mother for her physical acts of child-bearing, Jesus heaps more praise on her for her spiritual acts of prayer: he terms her blessed for hearing the Word of God and carrying it out (Luke 11:27-28). Yet it is patently impossible to carry out God's Word without a solid life of prayer.

At Calvary, Mary surely prayed beneath the Cross. Close union with her God would have been the only way she could have borne the slow excruciating death of her Son with such equanimity (John 19:25ff).

In the Upper Room, Mary remained in common prayer awaiting the descent of the Holy Spirit (Acts 1:14). It was doubtless her prayerful demeanor that enabled the Apostles and disciples to prepare to receive the Spirit well and become fearless witnesses to her Son and his Good News.

Application to Us

Praying with Mary covers three types of prayer as practiced first by the Church in the Liturgy: (1) praying to God with Mary; (2) praying to God in honor of Mary; and (3) praying to Mary. We should try to recite our Marian prayers in the same vein.

When we *pray to God with Mary*, we take cognizance of Mary receiving the Word of God and putting it into practice or repeat Mary's great canticle of thanksgiving, the *Magnificat*. We also identify ourselves with Mary in the offering of Christ's Sacrifice on the Cross or have recourse (at least indirectly) to Mary's intercession in heaven.

When we *pray to God in honor of Mary*, we celebrate the Virgin Mary by praising God for the participation of the Mother of Jesus in the major events of her Son's life. We also render praise to God for the special graces that prepared the Virgin Mary for her mission and for the rewards bestowed upon her in body and soul as well as for a number of events in the life of the People of God where Mary's action was particularly evident. Each time also provides us with an opportunity to have recourse to the intercession of the Mother of the Church so that her children might follow her example or enjoy her protection.

When we *pray to Mary*, we speak directly not to God but to Mary herself — to praise her, to congratulate her in words of the Gospel, and to directly beg for her intercession with her Divine Son and the Blessed Trinity.

However, it is most important to remember that in none of these forms is the prayer to Mary regarded by the Church as an end in itself. It remains completely suitable to serve the worship owed to the true God alone. The Father receives honor and praise for the wisdom of his purposes revealed to Mary. Through the honor paid to his Mother, the Son is better known and loved. And the action of the Holy Spirit in Mary and the Church is extolled and proclaimed.

In other words, Mary's mediation is not additional to that of Christ, since Mary and Christ are but one in the Mystery of his Mystical Body. She brings to those who pray to her the motherly aid of her own prayer, which merges with the supreme prayer of Christ the one Mediator.

Prayer to Our Lady of the Blessed Sacrament

Dear Mother Mary,
thank you for having given me the Eucharistic Christ
who offers himself to the Father
as the Victim of Calvary at every Mass,
who gives himself to us
as food in Holy Communion,
and who abides with us in the tabernacle.

For this reason we honor you
as Our Lady of the Blessed Sacrament.
Make us frequent apostles of the Eucharist
and so Eucharist-minded
that our very lives may be the Eucharist.

17

Our Lady of the Rosary

A Title Given Us by Mary

The title "Our Lady of the Rosary" is one that has been, so to speak, endorsed by Mary herself. For example, when she appeared to St. Bernadette in 1858 at Lourdes, she taught the unlettered teenager how to say the Rosary.

Later, when she appeared to the three young children at Fatima in 1917, Mary endorsed the Rosary, which the children were saying. Then when the children asked who she was, Mary replied, "I am the Lady of the Rosary."

This confirmed the Church's instruction on the Rosary as our Lady's Prayer, which had been highlighted by Pope Leo XIII when in his 1883 Apostolic Letter *Salutaris Ille* ("That Salvation") he decreed that the invocation "Queen of the Most Holy Rosary" should be added to the Litany of Loreto.

This invocation brings Mary before us as the woman who in the Rosary is contemplated and besought, framed in her true reality as Mother of God, and fully inserted in the Mystery of Christ.

Mary thus becomes the Mother who teaches her children a way of praying and reveals to them the secrets of the action of God as it has been accomplished in the fullness of time and as it continues to be offered throughout the centuries for every person who listens to her.

Saying the Rosary is a classic means to express one's devotion to Mary as well as a way to keep fresh and alive our faith in Jesus, our responsibility as his followers, our task to be his imitators and to offer leaven in the dough of the world and also the proper ecclesial dimension.

In short, the Rosary is a splendid prayer that teaches us to pray while it leads the soul to the contemplation of Mary, Mother of the Church and exemplar of the true Christian life.

What Is the Rosary?

The Rosary — in Pope Paul VI's felicitous phrase — is "a compendium of the Gospel." Indeed, it is a brief summary of the Life of Christ in the manner of St. Peter's discourse in the house of Cornelius:

"Jesus Christ is the Lord of all. You know what has taken place in all Judea, beginning from Galilee, after the baptism preached by John, that is, how God anointed Jesus of Nazareth with the Holy Spirit and power, and how he went around doing good and healing all those who were in the power of the devil — because God was with him.

"We are witnesses of all the things that he accomplished in the region of the Jews and in Jerusalem. They killed him by hanging him on a tree, but God raised him up on the third day and willed that he should appear, not to the whole people but to witnesses whom God had already chosen — to us, who ate and drank with him after he rose from the dead. And he commanded us to preach to the people and to testify that he is the one whom God appointed as judge of the living and the dead" (Acts 10:36-42).

The Rosary is a set form of prayers and meditations said with the help of a string of beads whereon to keep count of the prayers; the beads themselves are also called a Rosary. It consists of a string of beads divided into five sets (called decades), each of ten small beads and a larger one. A crucifix with two large and three small beads is always added but is not necessary.

Each decade is associated with one of twenty (originally fifteen) Mysteries of the Faith.

The method of saying the Rosary is to recite the Our Father on the large bead, the Hail Mary on each of the ten small beads, and the Glory Be to the Father on the large bead — all the while meditating on the pertinent Mystery, which belongs to one of four groups called Joyful, Luminous, Sorrowful, and Glorious Mysteries.

These meditations on events in the Life of Jesus and his Mother are of the essence of this devotion. Hence, it is not a mechanical repetition of the vocal prayers, but a loving dwelling on God's mercies, to which the prayers are a kind of accompaniment.

On the extra beads mentioned above, the Apostles' Creed and Our Father are said, once each, and the Hail Mary is said three times in total. Then at the end of the Rosary, frequently the Marian Prayer "Hail, Holy Queen" is added and also the Litany of Loreto.

The History of the Rosary

The origin of the Rosary is extremely obscure. According to the tradition of the Order of Preachers, accepted by a number of Popes since 1495, the Rosary was devised by St. Dominic himself, and used by him in his missionary work among the Albigensian heretics, in consequence of a vision in which our Lady revealed it to him.

However, scholars note that there was no uniform way of

saying the Rosary till a considerable time after St. Dominic's death, and his earliest biographers do not mention the prayer. Despite this point, the Rosary is very properly distinguished as Dominican. The friars of that Order gave it the form it now has and for centuries have zealously spread its use throughout the world, bringing blessings to countless souls and offering worship to God.

In truth, the Rosary was not born all at once but was the fruit of a lengthy evolution. By following this evolution we will better understand its spirit and open ourselves to search out the methods of reciting it that are included in the history of this prayer. In this way, we can be aided to make our use of it more effective.

Five centuries were necessary (from the twelfth to the sixteenth century) in order for the Rosary to arrive at the form it has today. The twelfth century saw the spread of the first (and Scriptural) part of the Hail Mary ("Hail Mary, full of grace, the Lord is with you" [Luke 1:28]; "blessed are you among women, and blessed is the fruit of your womb" [Luke 1:42]).

Previously these words of the Angelic Salutation had been in use but not with the frequency and repetitiveness that it came to assume when the "Psalter of Mary" was born. Its birth stemmed from the use monks made of the 150 Psalms of the Bible as is still done today in the Divine Office, now known as the Liturgy of the Hours. Those who were unlettered, monks as well as laypeople who could not read the Psalms, substituted 150 Our Fathers in their place.

In order to keep count of the Our Fathers, people made use of a corona, or crown, of 150 beads: the corona of Our Fathers. We should note that the use of such a corona with beads in order to count prayers is very ancient and is used not only by Christians but by other religions as well. In the second half of the twelfth century, 150 Hail Marys were substituted for the Our Fathers, and the "Psalter of Mary" was born.

The second part of the Hail Mary ("Holy Mary, Mother of God, pray for us sinners now and at the hour of our death") came into use only at the end of the fifteenth century. In the previous century, the Carthusian Henry of Kalkar had already subdivided the 150 Hail Marys into fifteen decades, set off from one another by the Our Father.

This subdivision had quickly met with great success and until 2002 constituted the series of fifteen Mysteries of the Rosary. In that year, as we shall see below, Pope John Paul II added a new series of Mysteries to the Rosary — the Luminous Mysteries.

As already mentioned, though St. Dominic (d. 1221) is not the author of the Rosary, which was in use before his time, he was a fervent propagator of it as were members of his Order. We might point out in particular the martyr St. Peter of Verona (d. 1252) who established a Confraternity of the Rosary wherever he preached.

Mystery and Meditation

We might also mention that the word "Mystery" used by the Church is subject to various meanings: (1) a revealed truth that we cannot fully understand; (2) the Divine Plan unfolded in the Life of Christ (see Ephesians 1:9; 3:9; *Constitution on the Church*, ch. 1); and (3) events in the Life of Christ.

The third meaning is the one that applies to the Mysteries attached to the Rosary. It goes back to the Apostolic Fathers of the Church such as St. Justin Martyr (d. 165).

Only after the fifteenth century did people begin to accompany the recitation of the Rosary with meditation on Gospel episodes. In the beginning there was a system of adding to the end of every Hail Mary a phrase concerning the episode being meditated on.

At the same period, the Dominican Blessed Alan de la Roche (d. 1478), in addition to widely spreading the "Marian Psalter," gave to it the name that became definitive for it: "Rosary of the Blessed Virgin Mary." He also established the subdivision in three parts of five decades each, suggesting that reflection take part on the Mysteries of the Incarnation (Joyous), of the Passion and Death of Christ (Sorrowful), and of the Glory of Christ and Mary (Glorious).

The multiplication of Confraternities of the Rosary contributed to the ever greater spread of Marian devotion as well as the prayer of the Rosary, which obtained official approval from St. Pius V in 1569. Such approval was only the first of a long series of Pontifical documents extolling this Marian prayer.

The Magisterium and the Rosary

St. Pius V, himself a Dominican, is the Pope of the Rosary, who approved the devotion and instituted the feast of the Rosary in 1572 on the occasion of the victory of John of Austria, over the invading Turks at Lepanto.

We can summarize his teaching as follows: (1) there is the need for prayer to overcome difficulties of wars and other calamities; (2) the Rosary is a simple prayer at the grasp of everyone; (3) this means has revealed itself as very effective against heresies and dangers for the Faith and has worked numerous conversions; (4) the recitation of the Rosary is recommended to the whole Christian populace.

From Gregory XIII to Leo XIII there are numerous Pontifical documents regarding the Rosary. Many of these concern the establishment of confraternities, discipline, privileges, etc. They do not always contribute new elements.

What they do show is a faith in the Rosary as an ecclesial means "for the exaltation of the Apostolic See and the Catholic Faith and the extirpation of heresy as well as the conservation of peace among Christian princes" (in the words of Clement VIII on January 13, 1593).

On March 12, 1869, Blessed Pius IX urged recitation of the Rosary for the good outcome of the First Vatican Council. Leo XIII (1878-1903), for his part, may be termed the equal of Pius V, with his 12 Encyclicals and five Apostolic Letters that develop Rosary themes.

This period also saw the birth of the practice of consecrating October to the Rosary, which — the same Pope said — is "the badge of our membership in the Faith and the compendium of the devotion that is due to Mary."

Indeed, Leo XIII did not spare voice or pen in singing the praises of the Rosary. Among his major and minor documents there are found 22 interventions in this regard for he regarded the Rosary as "an easy way to inculcate in souls the principal teachings of the Christian Faith."

The interventions of St. Pius X (1903-1914) and Benedict XV (1914-1922) on behalf of the Rosary are minor in tone. Pius XI (1922-1939), in his Encyclical *Ingravescentibus Malis* ("Amid Growing Evils"), urged Catholics to pray the Rosary in the hour of danger that threatened the world of his time. For he declared that this "Psalter of the Virgin" and "Breviary of the Gospel and of the Christian Life" is a very valid instrument to foster the Evangelical Virtues, nourish the Catholic Faith, and revive hope and charity.

Pius XII (1939-1958) wrote an Encyclical and eight letters on the Rosary and devoted numerous allocutions to it. The Rosary is "the summary of the whole Gospel, meditation on the

Mysteries of the Lord, an evening sacrifice, a crown of roses, a hymn of praise, a prayer of the family, a compendium of the Christian life, a secure pledge of heavenly favor, and a bulwark for the longed-for salvation."

In his 1951 Encyclical *Ingruentium Malorum* ("The Growing Evils"), the same Pope wrote: "We do not hesitate to affirm again publicly that we put great confidence in the holy Rosary for the healing of the evils that afflict our times. Not with force, nor with arms, nor with human power, but with Divine help obtained through the means of this prayer will the Church... be able to confront the infernal enemy."

John XXIII (1958-1963) honored the Rosary not only with his papacy but also with his whole life in which it was an essential component. His Apostolic Letter *Il Religioso Convegno* ("The Religious Meeting Place") presents the value and efficacy of the Rosary in a new language and is a veritable "summa" of the Rosary itself.

The Second Vatican Council (1962-1965), dealing with the Mystery of Mary, adverted to the practices of devotion to her: "This sacred Council ... stipulates for all the children of the Church... that practices and exercises of devotion toward Mary recommended by the Magisterium of the Church throughout the centuries should be highly esteemed" (*Constitution on the Church*, no. 67).

Pope Paul VI (1963-1978) alluded to the Rosary many times, reiterating that it was clearly approved by Vatican II and was a prayer for peace. He also issued a 1974 Apostolic Exhortation on Marian devotion (*Marialis Cultus*) in which he treated the Rosary at length and set forth its essential constitutive elements: (1) the contemplation of a series of the Mysteries of salvation, wisely distributed in [four] cycles; (2) the Our Father, which because of its immense value is at the basis of Christian prayer; (3) the litany-like succession of the Hail Marys according to a number fixed by tradition; (4) the doxology Glory Be to the Father, which concludes this devotion with the glorification of the one and triune God.

At the same time, Paul VI characterized the Rosary as a prayer that is grave and suppliant, lyrical and full of praise as well as adoration by reason of its constitutive elements. It also gives rise to pious exercises and inspires new formulations of prayers such as "Celebrations of the Word."

John Paul II and the New Luminous Mysteries

Following his predecessors, Pope John Paul II wrote and spoke much about Mary and the Rosary. On March 25, 1987, he issued an Encyclical entitled *Redemptoris Mater* ("The Mother of the Redeemer"), dealing with the Blessed Virgin in the life of the Church on her pilgrimage of faith.

On October 16, 2002, the Pope issued an Apostolic Letter entitled *Rosarium Virginis Mariae* ("The Rosary of the Virgin Mary") which provided an in-depth look at this time-honored Marian devotion and broadened the Mysteries that are contemplated in its recitation.

The late Pope suggested the addition of five new Mysteries from events found in the Public Ministry of Jesus, between his Baptism and his Passion, a part of his Life that was not covered by contemplation of the traditional Mysteries. He wrote:

"In the course of [the new] Mysteries we contemplate important aspects of the person of Christ as the definitive revelation of God. Declared the beloved Son of the Father at the Baptism in the Jordan, Christ is the one who announces the coming of the Kingdom, bears witness to it in his works, and proclaims its demands. It is during the years of his Public Ministry that *the Mystery of Christ is most evidently a Mystery of light*: 'While I am in the world, I am the light of the world' (John 9:5).

"Consequently, for the Rosary to become more fully a 'compendium of the Gospel,' it is fitting to add — following reflection on the Incarnation and the Hidden Life of Christ (*the Joyful Mysteries*) and before focusing on the sufferings of his Passion (*the Sorrowful Mysteries*) and the triumph of his Resurrection (*the Glorious Mysteries*) — a meditation on certain particularly significant moments in his Public Ministry (*the Mysteries of Light or the Luminous Mysteries*)."

The Pope listed five new Mysteries of Christ, making a total of twenty instead of the customary fifteen: (1) His Baptism in the Jordan, (2) His Self-Manifestation at the Wedding of Cana, (3) His Proclamation of the Kingdom of God, (4) His Transfiguration, and (5) His Institution of the Eucharist.

In doing so, the Pope made it possible for us to bring our prayer life and our daily life into closer touch with the Liturgical Year. It is true, of course, that we can say the Rosary simply without reference to any day, month, or season in the Liturgical Year. However, the Church is on record as saying that private or semiprivate prayers should proceed in accord with the major themes of the Liturgical Seasons.

These new Mysteries enable us to say the Rosary in accord with every season. We now, so to speak, have the Mysteries that go with Ordinary Time, which previously were lacking.

Praying the Rosary during the Liturgical Year

Our Rosary (and other prayers) to Mary could follow a pattern such as the following.

During *Advent*, we pray with Mary as the Immaculate Conception in expectation of the coming of her Son. During

Christmastime, we venerate Mary as the Mother of Christ and the servant of the Lord.

During *Lent*, we hail Mary as the collaborator with God and the witness of Christ's Passion. During *Eastertime*, we exalt Mary as the first among the redeemed, the first believer, and the witness of the power of the Spirit.

During *Ordinary Time*, Mary is always before us in our growth in faith — in the Ordinary of the Mass as well as in her feasts that occur throughout this time. We thus pray with the theme of each feast.

For example, on the *first Marian feast that occurs during this extended time*, that of Our Lady of Lourdes (February 11), we pray to Mary as the Mother who shows continual interest in the lives of her children on earth. And on the last, the Presentation of Mary (November 21), we pray to her as the exemplar of dedication to God.

By praying the Rosary in this way, we will always be praying with the mind of the Church and in perfect harmony with Christ in his Mysteries.

The Rosary and the Liturgy

In *Rosarium Virginis Mariae*, John Paul II spelled out clearly the relationship that the Rosary has with the Liturgy:

"There are some who think that the centrality of the Liturgy, rightly stressed by the Second Vatican Ecumenical Council, necessarily entails giving lesser importance to the Rosary. Yet, as Pope Paul VI made clear, not only does this prayer not conflict with the Liturgy, *it sustains it,* since [the Rosary] serves as an excellent introduction and a faithful echo of the Liturgy, enabling people to participate fully and interiorly in it and to reap its fruits in their daily lives" (no. 4).

The Rosary can be said to introduce its pray-ers to the Liturgy. There is a close relationship between the Liturgy and the Rosary: like the Liturgy, the Rosary has a communitarian character, is nourished by Sacred Scripture, and centers around the Mystery of Christ. The Rosary participates in the "Sacrifice of praise" to the Trinity.

The world-renowned liturgist Cyprian Vagaggini has stated in *The Theological Dimensions of the Liturgy*: "The Rosary in its formulas and its rites, though approved by the hierarchy, is not, at least as yet, approved as *official* prayer of the Church. The hierarchy alone by Christ's mandate are competent to judge what is official, namely the power which the Church, or rather Christ, considers in all respects as his own, in which, so to speak, he considers himself wholly engaged before God" (p. 116).

However, Vagaggini points out that the Rosary can be a public action of the Church under the right circumstances:

"The public and solemn recitation of the Rosary in a parish under the direction of the pastor, advised or actually imposed by the hierarchy, bishop, or Pope, is a public action of the Church herself and not only of the individual private believers or of a private group of believers in the Church" (p. 114).

Application to Us

It is clear from what has been said above that we should be devoted to the Blessed Virgin and that the Rosary should be part of our prayer life. In addition, we must say it by combining two elements: prayer and meditation.

The risk we run, because of how distracted we may get when praying, is to reduce the Rosary to a simple recitation of formulas and let our minds go off on their own, away from the meditation on the Christian Mysteries.

Our Lady of the Rosary

We must strenuously resist doing this, for it is meditation that is most important when saying the Rosary. Meditation engages thought, imagination, emotion, and desire. It deepens our conviction of faith, prompts the conversion of our heart, and strengthens our will to follow Christ — leading to the knowledge of the love of Jesus and ultimately union with him.

The Rosary can be said in many ways: e.g., with the help of beads or without them; by separating the decades and saying one of them at a time or by saying five decades at a time or even all twenty Mysteries at a time.

It can also be said in countless places: e.g., while walking in the street, riding a bus, or simply sitting in a waiting room. It can be said alone or with a group (e.g., within a family, a parish, or a larger assembly).

Pope John Paul II has declared: "Our heart can enclose in these decades of the Rosary events that comprise the life of an individual, a family, a nation, the Church, and all humanity. The Rosary beats to the rhythm of human life."

There are also other changes that can help in the recitation of the Rosary. For example, one can announce the Mystery with a brief Biblical reading or suggest some prayer intention for each decade. One may sing the Our Father or a Marian hymn before each Mystery and make use of slides to accompany the reflection. One can also conduct "Celebrations of the Rosary," true paraliturgies attuned to the Liturgical Season.

Prayer to Our Lady of the Rosary

> *Mary, Queen of the Holy Rosary,*
> *your Divine Son Jesus is the perfect Mediator*
> *between God and human beings,*
> *because he alone could in all justice merit*

*our reconciliation with God
as well as the graces that God would impart
after the reconciliation.
You are a Mediatrix in union with Christ
from whom your mediation draws all its power.
You merited the title of Unique Associate
above all by your union with Christ
in his redemptive sacrifice.
After Jesus, no one suffered as you did.
Now your action is primarily one of intercession.
In your contemplation of God,
you behold our needs with our prayers
and you beg God to grant these favors.*

*May the faithful recitation of my Rosary
be a sign of my gratitude to Jesus and to you
for all you have done for me
in bringing about my Redemption.
May my Rosary also be a means
of obtaining all the graces that I need
for the sanctification and salvation of my soul.*

18

Perfect Disciple of Christ

The Meaning of "Disciple" in the Ancient World

In the ancient world, every teacher possessed his company of disciples or learners. A disciple was a person who freely placed himself in the school of a teacher and wholeheartedly accepted the views and practices of the teacher.

The word is not found often in the Old Testament, but the idea is. The Prophet Elisha attached himself to Elijah (1 Kings 19:19ff) and a group of devout disciples surrounded Isaiah, receiving his witness and his revelation as a trust (Isaiah 8:16). More often the Sages or wise men had disciples whom they termed their "sons" (Proverbs 1:8, 10; 2:1; 3:1) and to whom they transmitted the traditional teaching.

However, neither the Prophets nor the Sages by their teaching took the place of the Word of God. Since the Word of God was the source of all wisdom, the ideal was not to attach oneself to a human master but to be a disciple of God. Thus, Divine Wisdom calls human beings to hear the Word and follow its lessons (Proverbs 1:20ff; 8:4ff, 32ff). Oracles of the end times announce that God will make himself master of hearts so that they will no longer need earthly masters (Jeremiah 31:31-34) but will be disciples of the Lord (Isaiah 54:13).

The Servant of the Lord, though charged to teach the

Divine injunctions (Isaiah 42:1, 4), waits each morning with an open ear and receives the tongue of a disciple (Isaiah 50:4). Hence, the Psalmist can pray "Lord, teach me!" (Psalm 119:12, 26f; 25:4-9).

After the return from the Exile, the Law became the primary object of teaching and the masters came to be called "doctors of the Law." They now added their own personal authority to the authority of the Word itself (Matthew 23:2, 16-22) when passing on the tradition that they received from their masters.

Christ's Requirements for His Disciples

The Greek word *doulé* is used 261 times in the New Testament, all in the Gospels and Acts of the Apostles, where it can usually be understood as *adherent, student, learner, or follower of a master or teacher.*

Apart from a few mentions about the disciples of Moses (John 9:28), of John the Baptist (e.g., Mark 2:18; John 1:35), or of the Pharisees (e.g., Matthew 22:16), the New Testament uses the word disciple solely for those who have acknowledged Jesus as their Master.

The word is not found in the New Testament Letters, but the idea is certainly there in the word *imitator(s)*. The disciples were to imitate, i.e., be the imitators of, their Master, so as to be recognized as disciples of the Master but also to learn the Master's teaching and then pass it on with some development. They would then be regarded as teachers with their own disciples.

Furthermore, use of the word disciple is not confined solely to those out of whom the Apostles were called (Luke 6:13). It is also used of an even larger group of people who come to hear Jesus and be healed by him (Luke 6:20).

And the first time Mark uses the term disciples, he adds

an explanatory phrase to it that indicates the meaning: "While Jesus was eating at Levi's house, many tax collectors and sinners were eating with him and his *disciples,* for there were many who *followed* him" (Mark 2:15).

In the Acts (11:26) the meaning is broadened to include *all Christians*: "It was in Antioch that the disciples were first called Christians." Finally, an even wider meaning is given disciples when in the next-to-last verse of Matthew the meaning is extended to include all potential Christians: "Go and make disciples of all the nations."

Most important of all, the basic characteristic of any disciple is to believe the teachings of the Master and teach them to others as the extension of the Master. So the two key words are to *believe* and *imitate* the Master.

It is obvious, then, that Jesus had unique requirements for his disciples.

First they need a *call* — initiated by Jesus (Mark 1:17-20) and ultimately by the Father who gives Jesus his disciples (John 6:39; 10:29; 17:6, 12).

Secondly, the disciples must have *a personal attachment to Jesus*. They are to follow Jesus — to fashion their conduct on his, to listen to his lessons, and to conform their lives to his (Mark 8:34f; 10:21; John 12:26). They are not bound to a doctrine but to a *person*; they cannot leave him who is for them more than father and mother (Matthew 12:46-50).

Thirdly, the disciples of Jesus are called to *share the destiny of their Master*: to carry his Cross (Mark 8:34), to drink his cup (Mark 10:38f), and finally to receive the Kingdom from him (Matthew 19:28f; Luke 22:28ff; John 14:3).

It is obvious that Mary, the mother of Jesus, fulfilled all three of these characteristics and was fully qualified to be called a disciple.

The Title and Scripture

The Second Vatican Council affirmed Mary's cooperation "in the salvation of human beings with free faith and obedience" (*Constitution on the Church*, no. 56). "The Blessed Virgin *advanced in the pilgrimage of faith* and preserved her union with her Son unto the Cross" (Ibid., no. 58).

This theme underlines the idea of Mary as the Perfect Disciple of Christ: "[Mary] is worthy of imitation because she was the first and the most perfect of Christ's disciples" (Paul VI: *Marialis Cultus*, no. 35).

In Matthew (12:46-50), there is a passage that describes how Jesus, while teaching, is visited by his Mother and his relatives. He says to those who bring him the news of their appearance: "Who is my Mother and who are my brothers and sisters?" And extending his hands toward his disciples, he declares: "Behold my Mother and my brothers and sisters. For whoever does the Will of my Father who is in heaven is my brother and sister and Mother."

Hence, for Jesus the relation of discipleship is closer to his heart than family ties themselves. Such a relationship originated in doing the Will of the Father; hence, doing the Father's Will is greater in itself than being the Mother of Jesus.

It is Luke, above all, who sketches the figure of Mary as *disciple*, after having beautifully delineated her as Mother of the Son of God made Man. He places this episode immediately after the Parable of the Sower and of the Seed that falls on different terrain (see Luke 8:4-15).

In doing so the Evangelist intends to show that the passage in question must be illumined by the parable. The climax is the affirmation of Jesus put in a positive rather than a negative manner: "My Mother and brothers and sisters are those who hear the Word of God and put it into practice" (Luke 8:21).

All this is suitably applied to Mary, who has welcomed the Word of God, becoming the first believer of the Church. Indeed, in Acts 1:14 Luke numbers Mary among the members of the first community of believers after Christ's Resurrection.

The Infancy Narrative also portrays Mary as a believer: "I am the handmaid of the Lord. Let it be done to me according to your word" (Luke 1:38). Hence, Mary verifies in her person the definition of a disciple of Christ.

In the account of the Visitation, Luke associates Mary with the idea of following and discipleship. The words "And blessed is she who has believed in the fulfillment of the words of the Lord" (Luke 1:45) form the basis for the greeting uttered by Elizabeth: "Blessed are you among women, and blessed is the fruit of your womb" (Luke 1:42).

Then in 11:27-28, Luke underscores the fact that being a disciple constitutes for Jesus a higher relationship than family ties: "Rather blessed are they who hear the Word of God and put it into practice."

Both the quotation of Elizabeth and that of the woman in the crowd praise Mary's physical motherhood. Yet both the praise uttered by Elizabeth and the praise falling from Jesus' lips stress perseverance in hearing and in preaching the Word of God.

Luke 11:28 has parallels in two passages from the Infancy Narrative: "Mary preserved all these things in her heart and meditated on them" (Luke 2:19); "His Mother preserved all these things in her heart" (Luke 2:51).

Hence, Luke considers the Mother of the Lord as the true disciple from the moment that she verified two conditions of being a disciple — hearing the Word and carrying it out in her life.

Even in the scenes at Cana and on Calvary, described by John, Mary — under the name of "Woman" — transcends her function as Mother and assumes the name of disciple. On Calvary, for example, she becomes the Mother of the ideal disciple, presenting herself at the same time as the model both of Mother and of disciple.

The Title and the Fathers

The early Fathers singled out for praise Mary's faith at the Annunciation, as Elizabeth had done in Scripture. Mary was prominent among the Poor of the Lord and embodied believing Israel for she believed the Election, the Covenant, the Promises, and the Law, which was the Word of God transmitted in writing and tradition.

Thus, St. Ambrose (d. 397) declared: "You see that Mary has not doubted but believed." St. Augustine (d. 430) said repeatedly that Mary "conceived by faith": "Holy Mary clearly carried out the Will of the Father, and therefore it is a greater thing for her to be a disciple of Christ than to be his Mother. She is more blessed in being a disciple of Christ than in being the Mother of Christ."

In later times, other great Fathers and Doctors continued to praise Mary's faith. One of the greatest of these encomiums comes from the pen of St. Alphonsus Liguori, the Marian Doctor par excellence, in his master work *The Glories of Mary*:

"She saw her Son in the crib at Bethlehem and believed that he was the Creator of the world. She saw him flee from Herod and believed that he was the King of kings. She saw him born yet believed him to be eternal. She saw him poor and in need of food and believed that he was the Lord of the universe.

"She saw him lying on the straw and believed that he was omnipotent. She observed that he did not speak and yet believed that he was filled with infinite wisdom. She heard him cry and believed that he was the joy of paradise. Finally, she saw him in death, despised and crucified, and even though faith wavered in others, she remained firm in her conviction that he was God."

The Title and the Magisterium

It is mainly in modern times that the Magisterium of the Church has spoken specifically about Mary as the perfect disciple of Christ. St. Pius X in his Encyclical on the Fiftieth Anniversary of the proclamation of the Dogma of the Immaculate Conception (*Ad Diem Illum Laetissimum* ["On That Joyful Day"]) hinted at it by stressing Mary's great faith:

"Since the Son of God made Man is the 'author and finisher of faith' (Hebrews 12:2), it surely follows that his Mother most holy should be recognized as participating in the Divine Mysteries and as being a guardian of them, and that upon her as a foundation — the noblest after Christ — rises the edifice of the faith of all centuries."

As we have already mentioned, Vatican II extolled the Blessed Virgin as cooperating in the work of salvation through free faith and obedience. At the same time, it made her faith the basis of the Mary-Church typology (*Constitution on the Church*, no. 58).

It was Paul VI, however, who really stressed the fact of Mary's perfect discipleship and what it means to the faithful. In his Closing Discourse to the Third Session of the Second Vatican Council he declared:

"In her earthly life Mary realized the perfect figure of the disciple of Christ, mirror of all virtues, and incarnated the evangelical Beatitudes proclaimed by Christ. Therefore, in her the whole Church in the incomparable variety of life and works attains the most authentic form of the perfect imitation of Christ."

Later in his Apostolic Exhortation *Marialis Cultus* (no. 35), he wrote:

"Mary is held up as an example to the faithful for the way in which, in her own particular life, she fully and responsibly accepted the Will of God (see Luke 1:38), because she heard the Word of God and acted on it and because charity and a spirit of service were the driving force of her actions. She is worthy of imitation because *she was the first and the most perfect of Christ's disciples.*"

A bit earlier, in his 1967 Apostolic Exhortation *Signum Magnum*, the same Pope had described Mary's faith in more detail:

"If we then contemplate the Virgin of Nazareth in the halo of her prerogatives and of her virtues, we will see her shine before our eyes as … the summit of the Old Testament and the dawn of the New, in which the 'fullness of time' (Galatians 4:4) was realized, which was preordained by God for the mission in the world of his only-begotten Son.

"In truth, the Virgin Mary, more than all the Patriarchs and Prophets, more than the 'just' and 'pious' Simeon, awaited and implored 'the consolation of Israel … the Christ of the Lord' (Luke 2:25-26) and then greeted his advent with the hymn of the *Magnificat* when he descended into her most chaste womb to take on our flesh" (Part II, no. 3).

Finally, Pope John Paul II, in his Encyclical *Redemptoris Mater*, nicely summarized the reasons behind the title:

"Without any doubt, Mary is worthy of blessing by the very fact that she became the Mother of Jesus according to the flesh…, but also and especially because already at the Annunciation she accepted the Word of God, because she believed it, *because she was obedient to God*, and because she 'kept' the Word and 'pondered it in her heart' (see Luke 1:38, 45; 2:19, 51) and by means of her whole life accomplished it.…

"Through faith Mary continued to hear and to ponder

that Word, in which there became ever clearer, in a way 'that surpasses knowledge' (Ephesians 3:19), the self-revelation of the living God. Thus in a sense Mary as Mother became the *first disciple of her Son*, the first to whom he seemed to say: 'Follow me,' even before he addressed this call to the Apostles or to anyone else (see John 1:43)" (no. 20).

The Great Believer or The First Among Believers

Basically, then, this title is tantamount to one that would read "The Great Believer." Mary was the perfect disciple of Christ because she had faith beyond all telling. Perhaps Cardinal Joseph Ratzinger (before becoming Pope Benedict XVI) has put this aspect of our Lady best by the following lines:

"Mary is the great believer who humbly offered herself to God as an empty vessel for him to use in his mysterious plan. Without complaint she surrendered control of her life; she did not try to live according to human calculation but put herself completely at the disposal of God's mysterious, incomprehensible design.

"All she wanted to be was the handmaid of the Lord, the instrument and servant of the Word. Therein lies her true fame: that she remained a believer despite all the darkness and all the inexplicable demands God made on her.

"She believed even in the face of certain incomprehensible facts: that she should carry her Creator in her womb; that the Child growing there should be the Lord; that he who was the source of Israel's salvation should be regarded by his fellows as deranged; that he should brush her aside, first as a twelve-year-old and again at the beginning of his Public Life; that he who was to bring salvation and healing to Israel should be executed by that same Israel.

"Today God is still mysterious; indeed he seems to have a special kind of obscurity in store for each person's life. But could he ever render any life as dark and incomprehensible as he did Mary's? 'Blessed are you who have believed' (Luke 1:45), even when this faith became a sword that pierced her heart.

"This is the real reason for her greatness and her being called blessed: she is the great believer."

Application to Us

In the above-mentioned *Signum Magnum*, Paul VI also held up the Virgin Mary as a model for all of us. "'Therefore, I beg you, be imitators of me as I am of Christ' (1 Corinthians 4:16). These words, and with greater reason than the Apostle Paul to the Christians of Corinth, can be addressed by [Mary] the Mother of the Church to the multitudes of the faithful, who, in a symphony of faith and love with the generations of past centuries, acclaim her as blessed (see Luke 1:48). It is an invitation that we have a duty to heed docilely" (Ibid.).

In imitating Mary's faith, we must be aware that even for her it was not an easy one to attain. Basically, it was the result of her Motherhood being both Divine and virginal as well as her willingness to live with the Mystery. The latter aspect is what is missing from our faith. In our day there seems to be no room for this type of religious Mystery as a result of our technological culture.

Hence, Mary can teach us to strive to attain the deepest meaning of things rather than the materialistic meaning. The sense of Mystery lies in the capacity that things have to point beyond themselves.

Surely, Mary's faith is never definitive; as the Council said, "she advanced in the pilgrimage of faith" (*Constitution on the Church*, no. 58). She had constantly to reform it with every episode of her life by meditating on the Word of God.

The same is true for us. We must continually renew and reform our faith based on the events of our life and our meditation on the Word of God. Only in this way can we avoid a faith that is dead and attain a truly living faith.

Finally, Mary's faith was one that affected her "whole being," her existence and her way of life. Indeed, a true description of Mary is not "a woman and a believer" but a believing woman. All that she is, even under the purely human sphere, arises from her faith. If she is "blessed among women," as Elizabeth greets her, it is not because she is biologically the Mother of God but because she has had the courage to believe what is above belief (see Luke 1:45).

In the same way, we should strive to be believing persons, living our faith every moment of our lives. We will then be true disciples of Christ, pursuing our pilgrimage of faith unto the glory of the Lord reserved for God's true and faithful servants.

Prayer to Mary, Perfect Disciple of Christ

O Mary,
you are rightly called blessed,
for you received God's Son in your virginal womb.
But you are more blessed because,
as a disciple of the Incarnate Word,
you eagerly sought to know God's will
and faithfully carried it out.

Help us to imitate you
in receiving the saving Word of God,
so that by the power of the Holy Spirit

*it may speak to us in our daily lives
and bring forth a rich harvest of holiness.
Thus, we may be true disciples of Christ,
eagerly hearing his words
and putting them into practice.*

19

Queen of Angels

Mary's Queenship

The title "Queen" is often found in invocations to the Blessed Mother that are intended to stress Mary's spiritual greatness and her place in the Divine Plan, while inspiring in us respect, dependence, and unlimited trust in her. It is a title that does not wish to inculcate worldly modalities of power or relationships of absolute subjection but to underline a superiority conferred on Mary by God himself, which redeemed her in a unique and complete way and rendered her Mother of his Divine Son.

Thus, Mary is "Queen of the Angels" and "Our Lady of the Angels" because in her role as Mother of God she is superior to every other creature, even the Angels who are pure spirits created by God to worship and serve him.

This title brings to our mind the Mystery of the "hereafter," of that eternal Kingdom about which we have only an obscure knowledge based on the Word of God, which indicates how and when our human history will come to an end. It recalls for us "heaven," where Mary already lives her infinite glory with her own body and where those we call "the dead" also live.

The Crowning of Mary as Queen of Heaven and Earth is the Fifth Glorious Mystery of the Rosary. One of its purposes is to highlight the bodily aspect of the Assumption and to record the final moment of our Lady's Assumption into heaven most likely resulting from the allegorical interpretation of a few Scripture texts.

In the Liturgy of the Hours, the Church has included the splendid words of St. Amadeus of Lausanne (d. 1159): "When the Virgin of virgins was led forth by God and her Son, the King of kings, amid the company of exulting Angels and rejoicing Archangels, with the heavens ringing with praise, the prophecy of the Psalmist was fulfilled in which he said to the Lord: 'At your right hand stands the Queen, clothed in gold of Ophir' (Psalm 45:10)."

The text of Song of Songs 4:8 in the Vulgate reads: "Come from Lebanon, my bride,... and you shall be crowned...." The text of the Book of Revelation 12:1 reads: "A great sign appeared in the sky, a woman clothed with the sun, with the moon under her feet, and on her head a crown of twelve stars."

Pope Pius XII stated in the Encyclical *Ad Caeli Reginam* ("To the Queen of Heaven"): "Sacred art, founded on Christian principles, faithfully expresses the simple and spontaneous piety of the faithful. Ever since the Council of Ephesus [431 A.D.] it has pictured Mary as Queen and Empress, seated on a royal throne, adorned with royal emblems, crowned with a diadem, surrounded by Angels and Saints, and dominating not only the forces of nature but also the evil influence of Satan."

The coronation of Mary was discussed by a few of the Fathers, e.g., St. Gregory of Tours (d. 594), but only in the Middle Ages when the cult of Mary was at its zenith did it become a frequent theme.

In the twelfth century, Christian art portrayed Mary as seated at her Son's right hand with a crown on her head. And by the next century Mary was shown as being crowned Queen by Christ the King. At times Mary is portrayed as kneeling before

God the Father to receive the crown or being crowned by the three Persons of the Trinity.

From the end of the sixteenth century in the West, the practice became widespread for the faithful, both religious and laity, to crown images (pictures or statues) of the Blessed Virgin. The Popes endorsed this devout custom and on many occasions, either personally or through bishop-delegates, carried out such a coronation.

The growth of the custom led to the Church's composition of a special rite for crowning images of Mary, and in the nineteenth century it was incorporated into the Roman Liturgy. By means of this rite the Church proclaimed that Mary is rightly regarded and invoked as Queen. The rite was revised in 1981 as part of the *Roman Ritual* under the title *Order of Crowning an Image of the Blessed Virgin Mary*.

For more about the Queenship of Mary, see chapter 21: "Queen of Peace."

Church Teaching about Angels

Angel is a word that comes from the Greek meaning "messenger" and denotes free spirits not dependent on matter who are created to honor and serve God. The profession of faith of the Fourth Lateran Council (1215) states:

"God from the beginning of time made at once out of nothing both orders of creatures, the spiritual and the corporeal, that is, the angelic and the earthly, and then the human creature, who as it were shares in both orders, composed as he is of spirit and body."

Angels are personal and immortal creatures with intelligence and will, and surpass in perfection all visible creatures. They have Christ as the center of their world and are his Angels.

Angels have been present throughout the History of Salvation, announcing this salvation and aiding the accomplishment of the Divine Plan. They shut up the earthly paradise (Genesis 3:24), protected Lot (Genesis 19), saved Hagar and her child (Genesis 21:17), stopped Abraham from offering his son (Genesis 22:11), communicated the Law (Acts 7:53), led the People of God (Exodus 23:20-23), announced births and vocations (Judges 6:11-24; 13:1-23), and assisted the Prophets (1 Kings 19:5-8; Isaiah 6:6-7), to cite just a few examples. Lastly, Gabriel announced the birth of the Precursor of the Messiah and that of Jesus himself (Luke 1:11-20, 26-38).

From the Incarnation to the Ascension, the life of the Word of God is surrounded by the adoration and service of Angels. When God brings the Firstborn into the world, he says: "Let all God's Angels worship him" (Hebrews 1:6). Their song of praise at Christ's birth forever resounds in the Church's praise: "Glory to God in the highest!" (Luke 2:14).

They protect Jesus in his infancy (Matthew 1:20; 2:13, 19), minister to him at the end of the temptations by Satan in the desert (Matthew 4:11), strengthen him in his Agony in the Garden (Luke 22:43), and are with him at his Ascension (Acts 1:11). They also evangelize by proclaiming the Good News of Christ's Incarnation and Resurrection (Luke 2:8-14; Mark 16:5-7), and they will be present at Christ's Second Coming, which they will announce, to serve at his judgment (see Acts 1:10-11; Matthew 13:41; 24:31; Luke 2:8).

The Angels in Human Life and in the Church

From infancy to death human life is surrounded by the watchful care and intercession of Angels as indicated by Scripture (e.g., Matthew 18:10; Luke 16:22; Psalms 34:7; 91:10-13).

The word Angel here can be used in two ways. In the first case, it refers to all the heavenly spirits without distinction of rank or choir. In the second, it denotes only the spirits of the lowest rank or choir, those who act as God's messengers to humans.

Scripture also seems to imply a different order or rank for the Angels mentioned and thus a different function in the heavenly court. The different orders have been called choirs, and from the third century the Church Fathers have acknowledged nine choirs of Angels.

By the sixth century, these nine choirs were divided into three hierarchies: (1) Seraphim, Cherubim, and Thrones, which belong to the supreme hierarchy; (2) Dominations, Virtues, and Powers, which belong to the middle hierarchy; and (3) Principalities, Archangels, and Angels, which belong to the lowest hierarchy.

The whole life of the Church also benefits from the mysterious and powerful help of Angels. The Angels are mentioned in various parts of the Mass. They are invoked at the Blessing of Incense and in all the Prefaces, and our voices are joined with theirs in the singing of the Sanctus: "Holy, Holy, Holy."

The Glory to God is known as the Angelic Hymn since it was sung by the Angels at Christ's birth.

After the Consecration in Eucharistic Prayer I, the aid of the Angels is invoked: "Almighty God, we pray that your Angel may take this sacrifice to your altar in heaven." This implies that the Angels surround the priest and the altar, uniting with the assembly in adoration of the Victim on the altar, Jesus Christ himself.

Then one of them carries and presents the Sacred Gifts of the earthly altar to God the Father so that they may be accepted by him with kindness since they constitute the Sacrifice of Praise of the Church Triumphant.

Mary's Awareness of the Angelic World

Mary grew up in a world in which Angels formed part of the structure of life. She learned that they had intervened in the past history of the Jewish people. They had helped promulgate the Law (Acts 7:38; Galatians 3:19) and protected God's faithful as avengers (Exodus 23:20; 2 Kings 19:35; Psalm 78:49; Daniel 10:13). They also watched over human beings (Tobit 3:17; Psalm 91:11; Daniel 3:49f), presented their prayers to God (Tobit 12:12), and presided over the destinies of nations (Daniel 10:13-21).

Mary discovered other things too. Since the time of Ezekiel Angels explained to the Prophets the meaning of their visions (Ezekiel 40:3f; Daniel 9:21ff; Zechariah 1:8f). And they received names corresponding to their functions: Raphael, "God heals" (Tobit 3:17; 12:15); Gabriel, "Hero of God" (Daniel 8:16; 9:21); and Michael, "Who is like God?" (Daniel 10:13, 21; 12:1).

Hence, Mary was well aware of the Angelic world and its presence in the world of human beings. She was also acquainted with the "Angel of the Lord," present in the ancient Biblical narratives (Genesis 16:7; 22:11; Exodus 3:2; Judges 2:1), who is no different from Yahweh himself and manifested himself on earth in visible form (Genesis 16:13; Exodus 3:2). For God could not allow creatures to see his face (Exodus 33:20) since he lives in light inaccessible.

At the same time, Mary also knew of two Old Testament Messianic texts that spoke of a Woman who was to help overthrow God's ancient enemy (a fallen Angel) by giving birth to the Messiah King while remaining a virgin (Genesis 3:15; Isaiah 7:14).

Queen of Angels

Mary's Experience of Angels in Her Life

In her own life, Mary experienced the coming of Angels as messengers from God and helpers on earth. She did so first during the Conception and Infancy of her Son Jesus. At the Annunciation (Luke 1:28-36), the Archangel Gabriel announces to her that she will be the Mother of the Messiah who will be the Son of God. In the light of her knowledge that Angels were from God, she believes the Angel's message and consents to become the Mother of God's Son.

Later, she will hear from Joseph of the messages he receives via the Angel of the Lord concerning her mode of conception and, after Jesus' birth, concerning the way to outwit the wicked Herod (Matthew 1:20-21; 2:13, 19-20). At the Visitation, Mary meets her cousin Elizabeth who also benefited from an Angelic mission (Luke 1:11-25).

After the birth of Jesus, shepherds alerted by an Angelic choir came to meet the Child and to tell Mary and Joseph what had been told to them about him (Luke 2:8-17). "Mary preserved all these things in her heart and meditated on them" (Luke 2:18f) — including the appearance of the Angels!

Mary was also familiar with Angels by the fact that Jesus mentioned them at various times in his preaching. In addition to having intimate dealings with Angels (Matthew 4:11; Luke 22:43), Mary's Son spoke about them as real and active beings. He showed that they watch over human beings and always view the face of his Father (Matthew 18:10), which no human can do. Moreover, their life escapes subjection to the flesh (Matthew 22:30).

They are at Christ's service, and he can call upon their intervention at the time of his Passion (Matthew 26:53). They will also be the executors of the Last Judgment (Matthew 13: 39, 49; 24:31), and they always share in the Divine Joy when sinners repent (Luke 15:10). Hence, Mary was well versed on the subject of Angels.

Angels at Mary's Assumption

Perhaps Mary's fullest encounter with Angels took place at the Assumption. The Apocryphal Books about the Assumption assign an important place in the event to Angels, especially Michael. The Ethiopic *Book of Rest* states that many Angels accompanied Jesus and Michael to the scene of Mary's death. Her soul was entrusted to Michael, and her body was buried. After three days, our Lord and Michael returned, accompanied by countless Angels. Then Christ gave a sign and Michael spoke with the voice of the faithful Angels.

"The Angels came down in three clouds, and their number above the cloud appeared to be ten thousand before the Savior. And our Lord told them to bear Mary's body in the clouds.... And when they had reached paradise, they placed Mary's body by the tree of life. And they brought her soul and placed it on her body. And the Lord sent the Angels back to their own place."

Other versions of this Book have Mary in conversation with Michael, who links to Mary's person the paramount event in Jewish salvation history — the Exodus. The preservation of the bones of the Patriarch Joseph are seen as a type of her bodily glorification.

Church Documents about Mary and Angels After the Eighth Century

From the eighth century onward, we have further evidence of Mary's relationship to Angels. An eighth-century liturgical antiphon for the feast of the Assumption reads: "The holy Virgin Mary is exalted above the choirs of Angels to the heavenly kingdom."

The same subject appears in such hymns of the eleventh century as *Regina Caeli* ("Queen of Heaven"), *Ave Regina Caelorum* ("Hail, Queen of the Heavens"), and *Ave Domina Angelorum* ("Hail, Mistress of Angels") as well as in the title "Queen of Angels," pioneered by St. Fulbert of Chartres (d. 1028) and St. Anselm (d. 1099).

In the thirteenth century, St. Thomas Aquinas (d. 1274) notes that "the Blessed Virgin, as Mother of God, has a certain infinite dignity from the infinite Good who is God."

By the fourteenth century, Nicholas Cabasilas (d.1396) calls Mary the Mediatrix between God and Angels, and Theophanes of Nicaea (d. 1381) adds that Mary surpasses all the orders of Angels.

In the seventeenth century, St. Lawrence of Brindisi (d. 1619) describes Mary as exalted above all the Angels by Christ. And in that same century, the renowned Scripture scholar Cornelius A. Lapide (d. 1637) states:

"The Blessed Virgin is Mother of God, and therefore by far excels all the Angels, even the Seraphim and Cherubim. She is Mother of God, therefore most pure and holy; so much so that under God no greater purity can be imagined. She is Mother of God, and therefore whatever privilege has been granted to any Saints in the order of sanctifying grace she surpasses all."

The Church in official documents from the modern Popes has characterized Mary as "exalted above all the choirs of heaven" and as "Queen of Angels."

In the *Constitution on the Church* of Vatican II, Mary is described as "[surpassing] all other creatures in heaven and on earth" (no. 53), "exalted by the Lord as Queen of the Universe" (no. 59), and "by the grace of God exalted, after her Son, above all Angels and human beings" (no. 66).

Finally, in the revised Liturgy of Vatican II, Mary's Queenship of the Angels is clearly affirmed. In the Liturgy of the Hours, she is termed the "Queen of heaven and earth" (Invitatory for the Queenship of Mary, August 22) as well as hailed as "Queen of heaven" and "by Angels Mistress owned" (Marian Antiphons *Regina Caeli* and *Ave Regina Caelorum* at the conclusion of Night Prayer).

In the *Order of Crowning an Image of Mary*, the bishop prays: "[Mary] is exalted above the choirs of Angels." She is called "Queen of Angels" in the Litany of Loreto and the Litany in the *Order of Crowning an Image*, and in the latter she is also called "Queen of the universe." Lastly, in the *Collection of Masses of the Blessed Virgin Mary*, one of the Prefaces states: "You exalted [Mary] above all the choirs of Angels to reign with [Christ] in glory and to intercede for all your children, our advocate of grace and the Queen of all Creation" (Preface P 29 for the Mass of "Mary, Queen of All Creation").

Scriptural Basis of Mary's Heavenly Queenship of Angels

Sometimes we are tempted to believe that Jesus became incarnate only to save *human beings* who had fallen into sin. Angels and demons would seem to be outside the Mystery of Christ. Their creation, their trial, and their consequent state would all have been antecedent to and independent of the Incarnation.

However, the Bible indicates otherwise. The prologue to John's Gospel and the Christological hymns that begin the Letters to the Ephesians and the Colossians clearly state God's plan: "[Christ] is the firstborn of all creatures. In him all things in heaven [Angels] and on earth [human beings] were created, things visible and invisible...; all were created through him and for him" (Colossians 1:16).

Therefore, even the creation of pure spirits came about in Christ and for Christ, and in him all these were reconciled in

God, those in heaven (Angels) and those on earth (human beings), through the Blood of his Cross (see Colossians 1:19f).

Some theologians believe that only by the merits of Christ have the Angels been admitted into communion with the Mystery of the Trinity. Many of the Fathers made interesting statements in this regard, as for example St. Athanasius, who does not hesitate to say that even the Angels owe their salvation to the Blood of Christ.

In the light of the above, even the role of Mary with respect to Angels and demons becomes real and direct as a result of her participation in the Incarnation of the Word. Mary's title as Queen of heaven has more than merely an honorific ring. It expresses a real relationship that the Bible brings to light even though theology has yet to plumb its depths.

Application to Us

When we invoke Mary under this title, our eyes are opened to the infinite horizon of eternity, on heaven as the final destiny of glory that awaits us after our life on earth. Hence, we are enabled to see this present life in its true aspect. In this way, our daily lives take on new light and become the beginning of the "glory" of the Angels that Mary already enjoys and that is mysteriously present in us even now.

On our journey toward God in this life, God provides security for those who place their trust in him. We are strengthened by God and by Mary as well as the Angels and Saints of whom she is the Queen.

As we have seen, the Angels are always available to help us. They inspire us with faith and love at our liturgical gatherings so that we may worthily perform our worship. They prepare us inwardly for the reception of the Sacraments, for the Church calls on their aid.

Angels also help us in our warfare against the evil spirit. The New Testament urges us to have faith in God and faith in Christ and to make use of the armor of God. The Angels give us the help we need to resist evil.

We share with the Angels in the Divine life, and we are like them creatures of God. Hence, they long for our salvation so that we may join them in glorifying God and in enjoying the Beatific Vision. We should seek their assistance in order to repel the temptations of the evil one.

Angels also present our petitions to God by joining their supplications to our requests. It is, therefore, to our advantage to call upon them, especially in the time of trial and above all at the hour of death, so that they may defend us from the attacks of our enemies and lead our souls to heaven.

As we have seen, we also have a Guardian Angel, who keeps us in touch with heaven. We should love him and venerate him and pray to him with confidence. He is always our devoted friend, ever ready to help us on our way to heaven. In honoring him, we honor God whom the Angel represents on this earth.

Prayer to Mary, Queen of the Angels

> Mary, you are Queen of heaven and earth
> and Queen of the Angels.
> Make me your faithful servant on earth
> so that I may one day bless you in heaven.
>
> Help me to realize that in praising his Angels
> I honor their Creator,
> who saw fit to send his Angels
> to watch over his servants on earth.
> Grant that I may always be under their protection
> and frequently have recourse to their aid
> and one day enjoy their company in heaven.

20

Queen of Families

Meaning of the Title

On December 31, 1995, the Congregation for Divine Worship and the Discipline of the Sacraments sent a letter to the Episcopal Conferences of the world indicating that the Supreme Pontiff empowered them to insert the invocation "Queen of families" in the Litany of Loreto after "Queen of the most holy Rosary" and before "Queen of peace."

This is a relatively new Marian title, flowing quite naturally from the fact that Mary is "Mother of the Church." She is also Mother of the Domestic Church — i.e., the Christian family.

John Paul II concluded the Apostolic Exhortation *Familiaris Consortio* ("The Christian Family in the Modern World") with the words: "May Christ the Lord, the Universal King, the King of Families, be present in every Christian home as he was at Cana, bestowing light, joy, serenity, and strength."

By the side of the *King of Families* shines forth the *Queen of Families*. And it is once again John Paul II who gives us the meaning of this new invocation:

"Mary called herself the *'Handmaid of the Lord'* (Luke 1:38). Through obedience to the Word of God she accepted her lofty, yet not easy, vocation as wife and mother in the family of Nazareth. Putting herself at God's service, she also put herself at the service of others: a service of love.

"Precisely through this service Mary was able to experience in her life a mysterious but authentic 'reign.' It is not by chance that she is invoked as 'Queen of heaven and earth.' The entire community of believers thus invokes her; many nations and peoples call upon her as their 'Queen.' For her 'to reign' is to serve! Her service is 'to reign.'

"This is the way in which authority needs to be understood both in the family and in society and the Church.... The maternal 'reign' of Mary consists in this. She who was, in all her being, a gift for her Son has also become a gift for the sons and daughters of the whole human race, awakening profound trust in those who seek her guidance along the difficult paths of life on the way to their definitive and transcendental destiny" (*Letter to Women*, June 29, 1995).

The Family — First and Vital Cell of Society

The family has in recent times come under fire from all sides. Many secular voices claim it is antiquated, against progress, and a hindrance to self-fulfillment. They attribute all kinds of evils to its members: Oedipus complex; momism; physical, sexual, and verbal abuse; and unrelenting pressure on one another.

Yet these are all aberrations. The family is in reality a huge blessing that the Creator has bestowed on his creatures. The family is the beginning and basis of human society — its first and vital cell.

It is from the family that citizens come to fruition, and it is within the family that they find the first school of the social virtues that constitute the animating principle of the existence and development of society itself.

The relationships between the members of the family community are inspired and guided by the law of "free giving."

By respecting and fostering personal dignity in each and every one as the only basis for value, this free giving takes the form of heartfelt acceptance, encounter and dialogue, disinterested availability, generous service, and deep solidarity.

Thus, the family is the place of origin and the most effective means for humanizing and personalizing society. It contributes to building up the world by making possible a life that is really human — especially by guarding and transmitting virtues and values.

Today, we are confronted with a society that is becoming more depersonalized and standardized, and hence inhuman and dehumanized. The family, on the other hand, counters the anonymity of its members, by keeping them conscious of their personal dignity, enriching them with deep humanity, and actually placing them — in their uniqueness and unrepeatability — within the fabric of society.

The Christian Family — A Miniature Church

The Christian family plays an even more important part in the world's makeup. It builds up the People of God in history by participating in the life and mission of the Church.

The family represents and constitutes a miniature Church, which is the whole Body of Christ. It does so in three ways. (1) Its honest and moral expression combines the ineffable and inexhaustible harmonies of two separate beings into one life. (2) Its sacramental origin raises a fragile and violable natural love to the level of an inviolable and ever new supernatural love. (3) The law that governs it transforms the union from which it takes its origin into an exclusive and perennial society reflecting the union of Christ and his Church.

The family is thus the smallest cell of the Church. Hence,

like the Church, it is an evangelized and evangelizing community, which is ordained to the upbuilding of the Body of Christ.

Christian spouses and the Christian family have a "priestly" vocation and mission resulting from their baptismal priesthood of the faithful exercised in the Sacrament of Marriage. By this vocation, their daily lives are transformed into spiritual sacrifices acceptable to God through Jesus Christ.

This transformation is achieved in several ways. First, it is advanced by the spouses celebrating in common the Eucharist as well as the other Sacraments and offering themselves to the glory of God. It is also achieved by a life of prayer, including the Liturgy of the Hours, through prayerful dialogue with the Father, through his Son, in the Holy Spirit.

Family prayer enables its members to see family life in all its varying circumstances as a call from God and to live it in filial response to his call. The joys and sorrows in a family as well as the hopes and disappointments, births and birthday celebrations, wedding anniversaries, departures, separations and homecomings, important and far-reaching decisions, deaths of loved ones — all mark God's loving intervention in the family's history.

Family prayer enables the members to view these events for what they truly are and to react to them in the Christian way. They are then seen as suitable moments for thanksgiving, for petition, for trusting abandonment of the family into the hands of their common Father in heaven.

Furthermore, the Christian couple and the Christian family have the grace and the responsibility to share with the visible Church their liturgical, cultural, vision. That is, there exists a "domestic priesthood," which empowers and commits the couple and the family to glorify the Lord, to encounter him in prayer as a couple and family, and in and through the typical realities of conjugal and family existence as a whole.

Christian Parents: Educators in Prayer

Christian parents, as a result of their dignity and mission, have the specific responsibility of educating their children in prayer. They are to introduce the young minds to the gradual discovery of the Mystery of God and to personal dialogue with him.

In this respect, examples speak louder then words. By praying with the children, a father and mother can leave an indelible impression on their minds and hearts. A priest has stated that as a small child he witnessed his mother reciting the Rosary upon hearing of her own mother's death — and that example has never left him!

The words of Pope John Paul II on this point offer much food for thought:

"Mothers, do you teach your children the Christian prayers? Do you prepare them, in conjunction with the priests, for the Sacraments that they receive when they are young: Confession, Communion, and Confirmation? Do you encourage them when they are sick to think of Christ suffering, to invoke the aid of the Blessed Virgin and the Saints? Do you say the family Rosary together?

"And you, fathers, do you pray with your children, with the whole domestic community, at least sometimes? Your example of honesty in thought and action, joined to some common prayer, is a lesson for life, an act of worship of singular value. In this way, you bring peace to your homes and it is thus that you build the Church."

The Family and Liturgical Prayer

An important purpose of the prayer of the Domestic Church is to serve as the natural introduction for the children to the liturgical prayer of the whole Church.

This is true in preparing for the Liturgy and in extending it into personal, family, and social life. Hence, all the members of the family need to be introduced into participation in the Eucharist, especially on Sundays and Holy Days, and the other Sacraments, particularly the Sacraments of Christian Initiation of Children.

Parents must instill in their children that the Eucharist is the summit and fount of their Christian existence. It enables them to worship God fittingly, to encounter Christ personally, and to gain strength for living the Faith.

Children must be taught to cultivate a living faith in what is being done as they celebrate the Eucharist — and faith in the Father's acceptance of the act of worship on their behalf. They need faith in the Son's redemptive Passion and Resurrection as it is brought to them and faith in the Holy Spirit's sanctifying action, which brings Christ's saving grace to all.

Above all, children must be led to realize that they need a faith that discerns the importance of their personal participation. Each of them has something to give to every celebration, something that no one else in the community can offer. By their unique participation in each Eucharist, they bring Christ's power and love into their life situation.

Thus, their participation should be *full*, that is, as devoid of conscious distractions as possible. Their entire attention should be on the sacred action at hand.

It should also be *conscious*. They must strive to know what they are doing and do it with complete freedom and with the elimination of all routine.

Finally, it should be *active*. They should not merely be present as simple spectators. They should carry out the parts assigned to them at each Eucharist. They should put their stamp on the entire act of worship and make it their own.

The Family and the Liturgical Year

One of the most important things that the Domestic Church can teach the children is the meaning and function of the Liturgical Year. The Liturgy is the living memory of the Church, which is the community of witnesses to Christ. Through the Liturgy, the Church recalls the Mysteries of Christ.

In doing so, she is sustained by Christ the Son of God and enabled to span time. She feels the power of his Mysteries in her members who are thereby sanctified and inspired to act.

Over the course of centuries, the Church has structured this memory into a yearly cycle commemorating one or other event of her Savior's life. The primary function of this Liturgical Year is to prolong — by both public and private prayer — the worship of and true dialogue with the heavenly Father that Jesus achieved by his Life, Death, and Resurrection.

Living in accord with this year of the Church enables Christians to encounter this saving Paschal Mystery of Jesus in signs and to render fitting worship to the Father in Christ and through the Spirit. At the same time, it empowers Christians to lay hold of the saving benefits that Jesus obtained once and for all. It enables them to live in a Christian time, so to speak.

During the sacred Seasons of the Liturgical Year, the Church forms the faithful by means of the Liturgy, especially the Eucharist, as well as pious practices, instruction, prayer, and works of penance and mercy — many of which can take place in the home.

But the most important role in this liturgical formation is to be played by the faithful themselves. They are to make the most of the Church's time of grace. Through the sentiments to be inculcated in them during each Season, they can relive the Mysteries of Christ each day in their lives, ensuring that they are utilizing their time to the full.

The Family and Private Prayer

As preparation for the worship celebrated in church and as its prolongation in the home, the Christian family should make use of private prayer in its many forms.

"Prayer constitutes an essential part of Christian life. Prayer is the first expression of the inner truth of human beings, the first condition for authentic human freedom of spirit" (Pope John Paul II).

The family thus contributes to the authentic development of Christian life by its prayer. It not only teaches the members what to do in the service of society but also enables them to carry it out.

It teaches the children *what prayer is*: lifting up our minds and hearts to God so as to praise him, thank him, and ask for something. It teaches *why we pray*: because God is Lord and Father to us and because without prayer we cannot be saved. It teaches *what we should pray for*: that God may be glorified and all people may gain salvation.

The Domestic Church also teaches children *how* they should pray. They should do so:

(1) *with devotion*: praying from the heart and avoiding distractions;

(2) *with humility*: acknowledging their sinfulness and need for help;

(3) *with resignation*: leaving it to God as to when and how he will hear them;

(4) *with confidence*: trusting that God will hear them;

(5) *with perseverance*: continuing to pray even though their prayer is not heard at once or as soon as they would like.

The parents should also teach their children *when* to pray. The Church expressly encourages morning and evening prayer, reading and meditating on the Word of God, preparation for the reception of the Sacraments, devotion to the Sacred Heart of Jesus, grace before and after meals, and observance of popular devotions.

High on the list is the veneration of the Blessed Virgin Mary. And among the practices most recommended is the family Rosary. Since Mary is the Mother of Christ and of the Church, she is in a special way the Mother of Christian Families, Domestic Churches.

Reflection on the Christian family as a Domestic Church will give everyone a truer picture of the worth of each Christian family. It will indicate what a great responsibility is placed on Christian spouses, but also the surpassing graces to carry out their tasks that are part and parcel of the Sacrament of Marriage.

Mary, Mother of Every Christian Family

In an excellent 1973 Pastoral Letter entitled *Behold Your Mother*, the Bishops of the United States offered a good summary of this topic as shown by the following words.

"When Mary conceived and gave birth to Jesus, human motherhood reached its greatest achievement. From the time of the Annunciation, she was the living chalice of the Son of God made Man. In the tradition of her people she recognized that God gives life and watches over its growth.

[Mary might even have meditated often on the classic text from the Old Testament writer known as the Preacher:] "Just as you do not know the way of the wind or the mysteries of a woman with child, no more do you know the work of God who is behind it all" (Ecclesiastes 11:5; see Psalm 139:13; 2 Maccabees 7:22).

"Reverence for human life as sacred from the beginning is bound up with the correct understanding and use of sexual love. Abortion arouses in the Christian the same horror as the slaughter of the Innocents in St. Matthew's Gospel. Defenders of unborn life do well to appeal to the first part of the Hail Mary. Elizabeth's words, 'Blessed is the fruit of your womb' [Luke 2: 45], are true in a real sense of every unborn child.

"God called Mary and Joseph to sublimate the consummation of their married love in exclusive dedication to the holy Child, conceived not by a human father but by the Holy Spirit. When Mary said to Gabriel, 'How can this be since I do not know man?' (Luke 1:34), the Angel told her of the virginal conception. Joseph received the same message in a dream. Christian tradition from early times has seen St. Joseph as protector of the Christ Child and of his wife's consecrated virginity throughout their married life.

"Christian marriage is a sign of the union between Christ and his Church. Man and wife in mutual love, and in the children they welcome from God and care for, are a witness to the world of love of God and of their [neighbor].

"The offering of the bride's bouquet at our Lady's statue is an American Catholic custom that invites the Blessed Virgin into the life of the newlyweds. The conjugal chastity of a holy marriage is an answer to the neo-pagan degradation of human sexuality by pornography and by the glorification of promiscuity, divorce, and perversions.

"Parents and children will find renewed strength in the grace of Christ and in the example and assistance of the Blessed

Virgin, model of perfect purity and of self-surrender to God and neighbor.

"Christ was 'Man of Sorrows,' tortured and executed for the sins of [human beings]. Mary was 'Mother of Sorrows,' sharing her Son's sufferings even to Calvary. But there were also the joyous years at Nazareth, as her Son grew to adulthood, and something of the happiness of the Holy Family comes through in the Gospel preaching of Jesus with his tender examples from home life...."

Mary, Queen of the Home

"Mary is Queen of the home. As a woman of faith, she inspires all mothers to transmit the Christian Faith to their children. In the setting of family love, children should learn free and loving obedience, inspired by Mary's obedience to God.

"[Mary's] example of concern for others, as shown at the wedding feast of Cana, will exercise its gentle influence. 'He went down with them ... and was obedient to them.... [Jesus] progressed steadily in wisdom and age and grace before God and [human beings]' (Luke 2:51-52).

"This obedience of Jesus is emphasized throughout the New Testament: at Nazareth, throughout his ministry in which he sought only to do his Father's will, even unto death. The Gospel makes clear also Mary's obedience to the Law and to the traditional prayer life of her people.

"This is evident, for example, in her annual trip to Jerusalem for the Passover. Faithful to the Law of Moses, the holy couple brought Jesus to the Temple, his Father's house, for the presentation. Such obedience was the flower of Mary's faith. Because of it, God found her worthy to be the Mother of his Son.

"In her appearances during the Public Life, Mary showed

the same generous response to the Will of the Father made manifest in her Son. At the marriage feast of Cana, after her Son's mysterious reference to the 'hour not yet come,' Mary's reaction was to advise the waiters, 'Do whatever he tells you' (John 2:5).

"Family love builds on the Fourth Commandment, and in Jesus, Mary, and Joseph, parents and children have a powerful example of obedience to the Will of God.

Application to Us

"Family prayer, in whatever form it takes — meal prayers, night prayers, the family Rosary, attending Mass together — provides opportunities for prayer to the Blessed Virgin. Children forget many things when they grow up. They do not forget the manly piety of the father, the gentle devotion of the mother, and the love of Jesus and Mary as the support of the home, in sorrow and in joy....

"Because of the primacy of the spiritual in all that makes for renewal, top priority should be given to whatever may produce a sound 'family spirituality': family prayer, above all that which derives its content and its spirit from the Liturgy and other devotions, particularly the Rosary" (nos. 129-142).

In this way, the Virgin Mary, who is the Mother of the Church, also becomes the Mother of the church of our home. Thanks to her motherly aid, each Christian family can really become a "little church" in which the Mystery of the Church of Christ is mirrored and given new life.

The family members will take the Handmaid of the Lord as an example of humble and generous acceptance of the Will of God. And the Sorrowful Mother at the foot of the Cross will comfort the sufferings and dry the tears of those in distress because of the difficulties of their families.

Prayer to Mary, Queen of Families

Most Blessed Virgin Mary,
I choose you
for my Lady, Mother, and Advocate with God.
I dedicate myself and all who belong to me
to your service forever.
Bless me and all my family.
Never let any of us offend your Son.
In every temptation defend us.
Protect us in every danger.
Provide for us in the necessities of life.
Comfort us in sadness and sorrow,
and especially the final sorrow of death.
Grant that we may all enter heaven
to thank you and, in your company,
to praise and love Jesus our Redeemer
for all eternity.

21

Queen of Peace

A Modern Title

Scholars tell us that the title "Queen of Peace" has taken root in the twentieth century in place of the previous title "Help of Christians," which had to do with our Lady's role in the public life of nations.

From the beginning of the Church, Mary was invoked as a protectrix and ally of Christians in the battles against unbelievers: in the early attacks on Constantinople, during the Crusades, and in the wars for survival against the Turks. However, during the Middle Ages when wars began between Christians, the ideal of peace took on a higher and imperial value with Mary exalted as the Queen of Peace.

Twentieth-century Popes have made use of the title Queen of Peace. In 1883 Leo XIII made use of it in his Encyclical *Supremi Apostolatus* ("The Supreme Apostolate"). In 1917, Benedict XV inserted it as an invocation in the Litany of Loreto and he specifically related this act to the longed-for peace in that day:

"May this pious and ardent invocation rise to Mary, the Mother of Mercy who is all-powerful in grace!... May her loving and most merciful solicitude be moved to obtain for this convulsed world the peace so greatly desired! And may the ages yet to come remember the efficacy of Mary's intercession and the greatness of her blessing to her supplicants!"

Pius XII returned to the use of this title in a radio message for the 25th Anniversary of Fatima, as did Paul VI in his Encyclical *Christi Matri* ("The Mother of Christ").

An Outgrowth of the Title "Help of Christians"

Thus, the title "Queen of Peace" is a logical outgrowth of the title "Help of Christians." By helping Christians, Mary enables them to overcome their adversaries and bring about peace. However, such peace does not entail unpunished wrongdoing or unbridled freedom.

It means an orderly living together, guided and commanded by the Will of God. It also means orderly living within oneself in accord with God's Will. As Queen, Mary brings to the world the presence of Christ's truth, justice, and love.

Mary brought forth the Prince of Peace (Isaiah 9:5) amidst angelic chants of peace for all human beings. Peace is a blessing of Christ and does not come from the world; to pursue peace entails suffering and persecution (Matthew 10:34-39). It is peace of heart that puts anxiety and fear to flight, since it is the fruit of the complete teaching brought us by the Holy Spirit and partakes of the joy of heavenly hope (John 14:26-28).

Mary enables her clients to practice truth, justice, and love and so attain the inner peace of Christ for themselves. This is then manifested in a universal peace, without wars, disorders, or injustices, in which the Kingdom of Christ is propagated without barriers of any kind.

This title also flows from the cooperation of our Lady in the reconciliation or "peace" between God and the human family brought about by Christ:

(1) *in the Mystery of the Incarnation*: the lowly "Handmaid of the Lord" received God's word from the Angel Gabriel and conceived in her womb the Prince of Peace (see Luke 1:26-38), who restored our peace, reconciling in himself earth and heaven;

(2) *in the Mystery of the Passion*: the faithful Mother stood faithfully and fearlessly beside the Cross as her Son shed his Blood for our salvation and reconciled all things to himself in peace;

(3) *in the Mystery of Pentecost*: our Lady, the Daughter of Peace, joined in prayer with the Apostles as she awaited the coming of the Spirit of unity and peace, in love and joy.

Meaning of Queenship of Mary

The title of Queen was conferred on Mary by Christian Tradition from the beginning of the fourth century as an indication of her preeminence and power. Together with other royal titles it entered progressively into the usage of the People of God and eventually found expression in the Liturgy of the Hours (*Hail Holy Queen, Queen of Heaven*, etc.), in popular piety (Litany of Loreto, Fifth Glorious Mystery of the Rosary, etc.), and in Christian iconography that frequently depicts Mary's coronation.

In this connection, it is interesting to note that five of the last seven invocations added by Popes to the Litany of Loreto have the title "Queen" in them: "Queen conceived without original sin" (Pius IX, 1854); "Queen of the Most Holy Rosary" (Leo XIII, 1883); "Queen of peace" (Benedict XV, 1917); "Queen assumed into heaven" (Pius XII, 1951); and "Queen of families" (John Paul II, 1995).

The title became a common and accepted practice in the Church to the point that Pius XII, in 1954, instituted the liturgical Feast of the Queenship of Mary. On that occasion, the Pope issued the principal document of the Magisterium concerning our Lady's royal dignity, the Encyclical *Ad Caeli Reginam* ("To the Queen of Heaven") (October 11, 1954).

The Encyclical indicates that the Biblical foundations for the title are found in two texts of Luke: (1) the words of the Angel Gabriel predicting that the Son of Mary would reign forever (Luke 1:32-33) and (2) the words of Elizabeth, who greeted Mary with reverence and called her "the Mother of my Lord" (Luke 1:43). These texts show "clearly that because of her Son's royal dignity, [Mary] possessed a greatness and an excellence that set her apart."

The same document also reprehends the tendency to make Mary a "king of the feminine sex" and clearly states the Christological principle that Jesus Christ alone, God and Man, is King in the full, proper, and strict sense of the word: "The royalty of Mary is a participation in the royal dignity of Jesus Christ, but in a limited and analogical way." It includes three aspects or functions:

(1) *A preeminence, or primacy of excellence,* because the Blessed Virgin "surpasses in dignity all creation," according to the words of St. Germanus (d. 733): "Your honor and dignity surpass all creation; the Angels take second place to you in excellence."

(2) *A royal power,* which authorizes her to distribute the fruits of the Redemption: "The Blessed Virgin not only has been given the highest degree of excellence and perfection after Christ but also shares in the power that her Son and our Redeemer exercises over the minds and wills of human beings."

(3) *An inexhaustible efficacy of intercession with her Son and the Father:* "Mary has been made Queen of heaven and earth by God, exalted above all the choirs of Angels and all the Saints. Standing at the right hand of her only-begotten Son, our Lord Jesus Christ, she pleads strongly for us with a mother's prayers, and what she seeks she finds, nor can she ask in vain."

Finally, the Encyclical does not say whether Mary shares in legislative, judicial, or executive power because — as Pius XII said — "even less than that of her Son, Mary's royal sovereignty must not be understood after the manner of modern political life.... Mary's royalty is a superterrestrial reality that nevertheless searches souls and touches them in their profoundest spiritual and immortal being" (Allocution of November 1, 1954).

Reasons for Mary's Queenship

On March 21, 1981, the Church gave us a new rite for crowning an image of the Blessed Virgin Mary. Among other things this new rite makes the reasons for Mary's Queenship crystal clear. She deserves to be Queen because she is: (1) the Mother of the Son of God and the Messianic King; (2) the loving Associate of the Redeemer; (3) the perfect follower (or disciple) of Christ; and (4) the most excellent member of the Church.

(1) Mary is Queen because she is Mother of the Word Incarnate; because she "brought forth a Son who at the very moment of his conception was — by virtue of the hypostatic union of the human nature with the Word — even as man King and Lord of all things." And in this Incarnate Word "everything in heaven and on earth was created, things visible and things invisible, whether Thrones or Dominations, Principalities or Powers" (Colossians 1:16).

Mary is Queen also because she is the Mother of the Messianic King; because she bore a Son about whom the Angel said: "Great will be his dignity and he will be called Son of the Most High. The Lord God will give him the throne of David his father. He will rule over the House of Jacob forever and his Kingdom will have no end" (Luke 1:32-33).

The rite adds Elizabeth's salutation to Mary: "Who am I,

to have the Mother of my Lord come to me?" (Luke 1:43) as another Biblical indication of Mary's Queenship.

(2) The Blessed Virgin is Queen because she was associated wholeheartedly with Christ the Redeemer. By an eternal plan of God the Blessed Virgin is the New Eve, and she played a large part in the work of salvation by which Christ Jesus, the New Adam, redeemed us and purchased us for himself not with corruptible gold or silver but with his Precious Blood and made us into a Kingdom for our God.

(3) Mary is Queen because she was the perfect follower or disciple of Christ. This is a new theme and comes from the Book of Revelation (via Vatican II): "Be faithful until death, and I will reward you with the crown of life.... I will permit the victor to take his seat beside me on my throne just as I myself have won the victory and taken my seat beside my Father on his throne" (Revelation 2:10; 3:21).

The rite incorporates this theme (found in the *Constitution on the Church*, nos. 55-59) in a concise and concrete fashion. Mary consented to the Divine Plan and advanced in the journey of faith. She heard and kept the Word of God and faithfully preserved her union with the Son even to the Cross. She then persevered in prayer together with the Church and became proficient in the love of God.

(4) Mary is Queen because she is the "most excellent member of the Church," according to a felicitous phrase of the Council. She is "blessed among women" (Luke 1:42) and holds a preeminent place in the Communion of Saints for a twofold reason: her mission and her holiness.

Mary stands out in the chosen race, priestly people, and holy nation that is the Church because of the *singular mission* given her with regard to Christ and all members of his Mystical Body, and because of her copious virtues and fullness of grace.

Therefore, she deserves to be called the Mistress of human beings and Angels and the Queen of all Saints.

In fact, Mary's glory reverberates even outside the Church. She is the Daughter of Adam as well as our Lady. She is thus not only the joy of Israel and the splendor of the Church but also the glory of the whole human race.

An Understanding of Mary's Queenship in Accord with Our Time

The title Queen arose in cultures in which royalty was commonplace. In them there was a sense of royalty that was easily transferred to Mary. In our day, democracy is the dominant political ideology. Therefore, there is a need to express the teaching concerning Mary's Queenship in terms consonant with present-day culture. The following are some ways in which scholars say this may be done.

(1) Mary's Queenship should be inserted within the kingly status of the People of God (see 1 Peter 2:9; Revelation 1:6; 5:9; 20:4-6). As an excelling member of the Church, Mary the Queen proclaims the royal character of the other human beings, which is founded on union with Christ. In communion with all Christians, she participates in the Kingship of Christ.

Vatican II, in its *Constitution on the Church* (no. 36), spoke of this kingly function of the People of God as one of power for deliverance and service. This leads us to see that Mary is Queen because in her earthly life she fulfilled through Christ's grace a mission that she continues to carry out even more in heaven — a mission that has three aspects.

(a) Mary conquered the powers of evil from the first moment of conception. She was never under bondage to sin and always gave God's message her total consent. By her Assumption she already shares in Christ's victory even over the last enemy, death (see 1 Corinthians 15:26), and with Christ she works for the world's deliverance from sin.

(b) Mary understood her life as a service, in which consists royalty according to the Gospel (Luke 22:24-40). She did not construe her Divine Motherhood as expression of sovereignty but declared herself "servant of the Lord" (Luke 1:38), worshiping the one God and completely given to service for his plan of salvation.

(c) Mary accepted to render possible the realization of the Kingdom of God, welcoming the Angel's message concerning the Davidic Messiah who would reign forever over the house of Jacob (Luke 1:32-33). She knew that the oracle of Nathan (2 Samuel 7:12-16), to which Luke's text refers, envisaged above all the Messianic benefits of the religious order, such as peace, justice, piety, and deliverance. Thus, in accepting the King-Messiah, the Blessed Virgin accepted the Kingdom of God, which her Son would then purify of every nationalistic interpretation.

(2) The Queenship of Mary should take on a deeper Gospel inspiration. The Kingship of Christ is not expressed by the domination, imposition, and egoistic pursuits of a worldly kingship but in the rejection of violence and in the love and service of the truth, unto the total giving of self (John 18:36-37).

The Kingdom of God is the sovereignty of the Lord in human life (Matthew 7:21), a sovereignty that implies Divine filiation, universal brotherhood, and acts of "power" like cures and miracles.

In light of this, Mary is one who has inherited the Kingdom of God, because she shares in the power communicated by the Spirit for liberating the world from its evils (cures and conversions of life obtained at Marian shrines attest to this) and for bringing people to Divine filiation and Christian maturity.

(3) The Queenship of Mary should preserve its character of unique and motherly participation in Christ's kingly power. Mary was called to share in the power of Christ, in this authority and freedom of action to be exercised in perfect union with the Father's Will.

Hence, as Mother of the King par excellence whose Kingdom will have no end, Mary makes possible the marriage of the Word with humankind. She asks us to renew the Covenant with Christ (John 2:5), intercedes for us with her Son, and exercises a universal Motherhood toward disciples beloved by Jesus (John 19:25-27).

(4) The Queenship of Mary should be harmonized with the legitimate demands of the modern mentality. It must be divested of every appearance of authoritarianism or the kind of influence that would seem to jeopardize human freedom. Divine lordship is a lordship of love, and the glory of God is shown in his sovereign freedom to love and forgive.

Hence, the Queenship of Mary is the opposite of oppression and servitude, because it means her participation in a work that rouses hope and is expressive of a merciful and furthering love.

For the people of the first century, proclaiming Christ universal King was tantamount to saying all persons find in him alone the true answer to the question of their own identity. In similar fashion, Mary is Queen by exercising a role of leadership toward the People of God.

Thanks to Mary's prestige, her excellence as first Christian and type of the Church, she is a necessary point of reference for the faithful. In her they can find the secret to their own royal identity as children of God and the model for giving the Lord an ever greater place in their lives.

Application to Us

According to the New Testament, Christians are called to share in the Kingship of Christ: "If we have died with Christ, we shall also live with him. If we endure, we shall also *reign* with him" (2 Timothy 2:11-12).

Indeed, Christ himself mentioned this point when speaking with Peter: "Amen, Amen, I say to you, when everything is made new again, and the Son of Man is seated on his throne of glory, you yourselves will sit on twelve thrones to judge the twelve tribes of Israel" (Matthew 19:28).

"You are the ones who have stood by me faithfully in my trials. So now just as my Father has conferred a Kingdom on me I confer one on you; you shall eat and drink at my table in my Kingdom, and you shall sit on thrones judging the twelve tribes of Israel" (Luke 22:28-30).

The same conclusion can be drawn from the words of Christ in the Book of Revelation quoted above (Revelation 3:20-21).

Accordingly, the Second Vatican Council sets forth the requirements of the kingly office of the laity based on the royal dignity of the baptized: (1) sharing in Christ's Kingdom; (2) conquering sin; (3) serving Christ in others to bring them to him; (4) reigning by serving; and (5) showing concern for the spread of the Kingdom.

Mary is our Model in all of these requirements. Her Queenship should inspire us to follow her lead in a Queenship of service, as Pope John Paul II has so well indicated:

"[Mary] is glorified as 'Queen of the Universe.' She who at the Annunciation called herself the 'Handmaid of the Lord' remained throughout her life faithful to what this name expresses. In this she confirmed that she was a true 'disciple' of Christ, who strongly emphasized that his mission was one of service....

"In this way Mary became the first of those who 'serving Christ also in others with humility and patience lead their brothers and sisters to the King whom to serve is to reign' (*Constitution on the Church*, no. 36), and she fully obtained that 'state of royal freedom' proper to Christ's disciples: to serve means to reign!" (Encyclical *Redemptoris Mater*, no. 41).

While imitating her in this service, we can ask Mary to grant to the Church and the whole human family these favors:

(1) *the spirit of love,* so that we may live in peace as one family, united in love for one another;

(2) *the gift of unity and peace,* so that we may build up in our world the peace that Christ left us;

(3) *tranquillity in our times,* so that we may have true peace on earth and goodwill toward all.

Prayer to Our Lady, Queen of Peace

Most holy Virgin,
by your Divine Motherhood you merited
to share in your Divine Son's prerogative of universal Kingship,
and to be called Queen of Peace.
May your powerful intercession guard your people
from all hatred and discord among themselves
and direct their hearts in the way of peace.
Your Son came to teach us this way
for the good and well-being of all,
and his Church continues to guide our steps
along that same way.

Look kindly upon the efforts of Christ's Vicar
to call together and unite nations
around the only center of saving faith.

*Enlighten the rulers of our country
and of all countries on earth
to follow this path to peace.
Grant that there may be peace
in our hearts,
in our families,
and in our world.*

22

Seat of Wisdom

Wisdom in the Old Testament

The title "Seat of Wisdom" has been applied to Mary from the earliest times. Like many of her titles it has grown in meanings throughout the centuries. It has its basis in the Biblical concept of Wisdom — which in the Old Testament is expressed by the Law of Moses and in the New by the Person of Christ.

In the Old Testament, Wisdom is identified with the Mosaic Law, which documents the story of God's dealings with his chosen people. For example, Sirach 24:22 states: "All this [i.e., Wisdom and the observance of its dictates: see verses 1-2] is the book of the Covenant with the most high God, the Law that Moses has imposed on us, the heritage of the assembly of Jacob."

Baruch (4:1-4) says: "[Wisdom] is the book of the decrees of God, it is the law that subsists in the ages.... Blessed are we, Israel, because what is pleasing to God has been revealed to us."

At the same time, the translator of the Book of Sirach into Greek affirms that Israel is lauded as a people instructed and wise thanks to the many and profound teachings transmitted in the Law, the Prophets, and the Writings (Sirach, preface, 1-3). This shows that the "Law of Moses" embraces in practice all the Sacred Books of the Old Testament.

Furthermore this Wisdom is not any type of knowledge but

only religious knowledge. It reveals Divine thought and projects as manifested in the History of Salvation, i.e., all the marvels that God works in created things (Sirach 42:21-43:35; Wisdom 9:9) and in the lives of human beings, especially his chosen people (Sirach 44:1-50:24; Wisdom 9:18-19:22).

Wisdom in the New Testament

The New Testament shows us Christ as the Wisdom of God (1 Corinthians 1:24, 30). Indeed, he is the Master of Wisdom as well. He constantly makes use of the genres (proverbs, parables, and the like) and gives rules for life (Matthew 5-7), as the Sages did.

This aspect is set forth from the very childhood of Jesus with the Doctors in the Temple (Luke 2:40, 52). He himself alludes to it when he tells his audience that the Queen of the South rose up to hear Solomon's wisdom but one greater than Solomon is present and dispensing wisdom to them (Matthew 12:42).

Of old, Wisdom had been hidden in God while it ruled the universe, guided history, and was dispensed in the Law and in the teaching of the Sages. Now it is revealed in Jesus, in whom all the Wisdom texts find their fulfillment.

Furthermore, Christian Wisdom is not acquired by human effort alone but primarily through the revelation of God (Matthew 11:25ff). It is Divine, mysterious, and hidden, and impossible for human intelligence alone to fathom (1 Corinthians 2:7ff; Romans 11:33ff; Colossians 2:3).

This Wisdom is revealed by the accomplishment of salvation (Ephesians 3:10), but it can be communicated only by the Spirit of God to those who are open to his inspiration (1 Corinthians 2:10-16; 12:8).

Seat of Wisdom

History of the Title

One of the first to use the title "Seat of Wisdom" with reference to Mary was St. Augustine in the fourth century. By the tenth century the title is alluded to in Masses of Mary, Mother of the Incarnate Wisdom of God. The Readings are often from the Wisdom literature, especially Sirach and Proverbs.

In these texts, it is true that the Church listens primarily to the voice of Eternal Wisdom. However, it is evident that the Church also hears the voice of the Blessed Virgin Mary. For in these Readings, according to the common understanding of medieval writers, the Wisdom of God speaks in a certain sense in the person of the Virgin.

In the twelfth century, the title is taken up by St. Bernard. At the same time, in Morning Prayer of the Liturgy of the Hours as well as in Litanies in honor of our Lady, a number of titles are given her in praise of her close relationship with Eternal Wisdom: "Mother of Wisdom," "Fountain of Wisdom," "House of Wisdom," and "Seat of Wisdom" — with the last becoming the most common.

Scholars maintain that the title "Seat of Wisdom" celebrates (1) the maternal role of Mary, (2) her royal dignity, and (3) her incomparable Wisdom and prudence in the things of God.

(1) Through the Mystery of the Incarnation, the Wisdom of the Father was in his early years cradled in the arms of his Virgin Mother and seated on her lap. "For thirty continuous years [she] saw and heard him ... [and was] able to ask him any questions that she wished explained, knowing that the answers she received were from the Eternal God" (Cardinal Newman).

Indeed, as St. Pius X has stated, "Sharing as Mary did the thoughts and the secret wishes of Christ, she may be said to have lived the very life of her Son. Hence nobody ever knew Christ so profoundly as she did, and nobody can ever be more competent as a guide and teacher of the knowledge of Christ" (1904 Encyclical *Ad Diem Illum Laetissimum*).

(2) Mary was invested with royal dignity because the Child sitting on her lap was the Messianic King, "the Son of the Most High" to whom the Lord God gave the throne of his father David and who was to reign over the House of Jacob forever, and whose Kingdom would not end (see Luke 1:32-33 and Isaiah 9:6-7).

That Child is also the King visited by the Wise Men coming from afar, who found him with his Mother and adored him, offering him royal gifts (see Matthew 2:1-12).

(3) Mary was endowed with surpassing Wisdom and prudence because she is seen in the Gospel as a "wise virgin," who has chosen the better part, like Mary of Bethany (see Luke 10: 42), a "teacher of truth," who hands on to the Church the saving deeds and words of her Son, which she has treasured in her heart (see Luke 2:19, 51).

Mary's Words of Wisdom

The New Testament includes only seven instances wherein the words of Mary are noted. Six brief phrases plus the slightly longer *Magnificat* — her song of praise recorded in the first chapter of Luke's Gospel — are all that remain of our Lady's wisdom.

Few though they be, however, these seven phrases or "words" of Mary — like Christ's seven words on the Cross — give us a welcome glimpse into the very soul of the speaker.

Jesus reminds us that "from the fullness of the heart the mouth speaks" (Luke 6:45). And it is out of the overflowing treasures of thoughts and sentiments in her heart that Mary speaks. Her words are filled with meaning and sum up essential traits of her personality and religious functions.

Like the words of Jesus, Mary's words are "spirit and life" (John 6:63) for us. As St. Bernadine of Siena (d. 1444) puts it, "the Mother and Mistress of Wisdom speaks few words, but each one is permeated with a great depth of meaning. We read that the Mother of Christ spoke seven times, seven words filled with wisdom."

The first three of her words occur in the Gospel (Luke 1: 26-38) for the 4th Sunday in Advent (B), the Annunciation, and the Common of the Blessed Virgin Mary. The fourth occurs in the Gospel (Luke 1:39-56) for December 22nd, the Visitation, and the Assumption. The fifth occurs in the Gospel (Luke 2: 41-52) for the Holy Family (C), and St. Joseph. The sixth and seventh occur in the Gospel (John 2:1-11) for the 2nd Sunday in Ordinary Time (C).

Thus, the Liturgy brings Mary's words before us in the Mass texts at least once in every Season. In the Liturgy of the Hours, the fourth word — the *Magnificat* — is before us each day at Evening Prayer. As such, it is an apt reminder of the other words of our Lady (two of which — the first and the sixth — are in the Common of the Blessed Virgin Mary).

Power of Mary's Words

The Gospel account of the Visitation demonstrates very clearly that the words of Mary have a power all their own. At the sound of Mary's greeting to Elizabeth (which was undoubtedly the usual "Peace be with you"), the child in her cousin's womb leapt for joy, and Elizabeth was filled with the Holy Spirit.

A twofold effect took place at the sound of Mary's word of greeting: John the Baptist jumped for joy and Elizabeth was filled with the Holy Spirit. In the house of Elizabeth and her husband

Zechariah, the Incarnate Word distributed the first fruits of his gifts through his Mother.

Jesus thus made use of Mary's voice, as he would later make use of his own, to command demons, death, and life, and to perform miracles. In her earthly life as well as in her heavenly glory, our Lady is united with her Son in the bond of mercy, and it is through her that we reach Jesus.

Mary's words and her voice can still work wonders in today's world. They bring light, joy, and grace. Her voice is that of a Mother — light as a gentle breeze. It does not frighten but goes right to the heart and melts it with tenderness.

Besides revealing Mary's personality and role, her words hold special meaning for us. As the servant of God, she is the model for all Christians, since we are called to be servants of God. Meditation on her words and on her life will open up ways in which we can grow in our servanthood.

First Word: Childlike Wonder

"How can this be since I do not know man?" (Luke 1:34).

Mary utters this sentiment at Nazareth when the Archangel Gabriel announces to her that she is to be the Mother of God. Her reaction to this news of her exaltation is not one of self-acclaim or personal glory but one of honest amazement. How can God's call to motherhood be accomplished since she is and intends to remain a virgin?

This first word shows Mary's innate honesty. There is no room for dissembling or for hiding her true feelings in her relations with God. She freely expresses her amazement, consternation, and simplicity. Still, in a childlike way, Mary swiftly accepts God's invitation. Without hiding from the challenge, she seeks clarification only so that right action may follow. She acts with her eyes wide open.

This word of Mary tells us to look at life with our eyes wide open. At every moment and in every circumstance, God is calling out to us, too. Our task is to keep ourselves open to that call, no matter what it may entail. Our further task is to see God within the framework of our everyday lives.

Such a task means putting all our talents to work. God's call never comes to us in a vacuum. It reaches us in the framework of our ordinary lives — which should be both fully Christian and fully human.

Vatican II reminds us that modern human beings are in process of developing their personality and of increasingly discovering and affirming their rights. Since it has been entrusted to the Church to reveal the Mystery of God, who is the ultimate goal of humans, she opens up to them at the same time the meaning of their own existence, that is, the innermost truth about themselves: "Whoever follows after Christ, the perfect Man, becomes more fully human" (*Constitution on the Church in the Modern World*, no. 41).

In each circumstance, we have something to give that is exclusively ours. If we do not contribute it, no one else will, for no one else can. In building up the Body of Christ on earth, we must learn to discern the "signs of the times" and our roles in them. In this way, we will become the Christians God wants us to be — with the special nuances that he gave us to develop, explore, and fulfill for his glory and the salvation of souls, including our own.

Second Word: Obedient Service

"I am the handmaid of the Lord" (Luke 1:38).

As soon as Mary is assured by Gabriel that her virginity will remain intact since the unparalleled birth of her Son will occur through the almighty power of God, she has no reservation at all. She immediately identifies her state in relation to God — a devoted servant ready to provide zealous service.

This second word shows that Mary is totally open to God's Will for her. It thus testifies to Mary's certainty of God's supremacy and her unflagging obedience to his plan of salvation. At the same time, it brings out Mary's humility, selflessness, and commitment to true poverty.

This word encourages us to be completely obedient to God's call. For us, the best way to achieve this is in union with the Church. The Church is our link with Christ and God. Hence, we must remain deeply attached to her.

It is the specific function of the Church to Christianize all that is human. The energy for this process of Christianization is grace, the energy of Christ, found in the Sacraments, especially the Eucharist. This is the chief bond of union between the Incarnate Word and human beings.

The Church is indeed a "supernatural" organism — but in such a way that it is part and parcel of ordinary life. She enables the world to go on and all of us to take our rightful places in her. She does so by uplifting and encouraging us and by bringing Christ to us.

The Church is our bulwark of strength and hope, transforming the world through the Eucharist and showing us how to turn sadness into joy. We must be in tune with the Church, love the Church, and acknowledge that she is God's gift to us. And we must place all our love, our thoughts, and our service in her for she is the living sign of God's love for us, the Sacrament of Salvation.

Third Word: Biblical Knowledge

"Let it be done to me according to your word" (Luke 1:38).

Mary now goes further, putting her understanding into action. She consents to have what Gabriel has proclaimed be realized in her. At this stupendous moment, the Son of God becomes man. Mary thus helps set in motion the tremendous events called for in God's saving plan.

This third word indicates the depth of Mary's understanding and knowledge of God. Once assured of what God's call entails, she joyfully opts to become part of it.

Such an operative faith is the result of an active meditation on the Scriptures that set forth God's promises and their fulfillment in the history of the chosen people. It highlights Mary's familiarity with the Messianic tradition faithfully handed down over the centuries among the devoted servants of the Lord.

This word of Mary tells us that we must cultivate love for and interest in the Bible — the Book of Books — whose official interpreter for us is the Church. We must be willing to learn the characteristics of the Bible, the attitudes inculcated by the Bible, and the basic mentality endorsed by the Bible. This means becoming firmly convinced of the following.

(1) *God speaks to us in everyday words and actions* as well as through the printed words of the Bible. Every event and every conversation can be carrying a message from God to us — if we but train our heart and mind to see it.

(2) *We are part of a living History of Salvation.* We not only experience the History of Salvation but also collaborate in it — we "make" it.

(3) *God wants to be part of our lives.* He has a plan for each of us that is unique and unrepeatable. We are of great value to him.

(4) *God is with us in all we do and we live in his presence.* We are

never far from him, in whom we live and move and have our being.

Fourth Word: Joyful Praise

"My soul proclaims the greatness of the Lord" (Luke 1:46).

On visiting her cousin Elizabeth in the hill country of Jerusalem, Mary responds to the older woman's greeting of praise with a poetic passage extolling the God who has done such great things for her. This is known to all as the *Magnificat*, one of the most beautiful hymns of praise ever voiced.

The *Magnificat* (from the Latin verb for giving praise) is replete with allusions to the great deeds God worked for his chosen people in the Old Testament. It also points to even greater things to come, starting with the wondrous event in which Mary is taking part, the Incarnation of the Word of God.

This hymn that has been used by millions of Christians since its composition manifests Mary's keen mind, understanding spirit, joyous heart, concern for others, and love for God. It sets her apart as a woman of unshakable faith, unwavering hope, and uncommon love.

The poem is also reminiscent of several Old Testament hymns of praise — those of Miriam, Hannah, and Judith. In time, the glorious words uttered about Judith would be applied to Mary by the Church: "You are the glory of Jerusalem, the surpassing joy of Israel, and the splendid boast of our people" (Judith 15:19).

This fourth word reminds us that we are to offer spiritual worship for the glory of God and the salvation of human beings. For this purpose, we have been given the Holy Spirit, who calls and wonderfully prepares us for it. All we need do is tune in to the Spirit.

Thus, we can make all things in our lives "spiritual sacrifices acceptable to God through Jesus Christ" (1 Peter 2:5). This includes our works, prayers, and apostolic endeavors as well as our family lives, our daily occupations, our physical and mental relaxations, and even our hardships in life. We can offer these in the celebration of the Eucharist together with the offering of Christ himself. We can consecrate the world itself to God.

Fifth Word: Gentle Authority

"Son, why have you done this to us? You see that your father and I have been searching for you in sorrow" (Luke 2:48).

Twelve years after the birth of Jesus, Mary is separated from him during a trip to Jerusalem. After a frantic search, she and Joseph finally find him on the third day in the Temple and she voices her anguish.

This fifth word brings out Mary's gentleness and her acceptance of the responsibility and authority God has given her in life. At the same time, it shows that she shares the lot of all of us, experiencing trials and anxiety. And she bears it through faith.

This word is an apt reminder that we have a part to play in bringing about the Kingdom of God that Jesus proclaimed by the testimony of his life and the power of his words. Jesus now continues to fulfill this prophetic office until the complete manifestation of his glory. He does so through all Christians, so that the power of his message may shine forth in daily life.

Thus, we must (1) announce Christ through our living testimony as well as through our spoken word in the ordinary surroundings of the world; (2) join all other members of the Church in expressing consent to matters of faith and morals; and (3) utilize the special graces (charisms) that render each person suitable to take charge of diverse works and functions useful for the renewal and development of the Church (see 1 Corinthians 12:7).

Sixth Word: Tender Charity

"They have no more wine" (John 2:3).

Some twenty years after Jesus was lost in the Temple, at a wedding in Cana Mary notices that the bridal couple has run out of wine — a distinct embarrassment in those days. She hastens to intercede with her Son by telling him what happened and silently asking him to help.

This sixth word shows forth the greatness of Mary's heart. She attends to every detail and knows what she has to do. Her faith in her Son precedes and prepares for the miracle that will follow.

She shows that she is destined to play a role in the creation of the new People of God, the Messianic community that will gather around Jesus beginning with this first sign at Cana. Her role is to point the way to him by preparing the people through this miracle for the acceptance of his signs.

This word can serve as a reminder to us that Christ has now entered into the glory of the Kingdom and all things have been made subject to him. Moreover, Christ has communicated this kingly power to all his followers so that we may be constituted in royal freedom and by true penance and holy life may conquer the reign of sin in our own right.

Thus, we are called to serve Christ in our fellow human beings, so that we may by humility and patience lead them to the Kingdom.

We must learn the deepest meaning and value of all creation as well as its role in the harmonious praise of God. And we do so by assisting one another to lead holier lives each day. In this way, the world may be permeated by the Spirit of Christ, and it may more effectively fulfill its purposes in justice, charity, and peace.

All we need do is open our hearts and minds and cooperate with the grace of God. He will do the rest. He will give our lives a dimension they never had before, which helps us live them to the full and gives us a foretaste of heaven on earth.

Seventh Word: Deep Faith

"Do whatever he tells you" (John 2:5).

After informing Jesus of the bridal couple's problem at Cana, Mary turns to the waiters and bids them do whatever Jesus tells them. Her words correspond to the words of the chosen people when they promised to adhere to the Covenant of the Lord: "All that the Lord said we will do" (Exodus 19:8); "Tell us what the Lord, our God, tells you; we will listen and obey" (Deuteronomy 5:27).

This seventh word expresses Mary's faith and that of the whole people disposed to receive the revelation brought by Jesus. She exhibits the faith that has made her the first among believers. She shows that just as the Patriarch Abraham is the father of our faith, she is the Mother of our faith. She hears God's Word, meditates upon it constantly, and believes it with all her being — then she puts it into practice.

It is to this faith that Jesus alludes in his reply to the person who praises his Mother from a human standpoint. The woman says, "Blessed is the womb that carried you...." And Jesus replies, "Rather, blessed are those who hear the Word of God and put it into practice" (Luke 11:27-28).

This word is a call to us to have an operative faith, a faith that does not lie dormant but leads to works. In the time between

Christ's first and second Comings, the Church lives by faith and in the Mysteries of Christ's worship. These Mysteries are a working out and an explication of Christ's Paschal Mystery. They are accomplished through Word and Sacrament in the rites of the Church.

It is here that faith comes alive and reaches its fullness. Faith tells us that God is still God and that he communicates with us, that he sent his Son to save us, and that he has a plan in everything that happens to us. It is in this sense that John's words apply: "This is the victory that overcomes the world — our faith" (1 John 5:4).

Seven Words for Eternity

We see, then, that Mary's words have much to say to us. They sum up our Christian lives, and they can be called "Seven Words for Eternity." Like all words in Scripture, they have an astonishing quality of being well-nigh inexhaustible. Every time we come back to them, we learn something new. In this sense, they illustrate the qualities of the Word of God described by the Prophet Isaiah (55:10-11).

Thus, every time we return to Mary's words we can draw greater insights and spiritual understanding from them. It would be well for us to inscribe them on our hearts and keep them ever in our minds as the Sage indicates (Proverbs 6:20-23).

Her words will inevitably bring Mary to mind and lead us to call upon her. And Mary will lead us before the throne of her Divine Son. At his feet we will receive pardon and peace because Mary keeps putting in a word for us.

Mary Shared in the Wisdom of the Father

As we have already mentioned, Mary was the greatest representative of the "Poor of Yahweh," the pious Jews from ancient times who believed in the Lord and put their trust in him alone. Theirs was a "poverty of being" not simply one of money. They were the Remnant of whom the Prophets spoke, who would remain faithful to the Lord and inherit the promises he had made (see Isaiah 6:13; 37:31; Micah 4:6-7).

These pious ones, in keeping with the Wisdom of the Old Testament, which may be called the Wisdom of the Father, put their trust in the Lord. They knew that just as he had worked in the primeval darkness to produce all that exists, so the Lord worked on his "poor" to produce all that is good for them.

It was the Lord who had created a land for his people by uprooting the inhabitants of Palestine before them. And it was the Lord who had given them the Law through Moses.

Thus, Mary was very conversant with the Old Testament (the only Scriptures in her day). This knowledge is borne out by the *Magnificat*, our Lady's powerful prayer of praise and thanksgiving to God for all the great things he has done and continues to do for his people.

This prayer shows especially Mary's familiarity with the Psalms, which is reflected throughout this Magna Carta of the People of God. She was also familiar with the principal Messianic Prophecies in the Psalms. She knew the "Passion Psalm" (22) with its delineation of the Messiah's suffering for his people as well as the Songs of the Servant in Isaiah (52:13-53:12).

At the same time, she was aware of the prophecy about the Mother of the Savior in Genesis 3:15, known as the "Gospel before the Gospel," which referred to the Woman who would assist her Son the Messiah in overcoming the evil one. And she was also familiar with the prophecy about the Virgin Mother in Isaiah 7:14.

Mary Shared in the Wisdom of Her Son

During the time of her Son's life on earth, Mary undoubtedly shared in his Wisdom. She is shown pondering his childhood words at the Finding of Jesus in the Temple among the Doctors already mentioned.

She was also with him for all the Hidden Years when she undoubtedly spoke with him of many things and received the benefit of his Wisdom.

During the years of Christ's Public Ministry, Mary was exposed to his teaching and what people relayed to her about his sermons, for example, the great Sermon on the Mount, which is rightly regarded as dispensing the highest Wisdom for the ages.

Mary is specifically mentioned as being present at the Marriage Feast of Cana when Jesus, through her intercession, performed his first miracle. She heard his words about the Hour of Christ not having come and from other statements of Christ later on must have known that this bit of Wisdom was known only to the Father (see John 2:1-11).

Mary also appears in the account of the Coming of Jesus' Relatives (Mark 3:20-21) inserted within the account of the Unbelieving Scribes from Jerusalem who attribute Jesus' power over demons to Beelzebub (Mark 3:22-30). Some of his relatives are shown to lack belief in Jesus and to actually regard him as "out of his mind."

This is in keeping with Mark's emphasis on the Messianic Secret (on the incomprehension of Jesus' greatness).

Jesus is then alerted that his Mother and relatives are looking for him, which is the occasion for him to show that one who does the Will of his Father is as close to him as his nearest relatives (Mark 3:31-35 and parallels).

By these words Jesus shows that his Mother (who has been

shown to do always the Will of God: Luke 1:38) is the closest to him both naturally and supernaturally. It also represents another bit of Wisdom that Mary tucked away in her heart.

Mary is also alluded to in the account of the Woman in the Crowd Who Praises Jesus' Mother. Jesus stresses that faith and obedience to God come before all else, showing again that Mary is to be praised even more for her spiritual greatness than for her physical Motherhood of Jesus (Luke 11:27-28).

Finally, Mary shared Christ's Wisdom by partaking of his suffering during his Passion and Death and hearing his last seven words, among which was the word naming her the Mother of his followers (John 19:25-27).

Mary Shared in the Wisdom of the Holy Spirit

In the so-called Priestly Prayer before his Passion, Jesus promised his Apostles that they should not worry no matter what might come for the Holy Spirit would instruct them in all things and remind them of all that Christ had told them (John 14:26). In fact, he would guide them to all truth (John 15:13).

We may infer from this statement that the Holy Spirit dispenses the Wisdom of the Father and the Son. Thus when Mary in company with the disciples in the Upper Room was filled with the Holy Spirit, she shared in the Wisdom of the Spirit.

She who had been overshadowed by the Spirit at the Incarnation of the Word was once more filled with the gift from on high at the birth of the new People of God. Hence, Mary gained in Wisdom of the way to spiritual perfection, which is the way attributed to the Spirit.

This means that our Lady has a surpassing Wisdom about the spiritual life and the virtues and gifts of the Spirit. Hence, she can offer her children much help in becoming better spiritually.

Application to Us

Mary is the "Seat of Wisdom" in a twofold sense: (1) the carnal-biological sense, because she carried in her womb the Son of God, who is Wisdom incarnate; and (2) the ethical-spiritual sense, because she always embraced the Word of God, making it the object of a loving contemplation in her heart and seeking to penetrate its contents little by little, especially in its obscure aspects.

Thus, in accord with the teaching of Christ himself, Mary's beatitude does not consist primarily in bringing forth Jesus according to the flesh but in having had faith in the Word of the Lord.

This is also the vocation of the Church and all her members. We are all called to listen to and penetrate the meaning of the Scriptures. Our constant task is to apply the Scriptures to the signs of the times and the circumstances in which we live and act, especially when storms arise and all seems lost.

We must judge every event — whether it concerns the great story of the Church and the world or the little story of each believer — in the light of the prophetic Word of Jesus: "I am always with you" (Matthew 28:20); "I have told you these things before they come to pass so that when their hour has come you may remember that I have spoken them to you ... and thus you may believe" (John 14:29; 16:4).

Thanks to this openness to the wise Word of Christ every follower of his becomes (like Mary) the seat of the Divine presence: "If anyone loves me, he will keep my Word, and my Father will love him, and we will come to him and make our abode with him" (John 14:23).

Mary is the "Throne of Wisdom," the "Source of Wisdom," the "Shrine of Wisdom," and the "Sanctuary of Wisdom." Accordingly, as Pope Leo XIII said in his 1892 Encyclical *Magnae*

Dei Matris ("Great Mother of God"), she knows us and our needs perfectly:

"Nobody knows and comprehends so well as she everything that concerns us: what help we need in life; what dangers, public and private, threaten our welfare; what difficulties and evils surround us; above all how fierce is the fight we wage with the ruthless enemies of our salvation."

We should have frequent recourse to this Marian Wisdom to grow in Wisdom ourselves and to obtain help and consolation on our earthly pilgrimage to the Eternal Wisdom in heaven.

Prayer to Mary, Seat of Wisdom

Seat of Wisdom,
you became the great Mother
of the Divine Savior,
true Light of the world,
and uncreated Wisdom.
Help me also to receive that Wisdom of God
by learning from you
how to follow him
in poverty, chastity, and obedience
in keeping with my state in life.

Enable me to know the Faith
and to believe in all its teachings.
And may I carry out those teachings
every day of my life
so that I may one day enjoy that Wisdom
with you in heaven.

23

Temple of the Holy Spirit

The Temple Theme in Scripture

Sacred Scripture and the Liturgy speak of temples in various ways. The "Mystery of the Temple" was fulfilled in Christ Jesus (see John 2:19-22) in whom "the whole fullness of the Godhead dwells in bodily form" (Colossians 2:9).

The Church too is called a "holy temple": "You are fellow citizens of the Saints and members of God's household, built upon the foundation of the Apostles and Prophets, Christ Jesus himself being the cornerstone, in whom the whole structure grows into a holy temple in the Lord" (Ephesians 2:19-21).

Individual Christians are also "a temple of God" because God dwells in their hearts: "Do you not know that you are God's temple and that God's Spirit dwells in you?... God's temple is holy, and you are that temple" (1 Corinthians 3:16-17).

In a unique way, the Blessed Virgin is herself "a holy temple." For when she conceived the very Son of God in her immaculate womb, she became a true temple of the true God. In addition, when she cherished the Word of God in her heart (see Luke 2:19, 51), loved Christ so ardently, and faithfully kept his word, the Son and the Father came to her and made their home with her, in accordance with the promise of the Lord (see John 14:23).

Naturally, wherever the First and Second Persons of the

Trinity are, there also is the Third, the Holy Spirit. So Mary is also the temple of the Spirit!

The Title in the Fathers and the Liturgy

For the Fathers and the Liturgy, Mary has become the Holy of Holies. The feast of the Presentation of Mary in the Temple constitutes a tribute of glorification to Mary, considered as the new and true Temple of the Lord. Through the incarnation in her of God the Word, Mary has become in an eminent way the Temple of God. The ancient Temple of Israel contained a Divine Presence of a less real kind. It was the image of the Virgin Mary who offered earthly dwelling to God in her own body.

In the texts for this feast, the Byzantine Liturgy states: "The most pure Temple of the Savior, the most precious virginal Bridal Chamber, the sacred Treasure of the glory of God is today introduced into the house of the Lord, bringing with her the grace of the Divine Spirit."

And St. John Damascene (d. 749) declares: "O Virgin full of Divine grace, holy Temple of God that the spiritual Solomon, the Prince of peace, has constructed and dwelt in, and adorned not with gold or lifeless stones but rather with the Spirit."

For St. Jerome (d. 420), Mary is the "Temple of God, seat of the Holy Spirit." For Theophanes of Nicaea (d. 1381), Mary was "from the outset united to the Spirit, author of Life; and she did not taste the least particle of existence itself without participating in the Spirit, for participation in the Spirit had become for her participation in being."

In addition, Mary was given the title "Prophetess" by a good number of the Fathers. This would clearly allude to the action of the Holy Spirit upon her and within her!

The Contributions of Vatican II and Pope Paul VI

The principal affirmations of the Second Vatican Council concerning the relationship of Mary and the Spirit are centered upon the exemplary event of the Incarnation. Indeed, Mary is called Mother of the Word and "the Temple of the Holy Spirit" (*Constitution on the Church,* no. 53). This title, like similar titles (such as "Tabernacle of the Holy Spirit") used by the Fathers, indicates the Spirit's dwelling in Mary in a most singular and superior way to that in other Christians.

A second important affirmation is the consideration of Mary as "fashioned by the Holy Spirit and formed as a new creature" (Ibid., no. 56). The Council thus confirms the exalted holiness of Mary from the very first instant of her immaculate conception. And such holiness is the work of the Spirit who fashions Mary into a new creature.

A third affirmation concerns the consideration of Mary as "the image and most excellent model of the Church" (Ibid., no. 53). For the Church — in imitation of Mary and with the help of the Holy Spirit — is at one and the same time Mother, because she generates the children of God, and Virgin, because she keeps intact her faith, hope, and charity.

The Council also points to the event of Pentecost, in which Mary implores with her prayers the gift of the Holy Spirit upon the Church. Mary presents herself as the pray-er or intercessor. Hence, she is rightfully the model of all virtues.

For his part, Pope Paul VI wove together the contributions of the Fathers and the Council in his 1974 Apostolic Exhortation *Marialis Cultus* on "Devotion to the Blessed Virgin Mary" (no. 26):

"Theological reflection and the Liturgy have in fact noted how the sanctifying intervention of the Spirit in the Virgin of Nazareth was a culminating moment of the Spirit's action in the

History of Salvation. Thus, for example, some Fathers and writers of the Church attributed to the work of the Spirit the original holiness of Mary, who was as it were 'fashioned by the Holy Spirit into a kind of new substance and new creature.'

"Reflecting on the Gospel texts — 'The Holy Spirit will come upon you and the power of the Most High will cover you with his shadow' (Luke 1:35) and '[Mary] was found to be with child through the Holy Spirit.... She has conceived what is in her by the Holy Spirit' (Matthew 1:18, 20) — they saw in the Spirit's intervention an action that consecrated and made fruitful Mary's virginity and transformed her into the 'Abode of the King' or 'Bridal Chamber of the Word,' the 'Temple' or 'Tabernacle of the Lord,' the 'Ark of the Covenant' or 'the Ark of Holiness,' titles rich in Biblical echoes.

"Examining more deeply still the Mystery of the Incarnation, they saw in the mysterious relationship between the Spirit and Mary an aspect redolent of marriage, poetically portrayed by Prudentius: 'The unwed Virgin espoused the Spirit,' an expression that emphasizes the sacred character of the Virgin, now the permanent dwelling of the Spirit of God.

"Delving deeply into the doctrine of the Paraclete, they saw that from him as from a spring there flowed forth the fullness of grace (see Luke 1:28) and the abundance of gifts that adorned her. Thus they attributed to the Spirit the faith, hope, and charity that animated the Virgin's heart, the strength that sustained her acceptance of the Will of God, and the vigor that upheld her in the suffering at the foot of the Cross.

"In Mary's prophetic canticle (see Luke 1:46-55) they saw a special working of the Spirit who had spoken through the mouths of the Prophets. Considering, finally, the presence of the Mother of Jesus in the Upper Room, where the Spirit came down upon the infant Church (see Acts 1:12-14; 2:1-4), they enriched with new developments the ancient theme of Mary and the Church.

"Above all, they had recourse to the Virgin's intercession in order to obtain from the Spirit the capacity for engendering Christ in their own soul, as is attested to by Ildephonsus [d. 667] in a prayer of supplication, amazing in its doctrine and prayerful power:

"I beg you, holy Virgin, that I may have Jesus from the Holy Spirit, by whom you brought Jesus forth. May my soul receive Jesus through the Holy Spirit by whom your flesh conceived Jesus.... May I love Jesus in the Holy Spirit in whom you adore Jesus as Lord and gaze upon him as your Son."

Close Union of Mary and the Holy Spirit

Mary appears tied to the Holy Spirit by an objective, personal, and indestructible bond: the very person of Christ, whom together though in different ways they have generated. To regard Mary and the Spirit to be separated we would have to separate Christ himself, in whom their diverse operations have become concretized and objectified forever.

By his mere existence, every child proclaims that his father and mother have been united for an instant according to the flesh. Hence, the Child Jesus proclaims that the Holy Spirit and Mary have been united "according to the Spirit" and thus in an indestructible manner.

Even in the heavenly Jerusalem, the risen Christ remains the one who was "generated by the Holy Spirit and the Virgin Mary." Even in the Eucharist, we receive the one who was "generated by the Holy Spirit and the Virgin Mary."

In accordance with the words of the Angel to Mary, "The Holy Spirit will come upon you and the power of the Most High will overshadow you" (Luke 1:35), we see an indicative fact.

All those to whom Mary is sent after this descent of the Holy Spirit upon her are touched or moved by the Holy Spirit (see Luke 1:41; 2:27). It is certainly the presence of Jesus that the Spirit radiates, but Jesus is in Mary and acts through her.

Mary appears as the Ark or the Temple of the Spirit, as is suggested by the image of the cloud that overshadowed her. This recalls the luminous cloud that in the Old Testament was the sign of God's presence and of his coming into the Tabernacle (see Exodus 13:22; 19:16).

The Spirit Prepared Mary for Her Role in the Divine Plan

This title indicates quite clearly that Mary enjoyed the indwelling of the Spirit from the first moment of her conception. It was the Holy Spirit who prepared Mary for her role in the Divine Plan. He was with her from the very beginning — far before the moment of the Annunciation when she consented to become the Mother of the Son of God.

The Spirit was with Mary, making her the greatest representative of the Remnant, of whom the Prophets (inspired by the Spirit) spoke. This word referred to the portion of the chosen people who would remain faithful to God and inherit the promises he had made (see Isaiah 6:13; 37:31; Amos 5:15; Micah 4:6-7).

As time went on, this teaching about the Old Testament Remnant acquired Messianic overtones, which were fully realized only in the New Testament. The Remnant was a community of believers who had accepted the Messiah.

As we have already mentioned, in the New Testament this community included Mary's cousin Elizabeth and her husband Zechariah, the Shepherds at the crib, Simeon who prophesied about the Child Jesus and his Mother, and the aged Anna who praised God for the Messiah, as well as the afflicted, widows and orphans who put their trust in the Lord.

In her capacity as the greatest personage of this holy Remnant, Mary had a deep and full knowledge of the Old Testament. Accordingly, she was well aware of the Messianic Hope that was nurtured by the People of God and the prophecies that sustained it. All this (both prophecies and Mary's knowledge) was the work of the Spirit.

In addition, Mary was familiar with the pious women of the People of God, who foreshadowed her and painted portraits of her as the Mother of the Messiah.

It is important for us to realize that each of the portraits of the Old Testament was the work of the Holy Spirit. And Mary's knowledge of them was also the work of the same Spirit.

Hence, it is evident that the Spirit overshadowed Mary in more than the sense of conceiving Christ. He overshadowed her in her great knowledge of God's dealings with his People and in her own spiritual life. He dwelt in her as his Temple!

The Spirit Overshadowed Mary to Enable Her to Become the Mother of God's Son

Both Matthew (1:18-25) and Luke (1:26-38) indicate Mary's Motherhood of the Messiah as well as her fullness of grace. The first is the result of the Spirit's action because it is so stated. The second is implicitly the result of the Spirit's action because he is the Sanctifier.

Thus, the Holy Spirit was, from the first moment of Christ's conception, present with Mary, molding her into the holiest person of the People of God below her Son Jesus Christ. In the words of the Second Vatican Council:

"[Mary] is acknowledged and honored as the true Mother of God and of the Redeemer.... She is also the beloved Daughter of the Father and Temple of the Holy Spirit. Because of this gift of sublime grace, she far surpasses all other creatures in heaven and on earth....

"It is no wonder, then, that the usage prevailed among the Fathers to call the Mother of God 'all-holy' and 'free from every stain of sin,' as though fashioned by the Holy Spirit and formed as a new creature" (*Constitution on the Church,* nos. 53, 56).

It was this supernatural presence of the Spirit in Mary that enabled her to give wholehearted and free consent to become the Mother of the Savior. Then, even when events began to show the massive problems that would ensue (e.g., Joseph's inclination to "put her away"), that consent remained steadfast thanks to the grace of the Spirit.

The Spirit Proclaimed Mary's Divine Motherhood through Elizabeth

At the visit of Mary to her cousin Elizabeth, it was the presence of the Holy Spirit who caused Elizabeth's unborn son to leap for joy in her womb at the coming of Jesus the Savior in Mary's womb and who brought about the Baptist's sanctification from original sin before his birth. It was also the Spirit's grace that enabled Elizabeth to know and proclaim Mary's Motherhood of the Lord (Luke 1:39-45).

When Mary answered Elizabeth with the paean of praise found in the *Magnificat,* it was the Spirit who enabled her to give the capsule summary of the History of Salvation up to that point. And it was the same Spirit who inspired her to prophesy about future events in that Salvation History.

After Christ's birth, Mary's vision of God's victory over evil was made clearer by the Spirit. He led her to see that her role in the victory was to be filled with tears and suffering.

The first strong hint of this fact came to her in the flight into Egypt when Herod threatened the Child's life. It became even clearer when the Spirit impelled the aged Simeon to prophesy about Christ's victory and the sword that would pierce her soul in gaining it.

Thus, the Spirit was ever with Mary to inspire and assist her throughout her life — both during the Hidden Years and during the Public Life of her dear Son. In spite of loneliness, fear, and trials of every kind, the Spirit was always there to sustain her.

The Spirit Established Mary's Spiritual Motherhood at the Foot of the Cross

The Spirit was with Mary in the ordeal she underwent during the Passion of her beloved Son, especially when she met him bruised and bloodied carrying his Cross and when she stood at the Foot of the Cross.

Through the grace of the Spirit, she stood there firm in faith, strong in hope, and burning with love. She played many roles in the Mystery of Salvation and fulfilled in her person the prophecies of old.

She was the handmaid of the Redeemer, the Mother sharing his sufferings, united with the sacrifice of her Son, the High Priest, and helping to fill up in her flesh "what is lacking in the sufferings of Christ, for the sake of his Body, the Church" (Colossians 1:24).

She was the new Eve, fulfilling the prophecy of the saving role of the Woman. As the first woman, Eve, shared in bringing death, so the second Woman, Mary, shared in restoring life.

She was the Mother of Zion, acclaimed by all peoples in their cry: "All find their home in you" (Psalm 87:7), for she welcomed with a Mother's love all who had been scattered but were now gathered into unity by the Death of Christ (see John 11:52).

She was the image of the Church, which as it looks upon the Virgin draws inspiration from her courage and keeps constant faith with Christ her Bridegroom.

It was the Holy Spirit also who aided Mary's co-suffering in the drama of salvation and enabled her to put her own life on the line when her nation was brought low. He helped her endure the greatest of pains in bringing forth to new and Divine life the family of the Church, though she had brought forth her Son without the pains of childbirth under his power.

At the same time, the Holy Spirit enabled those whom Jesus, from the Cross, entrusted to Mary to be numbered among her adopted children.

The Spirit Descended on Mary and the Disciples at Pentecost

After Christ's Resurrection and Ascension, it was the Holy Spirit who first enabled Mary to keep the frightened and disappointed disciples together in prayer for nine days. Then on the tenth day he descended on them with his grace and strength in the form of tongues of fire.

The disciples exited the Upper Room like new persons, eager to preach the Gospel and to give their lives, if need be, for the Risen Lord. Mary shone forth as the Mother cherishing the infant Church in her love and as the supreme example of prayer in oneness of heart.

Thus, Mary was the Virgin filled with the Holy Spirit, for God had poured on her in abundance the gifts of the Holy Spirit. She who had been overshadowed by the Spirit at the Incarnation of the Word was once more filled with the gift from on high at the birth of the new People of God.

At the same time, Mary became, through the presence of the Spirit, the model for the Church. She became the model of prayer, praying with the disciples in oneness of mind and heart.

The one who waited in prayer for the coming of Christ was still at prayer as she called upon the promised Paraclete. The Spirit made her a model of harmony, unity, and peace; of obedience to the Holy Spirit; of watchfulness in waiting for the Second Coming of Christ; of faithful observance of the Word of God and eagerness to sow its seed.

At Pentecost, the Spirit also made Mary the model of liturgical worship. She became the exemplar of that sense of reverent devotion with which the Church celebrates the Divine Mysteries and expresses them in her life. For Mary is the Virgin who listens, the Virgin of prayer, the Virgin Mother, the Virgin who offers, the Virgin who keeps vigil for her Son.

The Spirit Works in the Hearts of Mary's Children

Paul says that when the designated time had come, God sent forth his Son born of a Woman, born under the Law, to deliver from the Law those who were subjected to it, so that we might receive our status as adopted children.

The proof that we are God's children is the fact that he sent forth into our hearts the Spirit of his Son who cries out "Father!" (Galatians 4:4-7).

It is that same Spirit who enables us to ask God to grant that we may enter more and more into the Mystery of his Incarnate Word and with him lead a hidden life on earth until, escorted by his Virgin Mother, we joyously enter his heavenly home.

Thus, it is through the power of the Holy Spirit and in and through service to her Son that Mary, during her life on earth, exercised her maternal activity toward us.

Secondly, Mary continues to live her Spiritual Motherhood:

"This Motherhood of Mary in the economy of grace continues without interruption until the perpetual crowning of all the Elect. Indeed, taken to heaven she did not set aside this mission of salvation, but by her manifold intercession she continues to obtain for us the gifts of eternal salvation" (*Constitution on the Church*, no. 62).

Thirdly, the purpose of Mary's maternal activity is to unite us with Christ so completely that each of us can say: "The life I live is not my own; Christ lives in me" (Galatians 2:20), so that Christ may be "all in all" (Colossians 3:11).

Fourthly, Mary's maternal function toward us is entirely the fruit of Christ's saving action. It flows from it and depends on it in everything. Christ makes associates of the very ones he saves, and first of all, in a singular manner, of his Mother whom he asks — and gives the means — to fulfill her maternal mission toward us.

Finally, Mary conceived the Word of God in her heart and flesh by the power of the Spirit who overshadowed her. It is by the same power of the Spirit, soul of her soul and life of her life, that she attains the spiritual fruitfulness that makes her our Mother.

Application to Us

We are accustomed to say that we "go to Jesus through Mary." In this maxim, there is an implicit conclusion that remains

Temple of the Holy Spirit

unvoiced: *in the Holy Spirit.* The Sanctifier cannot be absent wherever there is a question of sanctification (i.e., becoming Christlike and reaching Christ).

Just as Mary was a Temple of the Holy Spirit all her life, so are we called to be the same. The indwelling of the Spirit through grace is a great Christian teaching.

The Spirit comes to us as he came to Mary with *the theological virtues:* faith, hope, and charity; *the four cardinal virtues:* prudence, justice, fortitude, and temperance; *the seven gifts:* wisdom, understanding, counsel, fortitude, knowledge, piety, and fear; and *the twelve fruits:* charity, joy, peace, patience, benignity, goodness, longanimity, mildness, fidelity, modesty, continence, and chastity. Each of them is a way for us to become Christlike. Conscious of the Spirit, we should be totally open to his graces.

In this task, we are aided by Mary our Mother who is our model as Temple of the Holy Spirit. Certainly, she was careful never to "silence the Spirit" (1 Thessalonians 5:19), to use St. Paul's phrase. We should do likewise.

"In her maternal charity Mary cares for the brothers and sisters of her Son who are still journeying on earth" (*Constitution on the Church,* no. 62).

These words of the Second Vatican Council accord with the conviction we have when we ask Mary to pray for us, a conviction that is tantamount to the certainty that she knows us, sees us, and hears us. For it is by the same power of the Spirit who overshadowed her, who was soul of her soul and life of her life, that she attains the spiritual fruitfulness that makes her our Mother.

Prayer to Our Lady, Temple of the Spirit

Mary, Mother of Jesus
and my Mother,
I venerate you
as the Temple of the Holy Spirit.
You are the glory of Jerusalem,
the joy of Israel,
and the honor of our people.
As the valiant woman,
you crushed the head of the serpent
when you offered your Divine Son
to the heavenly Father
in the love of the Holy Spirit
for the salvation of the world.

Look upon me with your compassionate eyes
and behold my distress and my needs.
Help me never to lose the grace of God
or defile the temple of the Spirit,
that my heart may always remain his holy dwelling.
May I become his faithful child on earth,
as you were,
so that I may share his eternal glory in heaven.

24

Queen of All Hearts

The Culmination of All Marian Titles

It is rather fitting that the last Marian title in this series is *Queen of All Hearts*. In a sense, this title inculcates all the other titles of Mary.

Although it is a speculative title, it is even more a practical one. It leads us to have devotion to our Lady. That is not difficult for us to understand because its modern champion, St. Louis de Montfort, meant it to be used in a practical sense:

"Mary is the Queen of heaven and earth by grace as Jesus is the King by nature and by conquest. But as the Kingdom of Jesus Christ exists primarily in the heart or interior of man, according to the words of the Gospel, 'The Kingdom of God is within you' (Luke 17:21), so the Kingdom of the Blessed Virgin is principally in the interior of man, that is, in his soul.

"It is principally in souls that she is glorified with her Son more than in any visible creatures. So we may call her, as the Saints do, Queen of All Hearts" (*True Devotion to Mary*, no. 38).

Christ, the King of All Hearts

On December 11, 1925, Pope Pius XI issued the Encyclical on the Kingship of Christ under the Latin title *Quas Primas*. In it he explained the meaning of the Kingship of Christ and established an annual feast of Christ the King on the last Sunday in October to foster the awareness of Christ's dominion over all people and to establish peace among nations. In the renewed Liturgy of Vatican II, this feast is now celebrated on the Last Sunday in the Church Year, taking the place of the Thirty-Fourth Sunday in Ordinary Time.

The Pope stated that Christ has long been proclaimed King because of his preeminence over all creatures. He is said to reign in the *minds* of all human beings because of the keenness of his intellect and the extent of his knowledge, and because he is Truth itself and the source of all truth for all human beings.

He also reigns in the *wills* of people, for his own human will was ever perfectly and completely obedient to the Will of the Father. By his grace and inspiration, he so rules our free wills that they spring forward to the most noble endeavors.

Christ reigns, too, in our *hearts* by his love, "which surpasses knowledge" (Ephesians 3:19), while his mercy and kindness draw all persons to him; so that no one is loved so intensely and so universally as is Jesus Christ.

In virtue of the absolute rule over all creatures given him by the Father, Christ has authority in civil affairs. All human beings, whether collectively or individually, are subject to Christ. So there is no difference in this matter between the individual and the family (or the state). The salvation of society and the salvation of the individual are to be found in him.

Mary, the Queen of All Hearts

On October 11, 1954, Pope Pius XII issued an Encyclical on the Queenship of Mary under the Latin title *Ad Caeli Reginam*. The Encyclical sets forth texts from the Fathers of the Church connected with Sacred Scripture, taken up by theologians, and confirmed by the Popes — from St. Martin I (d. 656) to Benedict XIV (d. 1758) — as well as references to the Liturgy and popular prayers plus the contributions of Christian art and the custom of crowning images of Mary.

Then it goes on to illustrate the reasons for Mary's Queenship that flow from these documents: (1) Mary's Divine Motherhood; (2) her collaboration with Christ in the salvation of the world; and (3) her fullness of grace.

The Pope states that Mary enjoys a Queenship of Excellence: "Mary is raised by her dignity above all creation and comes first after her Son." She also enjoys a Queenship of Efficiency: "Not only has she been given the highest degree of excellence and perfection after Christ, but she also shares in the power that her Son and our Redeemer exercises over the minds and wills of human beings."

The Pope established the feast of Mary's Queenship on May 31 together with the consecration of the human race to the Immaculate Heart of the Blessed Virgin. In the renewed Liturgy of Vatican II, the feast of the Immaculate Heart of Mary is assigned to the Saturday following the Second Sunday after Pentecost, and the feast of the Queenship of Mary is established on August 22, one week after the Assumption.

In the light of the new insights of Vatican II, we can say that Mary is Queen because in her life on earth she fulfilled, by the grace of Christ, a mission that she continues to fulfill even more in heaven — a mission that has three aspects.

(1) From the moment of her Immaculate Conception, Mary conquered the powers of evil, conceding nothing to sin. Mary is the creature who had no part whatever with the way of sinners, in the sense that she was neither led astray nor divided by the influence of the devil.

Thus, Mary was never under bondage to sin, which constitutes a rift with God and with neighbor. In contrast to Eve, she paid heed only to the messenger of God and gave God's message her total consent. Through her Assumption, she already shares in Christ's victory even over the last enemy, death (1 Corinthians 15:26). And with Christ she works for the world's deliverance from sin.

(2) Mary chose to construe her life as a service, in which consists royalty according to the Gospel (Luke 22:24-40). She did not look upon her Divine Motherhood as expression of sovereignty but declared herself "Handmaid of the Lord" (Luke 1: 38), worshiping the one God and completely devoted to service for his plan of salvation.

(3) Mary consented to making the realization of the Kingdom of God possible, welcoming the Angel's message concerning the Davidic Messiah who would reign forever over the House of Jacob (Luke 1:32-33). The prophecy of Nathan (2 Samuel 7:12-16), to which Luke's text of the Annunciation refers, nourished Israel's hope.

However, among the religious circles of the Poor of the Lord to whom Mary belonged, that hope envisaged above all the Messianic benefits of the religious order, such as peace, justice, piety, and deliverance. In accepting the King-Messiah, the Blessed Virgin accepted the Kingdom of God, which her Son would later on purify of every nationalistic interpretation.

Meaning of the Title

Mary is our Queen whose dominion knows no limits. Jesus is King of the eternal centuries by nature and by conquest; through him, with him, and subordinated to him, Mary is Queen by grace, by Divine alliance, by conquest, and by particular election. And her Kingdom is as vast as that of her Son and God since nothing is excluded from her dominion.

Mary is our Queen who heals, cures, and leads us to salvation. Pope Pius XII said it was his intention in his Encyclical to show the world a truth that is capable of remedying its ills, of freeing it from its anguish, and of leading it toward the way of salvation that it so anxiously seeks.

Mary shares in Christ's reign over minds and wills. The Blessed Virgin has received not only the grade of excellence and perfection that is supreme after that of Christ himself but also some sharing of that efficacy by which her Son and Redeemer is rightly and properly said to reign over the minds and wills of human beings.

Mary rules over our hearts. Pius XII again stated that "Mary's Queenship is a supernal reality that at the same time penetrates the innermost hearts of human beings and touches all that is spiritual and immortal in their very essence."

Mary knows our innermost thoughts. The same Pontiff, in a radio message declared: "Let the sin-laden world take courage and know that a Mother's heart filled with mercy is pleading with her Divine Son for the needed grace of repentance and forgiveness. Let growing youth of both sexes know that a loving Mother's eyes are always on them. No path or circumstance is hidden from her anxious care."

By grace, Mary enlightens minds and strengthens hearts and wills. In another radio message Pius XII stated: "Mary's shining splendor is light and strength. It is a light that illumines the richness and the depths of the truths of Christian Faith. It is a force that overflows into the will and heart and makes them capable of translating that Faith into acts, even to the least detail."

All of us must be subject to Mary's queenly power and maternal love. In *Ad Caeli Reginam*, Pius XII calls upon all Christians to "glory in being subjects of the Virgin Mother of God, who, while wielding royal power, is on fire with a mother's love."

Mary's Divine Son, as King, draws all hearts to himself by his meekness and charity. We are naturally drawn to Mary our Queen and Mother. She is our "Mother Most Amiable," as we say in the Litany of Loreto. We are all attracted to goodness.

But Christ the King has also a direct power over our hearts by his grace. As St. Paul states, "It is God who works in you both to will and to do according to his will" (Philippians 2:13).

As Queen of All Hearts, Mediatrix of all Graces, and Spiritual Mother of all human beings, Mary has a direct power over our hearts. She exercises her Queenship over the interior of human beings. By her Queenly maternal mediation she brings us to will and to do things in accordance with God's good will.

The Liturgy has some beautiful things to say about Mary our Queen. The new Collection of Masses of the Blessed Virgin Mary, which the Church issued in our time, is a fine example. Combining parts of two of the fifty new Prefaces (Numbers 29 and 39) and adapting them slightly, we have a splendid encomium to our Lady:

"When the Son of God humbled himself to accept death on the Cross, the Father crowned him with glory and honor and seated him at his right hand as King of kings and Lord of lords.

"When the Blessed Virgin, the Father's lowly handmaid, endured with patient suffering the ignominy of her Son's crucifixion, he exalted her above all the choirs of Angels to reign with him in glory and to intercede for all his children, as our Advocate of Grace and the Queen of All Creation.

"Mary is the gracious Queen, who has herself uniquely known the Father's loving kindness and stretches out her arms to embrace all who take refuge in her and call upon her in their distress.

"She is the Mother of Mercy, always attentive to the voice of her children, seeking to obtain the Father's compassion for them, and asking his forgiveness for their sins.

"She is the Handmaid of the Father's love, never ceasing to pray for us to his Son, that he may enrich our poverty with his grace and strengthen our weakness with his power."

Application to Us

We must realize that Mary's royal power does not free us from the obligation to cooperate with God's grace. Her royal power is used to convert both sinners and those who have never known the Faith. But they must cooperate with grace. St. Paul says: "We beg you not to offer God's grace an ineffectual welcome" (2 Corinthians 6:1).

Thus, we must strive to be united with our Heavenly Mother with our whole heart and soul. Then she will use all the resources of her power and goodness on our behalf. She will reign completely in our hearts in order to establish the reign of her Divine Son. As St. Louis de Montfort indicated, "It was through the Blessed Virgin Mary that Jesus Christ came into the world, and it is also through her that he must reign in the world" (*True Devotion to Mary*, no. 1).

Indeed, the Saint longed for the day when Mary will be established as the Queen of All Hearts in actual fact, for he knew that then the Kingdom of God will be established everywhere on earth as well as in heaven.

"When will that day come ... when God's Mother is enthroned in people's hearts as Queen, subjecting them to the dominion of her great and princely Son? When will souls breathe Mary as the body breathes air?

"When that time comes wonderful things will happen on

earth. The Holy Spirit, finding his dear Spouse present again in souls, will come down into them with great power. He will fill them with his gifts, especially wisdom, by which they will produce wonders of grace....

"Lord, that your Kingdom may come, may the reign of Mary come!" (Ibid., no. 217).

It is then the task of all of us to let Mary reign in our hearts, so that we may be perfect children of God: "Be perfect as your Heavenly Father is perfect" (Matthew 5:48).

Under her maternal regency we enjoy the freedom of the children of God. Freedom from sin. Freedom to love God and to serve him. We are then in incomparably greater security than we could possibly be under our own direction.

It is in Mary that we find Jesus. In her we find all grace of the way and the truth, for she is our Mother, the Queen of All Hearts, the Queen par excellence.

Prayer to Mary, Queen of All Hearts

> O Mary, Queen of All Hearts,
> Advocate of the most hopeless cases,
> we have recourse to you,
> O Mother most pure and most compassionate,
> O Mother of Divine Love and full of Divine Light,
> consider our misery and our tears,
> our interior trials and our sufferings.
> Hear our prayers at your altar,
> where every day you give so many proofs
> of your love and power to heal both body and soul.
>
> Ask Jesus to cure us, pardon us,
> and grant us final perseverance.
> O Mary, Queen of All Hearts,
> we place all our confidence in you.

APPENDIX

Selected List of Marian Titles

This Selected List of Marian Titles is presented here to show the many titles that have been in use among Catholics. It is taken from the finest sources, including documents of the Church, the approved Marian Litanies (both those for public worship and those for private use), and the new Collection of Masses of the Blessed Virgin Mary.

The titles are arranged in alphabetical order letter by letter (not word by word). Thus, "Our Lady of Ransom" comes before "Our Lady of the Angels." The titles set off in boldface are those that are commented upon in this book.

A

Abyss of Suffering
Adam's Deliverance
Advocate
Advocate of Eve
Advocate of Grace
Advocate of Sinners
Advocate of the Church Militant
Advocate of the Most
    Abandoned Sinners
Advocate with Your Son for
    Your Children
All Chaste
All Fair and Immaculate
All Good
Allayer of Tempests

Altar of the Divinity
Anchor of Confidence
Anchor of Hope
Aqueduct of Grace
Archetype of Purity and Innocence
Ark Gilded by the Holy Spirit
Ark of the Covenant
Ark of the New Covenant
Associate of the Redeemer
Assumed by Your Son into Heaven
Assured Safety of the Faithful
Asylum of the Erring
August Mediatrix
August Mother of God the Son

B

Beauty of Virgins
Beauty of the World
Beloved Daughter of the Eternal Father
Beloved of God
Bereft of All Consolation
Blessed among All Hearts
Blessed among Women
Blessed and Most Blessed
Blessed by All Generations
Blessed Land Springing Forth the Savior
Blessed Mother
Blessed Queen
Blessed Spouse of God the Holy Spirit
Blooming like the Palm Tree
Bridal Chamber of the Lord
Bride of the Canticle
Bride of the Father
Bride of Heaven
Bride Unbrided
Bright as the Sun

C

Called Blessed by All Generations
Cancelor of Eve's Disgrace
Cause of Our Joy
Cedar of Mount Lebanon
Chamber of Spiritual Nuptials
Champion of God's People
Channel of Divine Graces
Chaste Virgin
Cheer and Comfort of the Dying
Chief Work of God
Chosen before the Ages
Chosen Bride of God
Chosen Daughter of Israel
Chosen Daughter of the Father
Cleanser of Sins
Comfort of Christians
Comfort of the Afflicted
Comfort of the Sorrowful
Comforter of the Afflicted
Conceived without Original Sin
Conqueror of All Error
Consolation of Adam
Consolation of Widows
Consoler of the Afflicted
Coredemptrix
Couch of Love and Mercy
Court of the Eternal King
Coworker of the Church Suffering
Created Temple of the Creator
Crimson Rose of the Land of Jacob
Crown of Martyrs
Crown of Virginity
Crowned with Twelve Stars
Cypress of Mount Zion

D

Daughter of Light Eternal
Daughter of Men
Daughter of Zion
David's Daughter
Deliverer from All Wrath
Deliverer of Christian Nations
Depositary of the Secrets of the Most High
Destroyer of All Heresies
Devoted Consoler of the Sorrowful
Devoted Spouse
Dispenser of God's Gift
Dispenser of Grace
Dispenser of Heavenly Treasures
Dispenser of the Gifts of the Redemption

Selected List of Marian Titles

Distinguished above All
Dove of Simplicity
Dwelling Place for Christ
Dwelling Place Meet for God
Dwelling Place of God
Dwelling Place of the Illimitable
Dwelling Place of the Spirit

E
Earth Unsown
Earth Untouched and Virginal
Eastern Gate
Embracer of Your Infant God
Envisioned by the Upright
Ever Green and Fruitful
Ever Virgin
Eve's Tears Redeeming
Exalted above the Angels
Exemplar of Christians
Eye of the Prophets

F
Fair as the Moon
Fastened to the Cross with Jesus Crucified
Filled with the Holy Spirit
Finest Fruit of the Redemption
Flawless Mirror
Fleece of Heavenly Rain
Flower of Jesse's Root
Foretold by the Prophets
Formed without Stain
Forth-Bringer of God
Forth-Bringer of the Ancient of Days
Forth-Bringer of the Tree of Life
Fountain of Beauty
Fountain of Gardens
Fountain of Light and Life
Fountain of Living Waters
Fountain of Salvation
Fountain of Tears
Fountain Sealed by the Holy Spirit
Fountain Sealed Up
Free from Every Stain
Friend of Those Who Live by the Evangelical Counsels
Fruitful like the Olive Tree
Full of Grace
Fullness of Grace to Overflow upon All

G
Garden Enclosed
Gate of Heaven
Gate of Paradise
Gentle Lady
Glorious Son-Bearer
Glory of Jerusalem
Glory of the Church Triumphant
Glory of the Holy Spirit
God's Eden
God's Olive Tree
God's Vessel
Golden Vessel
Graceful like the Dove
Gracious Lady
Greatest of Women

H
Handmaid of Divine Blessings
Handmaid of the Lord
Harbor of the Wrecked
Haven of the Shipwrecked
Healing Balm of Integrity
Health of the Sick
Help of Christians
Help of the Abandoned
Help of the Needy
Help of the Weak

Helper of All Who Are in Danger
Helper of the Redeemer
Holocaust of Divine Love
Holy Gate for the King of Heaven
Holy in Soul and Body
Holy Mary
Holy Mother of God
Holy Virgin
Holy Virgin of Virgins
Honor of Our People
Honor of the Sky
Hope of Christians
Hope of the Agonizing
Hope of the Despairing
Hope of the Hopeless
Hope of the Troubled
House Built by Wisdom
House of God
House of Gold

I

Image and Mother of the Church
Immaculate
Immaculate Conception
Immaculate from Your Creation
Immaculate Heart
Immaculate Lily Perfuming the Universe
Immaculate Mother
Immaculate Virgin
Incomparable Treasurer
Incorruptible Wood of the Ark
Impregnable Protection
Instrument of the Holy Spirit
Inventrix of Grace
Inviolate

J

Joseph's Spouse
Joy of All Saints
Joy of Israel

K

Key of the Heavenly Kingdom
Kingly Throne
King's Mother

L

Ladder of Heaven
Lady Most Chaste
Lady Most Venerable
Lamp Unquenchable
Leader of Virgins
Life-Giver to Posterity
Light Cloud of Heavenly Rain
Light in Darkness
Light of Confessors
Light of Nazareth
Light of the Despondent
Light of Those Sitting in Darkness
Lily among Thorns
Living Temple of the Deity
Living Temple of the Holy Spirit
Loom of the Incarnation

M

Madonna of the Streets
Market Place for Salutary Exchange
Mary the Dawn
Mary the Virgin
Mediatrix
Mediatrix after the Mediator
Mediatrix and Counciliatrix
Mediatrix Ever Pleading for Us
Mediatrix of All beneath the Sky
Mediatrix of All Graces

Selected List of Marian Titles

Mediatrix of People with God
Mediatrix of Salvation
Mediatrix of Sinners, Staunch and True
Mediatrix of the Mysteries of God
Mediatrix Reconciling Us to the Son
Mediatrix Set between Christ and His Church
Mediatrix to the Mediator
Mediatrix to Win Salvation for the World
Mediatrix Who has Found Favor with God
Medicine of the Sick
Minister of Holiness
Minister of Life
Mirror of Justice
Mirror of Patience
Mistress of the Heavens
Mistress of the Tribes
Model of Virtue
Moon Never Waning
More Beautiful Than Beauty
More Glorious Than Paradise
More Gracious Than Grace
More Holy Than the Cherubim, the Seraphim, and the Entire Angelic Host
Morning Star
Most Dutiful Daughter
Most Honored of Virgins
Most Humble One
Most Pure Virgin
Most Tender Mother
Mother Afflicted
Mother and Daughter of the Everlasting King
Mother and Mediatrix of Grace
Mother and Teacher in the Spirit
Mother and Virgin
Mother Bereft of Your Child
Mother Consumed with Grief
Mother Crucified in Heart
Mother Forsaken
Mother Inviolate
Mother Most Admirable
Mother Most Amiable
Mother Most Chaste
Mother Most Desolate
Mother Most Lonely
Mother Most Pure
Mother Most Sad
Mother Most Sorrowful
Mother Most Tearful
Mother of All People
Mother of Beautiful Love
Mother of Christ
Mother of Christ the King
Mother of Christians
Mother of Christ's Members
Mother of Consolation
Mother of Divine Grace
Mother of Divine Hope
Mother of Divine Providence
Mother of Eternal Glory
Mother of Fairest Love
Mother of God
Mother of Good Counsel
Mother of Grace
Mother of Human Beings
Mother of Jesus
Mother of Love and Indulgence
Mother of Mercy
Mother of Orphans
Mother of Our Creator
Mother of Our Head

Mother of Our Savior
Mother of Our Savior Crucified
Mother of Pardon and Remission
Mother of Perpetual Help
Mother of Purity and Grace
Mother of Reconciliation
Mother of Sorrows
Mother of the Church
Mother of the Golden Heights
Mother of the Heavenly and Earthly Church
Mother of the Living God
Mother of the Lord
Mother of the Mystical Body
Mother of the Orphan and the Destitute
Mother of the Savior
Mother of the True Solomon
Mother of the Unborn
Mother of Unity
Mother of Wisdom
Mother of Your Own Creator
Mother Pierced by the Sword of Sorrow
Mother Regenerating People in Christ with God
Mother Sorrowful
Mother Tearful
Mother Transfixed with the Sword
Mother Undefiled
My Body's Healing
My Soul's Saving
Mysterious Fountain
Mystical Rose
Mystical Stair of Jacob

N

Nature's Re-creation
Nature's Restoration
Neck of the Mystical Body
Never-Fading Wood
New Eve
Noblest-Born of the Christian Flock
Nourisher of God and Man
Nursing Mother of the Sick

O

Obtainer of the Divine Mercy
Olive Tree of the Father's Compassion
Only Bridge of God to People
Ornament of Carmel
Our Aid in Danger
Our Blessed Mother
Our Consolation at the Hour of Death
Our Hope
Our Lady
Our Lady of Akita
Our Lady of All Nations
Our Lady of Aparecida
Our Lady of Beauraing
Our Lady of Banneux
Our Lady of Cana
Our Lady of China
Our Lady of Consolation
Our Lady of Czestochowa
Our Lady of Divine Providence
Our Lady of Dolors
Our Lady of Ephesus
Our Lady of Fatima
Our Lady of Good Counsel
Our Lady of Guadalupe
Our Lady of Kazan
Our Lady of Kibeho
Our Lady of Knock

Selected List of Marian Titles

Our Lady of La Salette
Our Lady of La Trappe
Our Lady of La-Vang
Our Lady of Light
Our Lady of Loreto
Our Lady of Lourdes
Our Lady of Mercy
Our Lady of Montserrat
Our Lady of Mount Carmel
Our Lady of Nazareth
Our Lady of Perpetual Help
Our Lady of Pompeii
Our Lady of Pontmain
Our Lady of Ransom
Our Lady of the Angels
Our Lady of the Assumption
Our Lady of the Blessed Sacrament
Our Lady of the Cenacle
Our Lady of the Immaculate Conception
Our Lady of the Miraculous Medal
Our Lady of the Pillar
Our Lady of the Rosary
Our Lady of the Sacred Heart
Our Lady of the Snows
Our Lady of Victory
Our Light
Our Light in Darkness
Our Life, Our Sweetness, and our Hope
Our Mother, Sister, and Queen
Our Own Sweet Mother
Our Queen
Our Sister
Our Sure Rest
Our Sweetness

P

Paradise Fenced against the Serpent
Paradise of Innocence and Immortality
Paradise of the Second Adam
Paradise Planted by God
Partner in Human Redemption
Patroness and Protectress
Peace and Joy of Mankind
Pearl of Virgins
Perfect Disciple of Christ
Perfume of Faith
Perpetual Virgin
Petitioner of All Graces
Pierced with a Sword of Sorrow
Pillar of Faith
Preserved from All Sin
Pride of the Human Race
Promised to the Patriarchs
Propitiation of the Divine Wrath
Protectrix from All Hurt
Protectrix of the Forsaken
Protectrix of the World
Prudent Virgin
Purifier of Souls

Q

Queen Assumed into Heaven
Queen Conceived without Original Sin
Queen of All Creation
Queen of All Hearts
Queen of All Saints
Queen of All the Earth
Queen of Angels
Queen of Apostles
Queen of Confessors
Queen of Families

Queen of Glory
Queen of Heaven
Queen of Heaven and Earth
Queen of Life
Queen of Martyrs
Queen of Mercy
Queen of Patriarchs
Queen of Peace
Queen of Peace and Clemency
Queen of Prophets
Queen of the Most Holy Rosary
Queen of the Universe
Queen of Virgins
Queen Unconquered

R

Ready Helper of Those in Peril
Recoverer of a Lost World
Refuge in Affliction
Refuge in Time of Danger
Refuge of All the Unhappy
Refuge of Sinners
Refuge of the Forsaken
Regeneration of Life
Reparatrix
Reparatrix of Her Parents
Reparatrix of the Lost World
Reposing with Eternal Wisdom
Resort of the Lord
Resource of Mourners
Resplendent like the Sun
Restorer of the Ages
Rich in Mercy
Road Leading to Jesus
Rock of Constancy
Root of Jesse
Rose Ever Blooming
Royal Throne of the Eternal King

S

Safe Asylum amid the World's Dangers
Saluted by the Magi
Sanctuary of the Divine Trinity
Sanctuary of the Holy Spirit
Sanctuary of the Lord
Scepter of Orthodoxy
Seat of Divine Wisdom
Seat of Mercy
Seat of Wisdom
Second Eve
Secret Gift from Heaven
Serene like the Moon
Serene Virgin
Shelter of Orphans
Shield of the Oppressed
Sign of Tranquillity
Singular Vessel of Devotion
Sister and Mother
Solace of the Wretched
Source of Virginity
Sovereign Benefactrix
Spiritual Vessel
Splendor of the Church
Spotless Dove of Beauty
Staff of the Apostles
Star of the Sea
Star That Bore the Sun
Stay of the Falling
Strength of the Faithful
Strength of the Weak
Subduer of Hearts
Subduer of the Unbelieving
Sun never Setting
Suppliant All-powerful
Suppliant for Sinners
Support of Widows and Orphans

Selected List of Marian Titles

Surpassing Eden's Garden
Surpassing the Heavens
Surpassing the Seraphim
Sweet Flowering of Gracious Mercy
Sweeter Than Honey and the Honeycomb

T

Tabernacle of God
Tabernacle of God among Humans
Tabernacle of God Incarnate
Tabernacle of the Word
Temple Divine
Temple Indestructible
Temple of Divinity
Temple of the Holy Spirit
Temple of the Living God
Temple of the Lord
Temple of the Lord's Body
Temple of the Spirit
Terror of the Treacherous
The Purest and Loveliest of Creatures
Throne of Divine Clemency
Throne of Glory
Throne of the King
Tower of David
Tower of Ivory
Tower of Strength against Our Foes
Tower Unassailable
Treasure of the Faithful
Treasure of the World
Treasure-House of Life
Treasury of Immortality

U

Undefiled
Undefiled Treasure of Virginity
Undug Well of Remission's Waters
Unfailing Stream of Mercy
Unlearned in the Ways of Eve
Unploughed Field of Heaven's Bread
Untarnished Image of the Church
Unwatered Vineyard of Immortality's Wine
Uplifter of the Fallen

V

Vanquisher of Satan
Vessel of Honor
Victor over the Serpent
Virgin
Virgin Daughter of Zion
Virgin Gentle and Obedient
Virgin Inviolate
Virgin Most Faithful
Virgin Most Merciful
Virgin Most Powerful
Virgin Most Prudent
Virgin Most Pure
Virgin Most Renowned
Virgin Most Venerable
Virgin Mother
Virgin Poor and Humble

W

Wedded to God
Woman Clothed with the Sun
Woman Crowned with the Stars
Woman Transformed
Workshop of the Incarnation

This book was produced by ST PAULS/Alba House, the Society of St. Paul, an international religious congregation of priests and brothers dedicated to serving the Church through the communications media.

For information regarding this and associated ministries of the Pauline Family of Congregations, write to the Vocation Director, Society of St. Paul, 2187 Victory Blvd., Staten Island, New York 10314-6603. Phone (718) 982-5709; or E-mail: vocation@stpauls.us or check our internet site, www.vocationoffice.org

ST PAULS